I Came, I Saw

Norman Lewis was born in London. He has written thirteen novels and ten non-fiction works. He relaxes by his travels to off-beat parts of the world, which he prefers to be as remote as possible: otherwise he lives with his family in introspective, almost monastic calm in the depths of Essex.

NORMAN LEWIS

I Came, I Saw

'AN AUTOBIOGRAPHY'

PICADOR

First published 1985 by Hamish Hamilton Ltd
under the title *Jackdaw Cake*

This revised edition first published 1994 by Picador as
a Picador Travel Classic

This edition published 1996 by Picador
an imprint of Macmillan Publishers Ltd
25 Eccleston Place, London SW1W 9NF
and Basingstoke

Associated companies throughout the world

ISBN 0 330 34005 0

1 3 5 7 9 8 6 4 2

A CIP catalogue record for this book is available
from the British Library

Typeset by CentraCet Limited, Cambridge
Printed and bound in Great Britain by
Mackays of Chatham PLC, Chatham, Kent

Contents

Part One

I CAME, I SAW

Chapter One

WHEN I WAS first pushed by my mother into the presence of my Aunt Polly, the bandages had only been removed from her face a few days before to expose a patchwork of skin, pink and white, glazed in some places and matt-surfaced in others, dependent upon the areas of thighs or buttocks from which it had been stripped to cover her burns. The fire had reached every part of her and she spoke in a harsh whisper that I could hardly understand. She had difficulty in closing her eyes. Later I found that sometimes while asleep the lids would snap open. It was impossible to judge whether or not I was welcome because the grey stripe of mouth provided by plastic surgery in its infancy could hold no expression. She bent down stiffly to proffer a cheek and, prodded by my mother, I reached up to select a smooth surface among the puckerings, the ridges and the nests of tiny wrinkles, and touch it with my lips.

In the rear, the second aunt, Annie, wearing long white gloves, holding a fan like a white feather duster, and dressed as if for her wedding, waited smilingly. I was soon to learn that the smile was one that nothing could efface.

Dodging in and out of a door at the back of the hallway, the third aunt, Li, seemed like a startled animal. She was weeping silently, and with these tears I would soon become familiar. I was nine years of age, and the adults peopling my world seemed on the whole irrational, but it was an irrationality I had come to accept as the norm. My father, who wanted to be an artist, and

3

failing that a preacher, had been banished to England following irreconcilable personality clashes with my grandfather who feared and disliked such manifestations of the human spirit. Now, after years of an aggrieved silence, there were to be attempts to rebuild bridges. It was my grandfather's ambition to make a Welshman of me, so my mother had brought me to this vast house, with little preparation, telling me that I was to live among these strangers for whom I was to show respect, even love, for an unspecified period of time. The prospect troubled me, but like an Arab child stuffed with the resignation of his religion, I soon learned to accept this new twist in the direction of my life, and the sounds of incessant laughter and grief soon lost all significance, became commonplace and thus passed without notice.

My mother, bastion of wisdom and fountainhead of truth in my universe, had gone, her flexible maternal authority replaced by the disciplines of my fire-scarred Aunt Polly, an epileptic who had suffered at least one fit per day since the age of fourteen, in the course of which she had fallen once from a window, once into a river and twice into the fire. Every day, usually in the afternoons, she staged an unconscious drama, when she rushed screaming from room to room, sometimes bloodied by a fall, and once leaving a menstrual splash on the highly polished floor. It was hard to decide whether she liked or disliked me, because she extended a tyranny in small ways to all who had dealings with her. In my case she issued a stream of whispered edicts relating to such matters as politeness, punctuality and personal cleanliness, and by being scrupulous in their observance I found that we got along together fairly well. I scored marks with her by mastery of the tedious and lengthy collects I was obliged to learn for recitation at Sunday school. When I showed myself as word perfect in one of these it was easy to believe that she was doing her best to smile, as she probably did when I accompanied her in my thin and wheedling treble in one of her harmonium recitals of such favourite hymns as 'Through the Night of Doubt and Sorrow'.

Smiling Aunt Annie, who counted for very little in the household, and who seemed hardly to notice my presence, loved to dress up, and spent an hour or two every day doing this. Sometimes she would come on the scene attired like Queen Mary in a hat like a dragoon's shako, and other times she would be a female cossack with cartridge pockets and high boots. Once, when later I went to school, and became very sensitive to the opinions of my schoolfriends, she waylaid me, to my consternation, on my way home got up as a Spanish dancer in a frilled blouse and skirt, and a high comb stuck into her untidy grey hair.

Li, youngest of the aunts, was poles apart from either sister. She and Polly had not spoken to each other for years, and occupied downstairs rooms at opposite ends of the house, while Annie made her headquarters in the room separating them, and when necessary transmitted curt messages from one to the other.

My grandfather, whom I saw only at weekends, for he worked in his business every day until eight or nine, filled every corner of the house with his deep, competitive voice, and the cigar-smoke aroma of his personality. At this time he had been a widower for twenty-five years; a man with the face of his day, a prow of a nose, bulging eyes, and an Assyrian beard, who saw himself close to God, with whom he sometimes conversed in a loud and familiar voice largely on financial matters.

A single magnificent coup had raised him to take his place among the eleven leading citizens of Carmarthen, with a house in Wellfield Road. It was the purchase of a cargo of ruined tea from a ship sunk in Swansea harbour, which he laundered, packaged in bags dangerously imprinted with the Royal crest, and sold off at a profit of several thousand per cent to village shops and remote farming communities scattered through the hills. This had bought him a house full of clocks and mirrors, with teak doors, a wine cellar, and a wide staircase garnished with wooden angels and lamps. After that he was to possess a French modiste as his mistress, the town's first Model T Ford, and a valuable grey parrot named Prydeyn after a hero of the Mabinogion, too old by the time of my arrival to talk, but which could still, as it hung from a curtain rod in the drawing room, produce in its throat a passable imitation of a small, squeaking fart.

My grandfather had started life as plain David Lewis but, swept along on the tide of saline tea, he followed the example of the neighbours in his select street and got himself a double-barrelled name, becoming David Warren Lewis. He put a crest on his notepaper and worked steadily at his family tree, pushing the first of our ancestors back further and further into history until they became contemporary with King Howel Dda. For a brief moment the world was at his feet. He had even been invited to London to shake the flabby hand of Edward VII. But on the home front his life fell apart. The three daughters he had kept at home were dotty, a fourth got into trouble and had to be exported to Canada to marry a settler who had advertised for a wife, and the fifth, Lalla, an artist of sorts, who had escaped him to marry a schoolteacher called Bennett, and settled in Cardiff, was spoken of as 'eccentric'.

This was Welsh Wales, full of ugly chapels, of hidden money, psalm-singing and rain. The hills all round were striped and patched with small bleak fields, with the sheep seen from our house – as small as lice – cropping the coarse grass, and seas of bracken pouring down the slopes to hurl themselves against the walls of the town. In autumn it rained every day. The water burst through the banks of the reservoir on top of Pen-lan, sent a wave full of fish down Wellfield Road, and then, spilling the fish everywhere through Waterloo Terrace, down to the market. What impressed me most were the jackdaws and the snails on which the jackdaws largely lived. The snails were of every colour, curled and striped like little turbans in blue, pink, green and yellow, and it was hard to walk down the garden path without crushing them underfoot. There were thousands of jackdaws everywhere in the town, and our garden was always full of them. Sensing that my mad aunts presented no danger, they were completely tame. They would tap on the windows to be let into the house and go hopping from room to room in search of scraps.

Weekly the great ceremony took place of the baking of the jackdaw cake. For this, co-operation was forced upon my three aunts, as the ingredients had to be decided upon and bought: eggs, raisins, candied peel and sultanas required to produce a cake of exceptional richness. Li did the shopping, because Polly was supposed not to leave

7

the house and Annie was too confused to be able to buy what was necessary, put down her money, and pick up the change.

Each aunt took it in turns to bake and ice the cake and to decorate the icing. While they were kept busy doing this they seemed to me quite changed. Annie wore an ordinary dress and stopped laughing, Li ceased to cry, and Polly's fits were quieter than on any other day. While the one whose turn it was did the baking, the others stood about in the kitchen and watched, and they were as easy to talk to as at other times they were not.

On Saturday mornings at ten o'clock the cake was fed to the jackdaws. This had been happening for years, so that by half past nine the garden was full of birds, anything up to a hundred of them balancing and swinging with a tremendous gleeful outcry on the bushes and the low boughs of the trees. This was the great moment of the week for my aunts, and therefore for me. The cake would be cut into three sections and placed on separate plates on the kitchen table, and then at ten the kitchen windows were flung wide to admit the great black cataract of birds. For some hours after this weekly event the atmosphere was one of calm and contentment, and then the laughter and weeping would start again.

Polly did all the cooking, and apart from that sat in the drawing room, watched over by the parrot Prydeyn, crocheting bedspreads with the stiff fingers that had not been wholly spared by the fire. Li collected the instructions and the money left for her and went out shopping, and Annie dressed up as a pirate, harlequin, clown or whatever came into her head. My grandfather worked incessantly in his tea-merchant's business in King Street, returning as late as he decently could at night. On Sunday mornings, like all the rest of the community, he was hounded by his conscience to chapel, but in the afternoon he was accustomed to spend a little time with the Old English Game Fowl he bred, showed and – as the rumour went – had entered in secret cock fights in his disreputable youth. They were kept in wire pens in the back garden, each cockerel, or 'king' as it was known, separately with its hens. Show judges used to visit the house to test a contestant's ferocity by poking at it through the wire netting with a stick to which a coloured rag had been attached; any bird failing to attack being instantly disqualified.

The comb, wattles, ear-lobes and any loose skin were removed from the head and neck of these birds and there was frequently a little extra trimming-up to be done. Experience and skill were called for to catch and subdue a king in his prime and sometimes, like a Roman gladiator, my grandfather used a net. Once the bird was tied up and the head imprisoned in a wooden collar, he set to work in a leisurely fashion with a snip here and a snip there, using a special variety of scissors – known as a dubber – designed for this purpose.

The game cocks often escaped from their pens and strutted about the back garden on the look-out for something to attack. It was my Aunt Li and I who were their usual chosen victims. They had enormously long legs – so long that they appeared to be walking on miniature stilts. My grandfather and my Aunt Polly knew how to handle them and carried garden rakes to push them aside if necessary, but Li and I went in great fear of them. This they probably sensed, for any king that had managed to break out had the habit of lying in wait well out of sight until either of us came on the scene, when he would rush to the attack, leaping high into the air to strike at our faces with his spurs.

In the end Aunt Li and I formed a defensive alliance, and this brought us closer together. We based our strategy on cutting down the birds' numbers. Unlike normal chickens the game fowl laid only a few small eggs and had a short breeding season. Polly looked after the brooding hens and chicks, kept separate from the kings, and Li's method was to wait until her sister was out of the way, either while having or recovering from a fit, then take several eggs from the clutch under a sitting hen and drop them into boiling water for a few seconds before putting them back.

This promised to ease the situation in the coming year but did nothing to help us in our present trouble, so my aunt bought a cat of a breed supposed locally to be the descendants of a pair of wild cats captured in Llandeilo forest about a hundred years before. She brought it back in a sack one night, kept it in an outhouse without feeding it for three days, and then let it loose in the garden. At this time there were two or three game cocks at large, and the scuffle and outcry that followed raised our hopes, but in the morning the kings were still strutting through the flower beds ready for battle with all comers, and of the cat there was nothing to be seen.

As confidence and sympathy began growing between us, my Aunt Li and I took to wandering round the countryside together. Li was a small woman, hardly any bigger than me. She would wet me with her tears, and I would listen to her sad ravings and sometimes stroke her hand. One day she must have come to the grand decision to tell me what lay at the root of her sorrow. We climbed a stile and went into a field and, fixing her glistening eyes upon me, she said, 'What I am going to tell you now you will remember every single day of your life.' But whatever she revealed must have been so startling that memory rejected it, for not a word of what was said remains in my mind.

The Towy River made and dominated Carmarthen, and it was always with us whenever we went on our walks, throwing great, shining loops through the fields, doubling back on itself sometimes in a kind of afterthought to encircle some riverside shack or a patch of sedge in which cows stood knee-deep to graze. In winter the whole valley filled up with floods, and people nervously remembered the prophecy of the enchanter Merlin that the floods would eventually engulf the town where he was buried. For my aunt they offered endless excitement, with the drowning sheep and cattle carried away on the yellow whiplash of the river's current disappearing beneath the surface one after another as it swept them towards the sea, and the coracle men spinning in whirlpools in their black, prehistoric boats as they prodded at animals with their poles, trying to steer them to safety.

In summer the people of Carmarthen went on trips to the seaside at Llanstephan, at the river's mouth. There was no more beautiful, wilder or stranger place in the British Isles, but the local Welsh no longer saw the beauty, and familiarity and boredom drove all who could afford it further afield for such outings to Tenby, which was certainly larger and jollier. The Normans had built a castle in Llanstephan in about 1250, and there was an ancient church, and a few Victorian cottages, but apart from this handful of buildings, little in this landscape had changed for thousands of years. Here the Towy finally unwound itself into the sea, its estuary enclosed in a great silken spread of sand occupying a third of the horizon, to which our century had added not a single detail but the bones of two foundered ships in the process of digestion by mud.

For the villagers a shadow hung over this scene. On fine Sundays and holidays throughout the summer, miners and their families would descend upon them. The train brought them from the hellish valleys to Ferryside across the estuary, and from Ferryside they would cross by boat to take joyous possession of the sands. At first warning of this invasion the people of Llanstephan made a bolt for their houses, slamming their doors behind them, drawing their curtains and keeping out of sight until six hours later the turn of the tide released them from their misery.

The miners were despised and hated by the villagers of Llanstephan just as were field labourers by their more comfortable fellow countrymen in England in those days. To the villagers they were no better than foreigners, people whose habits were beyond their understanding, in particular the frantic pleasure they showed, and their noisily offensive good humour released into the calm and sober environment of Llanstephan on a Sunday afternoon. When I saw my first miners come ashore in Llanstephan, I asked my aunt if they were dwarfs, so reduced in size had these Welshmen – identical in stock with those of Llanstephan – become after three generations of lives spent underground.

In Carmarthen and its surrounding villages people were obsessed with relationships, and practically everyone I met turned out to be a cousin, four, five or even six times removed. Cousins who were old – say over thirty – were respectfully known as aunties or uncles, and one of the reasons for our trip to Llanstephan was to see an Auntie Williams who lived in the first of the line of cottages along the sea front. All of these were like little houses from a child's picture book, with old-fashioned gardens full of rosemary and honeysuckle, tabby cats everywhere, and fantail pigeons on the roofs.

Auntie Williams was a little Welsh woman of the kind they still showed on picture postcards, wearing black, steeple-crowned hats, and although the old witch's hat had gone she still wore the shawl that went with it in all weathers. She was famous for her 'early-red-apple' tree, perhaps the last of its kind, which bore its ripe, brilliantly red fruit as early as August, and also for her husband, once a handsome man – as proved by the large coloured photograph in her front room, taken in uniform shortly before the battle of the Somme in which most of his lower jaw had been shot away. These days he wore a mask over the lower part of his face, and a tube protruding from his right nostril was fixed behind his ear. On my first visit he was with us for lunch, dressed in a jaunty check jacket. Auntie Williams had boiled a sewin, mixing a scrap of pink fish well chewed by her into the gruel she fed her husband through the tube, and gently massaging his throat as it went down. Everybody in Llanstephan admired him for the cheerfulness with which he had suffered his disability, and he had published a little philosophical book designed to help others to bear with such handicaps.

The finish of the meal, joined by two more neighbouring aunties, was spoilt by the arrival of the ferry boat, bringing the miners and their families. They came unexpectedly, as the jetty had been put out of action by the villagers in the preceding week. But the villagers had underestimated the miners' determination to enjoy themselves, as with tremendous effort they dragged the heavy boat clear of the water and onto the sand.

Until this calamity, the three Llanstephan aunties, hard to tell apart with their round country faces and polished cheeks, had been full of smiles, and by Uncle Williams' gestures and noises he too had seemed brimful of good humour. Aunt Li, whose vacant expression signified for me that for once she was not actually unhappy, was teasing a small crab she had found in a pool. Now, suddenly, as the mining families climbed down from the boat and advanced towards us, a great change came over our family gathering. The miners' children, shrieking with delight, scampered ahead, and the miners and their wives trudged in the rear over the wet sand, carrying their boots and shoes, their little parcels of food, and two bulky packages. Watching this advance, the Llanstephan aunties' kindly, homely faces became those of different barely recognizable people. My Carmarthen relations laughed and wept in their meaningless way, or – in the case of Polly – were unable to produce a facial expression of any kind, but they had at least spared me the spectacle of anger, which was frighteningly new. The soft singsong Welsh voices had lost their music and fallen flat, as they talked of the wickedness of miners. It was a local theory, supported by the chapels, that poverty was the wages of sin – and the miners looked poor enough. Their women, it was thought, who often worked alongside their men, were driven into the mines not by hunger but shamelessness, and discussing this aspect of the mining life the Llanstephan aunties made the loading up and manoeuvring of coal trucks in near darkness a thousand feet under the earth seem a carnal indulgence.

Uncle Williams went into the house and came back with a placard, which he fixed to a post by his wall. It said, 'Remember the Sabbath Day, to keep it Holy', but the miners ignored it. Their children were everywhere, screaming with glee. They threw wet sand at each other, dug up cockles, dammed the little streams flowing on the beach, and even came to stare open-mouthed over the garden walls. When no one was watching I sneaked away to try to join forces with them, but we did not easily mix. Immersed in their games, they ignored me, and I was too shy to speak.

Presently a miner beckoned to me. He and his wife were setting out their picnic on a cloth spread over the dry sand. The man was short but very strong-looking, with bowed legs, and a snake tattooed on each forearm. He asked me my name, and I told him, and his wife looked up and smiled and gave me a slice of cake. 'Sit you down,' she said, and I was just going to when Auntie Williams spotted me and let out a screech. 'Come you back by here.'

I went back and Auntie Williams said, 'What she give you, then?' I showed her the cake and she took it away and threw it to the pigeons. Wanting to get away from her I went over to Li, but she was no longer blank-faced as she had been when I left her, and for me that meant that something had upset her. She had lost her crab, and I thought it might be that. 'Like me to find you another crab, Auntie?' I asked, but she shook her head.

On the beach, sandwiches had been passed out to the children. The man who had spoken to me opened a bottle of beer. He drank from the neck, and passed it to his wife. The couple who had been carrying the two brown paper parcels untied the string and unwrapped them. One of the parcels had held the box part of a gramophone, and the other the horn, and these they fixed together. We watched from our chairs under the apple tree while this was going on. No one spoke but I could feel the astonished horror. The people who had brought the gramophone wound it up and put on a record and soon a little thin, wheezing music reached us between the soft puffs of breeze, and the squawking of the herring gulls flopping about overhead.

The people in the cottage next door had come out into the garden to watch what was going on and one of them, a man, shouted a protest. Uncle Williams stood up, picked an apple and threw it in the direction of the couple with the gramophone, but with so little force that the apple hardly cleared our low wall. His example gave great encouragement, though, to the others, and the man who had shouted from the garden next door threw a small stone. My feeling was that he never really intended to hit anything, and the stone splashed in a beach puddle yards from the nearest of the miners, who gave no sign of realizing what was happening and went on eating their sandwiches and drinking their beer, never once so much as looking in our direction. Next a bigger stone thudded on the sand, and there were more shouts from the cottages, and two or three children who had gone off to collect shells gave up and went back to join their parents.

More shouts and more stones followed – all the stones thrown by men whose aim was very bad, or who otherwise weren't trying. After a while the miners began to pack up, taking their time about it, and paying no attention at all to the villagers who were insulting them.

The gramophone was taken apart and parcelled up as before, and everything they had brought with them packed away; then, without looking back, they began to move towards the ferry boat, and within half an hour they had managed to push the boat into the water and that was the last of them.

Uncle Williams took down the placard and put it away, and his wife put on the kettle for tea. Nobody could find anything to say. The weather experts who could tell by the look of the seaweed had promised them a fine afternoon, but the miners had ruined their day. Li suddenly got up and said she was going home. 'We got an hour still to wait for the bus, Auntie,' I said. 'Never mind about the bus,' she said. 'I'm leaving now,' and she was off, marching down the path, and I could see by the way she was walking, with her head thrown back and slightly to one side, that something had upset her, although there was no way of saying what it was. I'd seen enough of her by then to know that it wasn't the miners being there that bothered her – in which case it could only be something one of the Llanstephan relations had said or done that was to blame. But what was it? I couldn't guess. There was no telling the way things took Aunt Li.

I ran to catch her up. It was six and a half miles to Carmarthen but she was a fast walker, and I expected we'd beat the bus.

Chapter Two

IN THE AUTUMN I was sent to local day school, the Pentrepoeth at which my father had suffered some thirty-five years before. He had been there in the days when the Welsh had decided to anglicize themselves, and he was caned for speaking the native language in a master's presence. By my time a swing of the pendulum had occurred, and some lessons were conducted in Welsh of which I was unable to understand a word. For this I received a mild cuffing, not only to cure me of idiocy, but to punish what was suspected as stubborn muteness or malice. The fact was that life in Wellfield Road had had the effect of practically silencing me in the presence of adults. The master was a fourth or fifth cousin of mine, as he mentioned to me reproachfully, but this had no effect on his treatment of me. He would appeal to the schoolchildren. 'Not understanding a word I say to him, he is. What do you call a boy that cannot even respond when spoken to? What is the name for him?' All the children would shout with delight, 'Dickie Dwl, sir' (stupid Dick). 'That's right, boys, and that is what his name shall be, Dickie Dwl.' I was then sent down to the infants' school in the effort to force a little Welsh into me. This was quite unsuccessful.

The harsh winter that year was a good time for me. In South Wales the winters are expected to be mild and wet, but this was an arctic exception, throwing out challenges and imposing strains, and many people – as did my family – found it wholly beneficial to battle with the elements, distracted in this way from other troubles.

Where the floods had been, vast sheets of ice covered the fields. Most of the services gave in, the electricity failed, and the water mains froze up. Farmers snowed up in their hill farms were unable to bring food to the market, and Pen-lan loomed over us like a Himalayan ice-peak, the sheep dying in snowdrifts on its slopes.

It was an emergency that had a tonic effect in Aunt Polly's case too, and she bustled about endlessly organizing supplies of fuel and food and badgering reluctant workmen to trudge through the snow up to the house to repair the damage done by storm and flood.

I soon noticed a slackening in the severity of her fits, and although she still continued to suffer one a day, she was much quieter, and the attacks were of shorter duration. Some time in the afternoon the inevitable symptoms, the silence and the withdrawal would appear, and Annie and Li would set about putting in hand the usual security precautions, which included locking the door of any room in which a fire was burning. Fits happened once in a while in Polly's bedroom, or in the bathroom – but more often either the kitchen or the breakfast room was chosen. I went in mortal fear of seeing Aunt Polly's face when she was having a fit. Before entering any room I would push open the door, inch by inch, until I could see what was going on, and it always happened that if Polly was there and in trouble, I soon spotted her feet which were small and neat sticking out from behind the sofa or an armchair, whereupon I silently closed the door and slipped away.

My grandfather had arranged for two layers of under-felt for the breakfast room carpet and well-padded furniture to help break the almost routine fall. There was little to be done to minimize the dangers of the kitchen, and it was here that Polly had fallen twice into the fire. I was astonished that she had not been burned to death, for as far as I could judge a fit could last up to a half hour, and during this time she was left to lie where she was. When a fit was in progress she made no sound, although after it was over she sometimes screamed. This final scream, when it occurred, was a good sign for Grandfather, for it meant that for two or three days afterwards the seizures would be less violent, and Polly would be active about the house and garden, able to discuss family matters in her damaged, whispering voice. The long, hard winter muffled this outcry, but with the thaw, the putting-out of candles and oil lamps, the water running through the taps, and the goods delivered again to the door, my good times were over and tensions began to build up once more.

As soon as the town came out of the coma of that winter my grandfather embarked on his last romance, a disaster involving the Parisian modiste who had opened up in business a few yards from his King Street establishment. Of the facts of the case I knew nothing until told by my mother some years later. I was aware of a family upheaval but there was nothing unusual in that apart from its magnitude, and that for the first time I saw my grandfather under physical assault by his daughters. The modiste, according to my mother, was thirty-five years younger than the old man, and turned the head of every male in town, and what my mother could not understand – and I heartily agreed with her – was what such a creature would be doing in a grey little, milk-swilling, psalm-singing place like Carmarthen? Her story was that my grandfather had picked the girl up on Paddington

Station on one of his trips to London, and had let her
persuade him to set her up in business.

The luckless young modiste, said my mother, was
harried by Annie and Li from pillar to post. I was able to
describe to her an episode I had witnessed of this persecution when, in King Street, my Aunt Li had once left
me to rush at a woman passer-by, tear the hat from her
head and trample it under her feet.

I was to see this same woman once more on the day
she called at the house. My grandfather was at his
business and she had come for a meeting with Aunt
Polly, in the hope, perhaps, of winning her over. She
was kept waiting in the hall where, with long practice at
self-concealment, I had placed myself out of sight. Polly
had had a fit an hour or so before, and was given time to
get over it before being told about the visitor. Then –
half the girl's size – she came into sight, still twitching a
little and eyes staring, walked straight up to her and
struck her in the face.

It was the last I ever saw of the girl from Paris, but
her presence and the guilt and shame the liaison generated
must have been manna to the congregations of the town's
many chapels. There had been some talk of my grandfather becoming mayor, but little more was heard of
this, and when I brought the matter up with Aunt Polly
I was told that there had been some trouble over his
refusal to join the Church of England. After that even his
position in his chapel seemed on the wane where, probably because of a voice of irreplaceable power, he
remained precentor, but ceased to be deacon. His friend
and protector had been Lord Kilsant, with whom he had
conducted certain discreet business transactions, and who

had encouraged him when he applied for a grant of arms and advised him on his choice of emblem (which included a teapot emblazoned on a shield). Now the man with whom Grandfather had been seen walking arm and arm with down King Street on his way to the Liberal Club turned out to have master-minded a financial swindle in the City of London for which he was tried and sent to prison. And worse was to follow when there were widespread allegations that the origins of an outbreak of the 'bad sickness' (as gonorrhoea was always known), soon reaching epidemic proportions, had been tracked down to the presence of the French girl in the town.

My grandfather turned for solace to his game cocks, encouraged perhaps to do so by an exceptionally successful breeding season in the previous year, before Li had had the idea of parboiling the eggs. This had produced a king of which he was very proud, and though I had good reason to detest game cocks, I had to admit that this was a handsome if terrifying bird. I had never seen a cock before with such beautiful plumage, with shining wine-coloured feathers, streaked and shot, according to the light, with the deepest of blue. Grandfather had mentioned to someone when I happened to be in the room – he never in all the months that I lived in the house addressed a word to me – that he had been penalized at the Carmarthen show for breeding birds with legs that were too long. This one, although it reached to my waist and could comfortably peck me in the face, was a little shorter, exactly as demanded at this time by the changing fashion in poultry. It was fed on chopped up fillet steak, barley sugar, aniseed, ginger, rhubarb and yeast mixed with 'cock bread' made from oatmeal and eggs to which a little cinnamon was added.

The bird's great moment arrived when it was 'dubbed'. While Aunt Polly held the king by the legs, my grandfather opened its beak with one finger in its mouth and the thumb at the back of the head, then with a single cut removed the comb, very close to the skull. Next the ear-lobes and wattles went, the whole process timed by a stop-watch to last not longer than a minute. My grandfather claimed that the king felt no pain. As soon as the operation was over a few grams of corn were thrown to it, and now came the supreme moment, for a future champion would show 'eagerness' at this point – as did Grandfather's bird – by swallowing its own comb.

This bird showed an inexhaustible energy that caused it to break into a skip as it strutted round its pen, and it was this skipping, its swaggering walk, its fiery red eye and the way it hurled itself at the wire when provoked which entranced the experts that came to see it. My grandfather completed the entertainment by throwing it a sizeable rat, only partially disabled, which it soon despatched. A bird of this calibre, someone told me, could drive a spur right through a quarter-inch-thick wooden board, and had been known to kill weasels, and even a fox. The opinion was that my grandfather had bred a winner, and he was advised to bypass the local shows and groom the king for the Royal Agricultural Hall, London, or the Crystal Palace, where it was certain to receive the award for the best in its class, if not the show.

With the coming of spring Aunt Polly's condition worsened, as if the sickness she suffered from was bent on making up for time lost in the calm of the winter. She locked herself in her bedroom for more than a week, and made no reply to appeals by my grandfather, shouted through the keyhole, or the messages – to which a decorative biblical text was sometimes pinned – pushed under the door. Sometimes I was awakened in the night by the sound of a lavatory flushed, the faint crunch of boards, and the squeak of the door of the kitchen, over which I slept. The doctor was called in and he and my grandfather sat together in the drawing room under floating turbans of cigar smoke, while the old grey parrot crawled over the furniture making its farting noises, and a number of tall clocks ticked the wrong time. Our doctor was another cousin, and inbreeding had given him and my father almost identical faces. I wandered into the room out of curiosity and neither man bothered to look up. On a previous occasion, the doctor had shaken his head out of sympathy when I had had nothing to say in reply when spoken to, and probably assumed that I was deaf and dumb.

'What do you suggest?' my grandfather asked.

'You'll have to put her away, for your sake as well as her own.'

Grandfather shook his head.

'There's no telling what could happen. Nothing I can give her will do any good. If she stays here don't hold me responsible for whatever happens.'

He put down a paper to be signed, but my grandfather pushed it away.

There was a long discussion about the worsening relationship between Polly and Li, and the doctor said that it was impossible for the two women to go on living under the same roof together.

My grandfather told him that if anybody had to go, it would be Li. Polly was his first born, and his favourite – although he did not admit to this.

The only person in the world whom Polly claimed to love, and who could bring her to her senses at times like this, was my mother, but for some weighty reasons of her own, this was an occasion when my mother was unable to leave the family home in Enfield and come to the rescue. In the last resort, and taking the view that even should the attempt fail there was nothing to be lost, my grandfather persuaded his only married daughter, Charlotte, who lived in Cardiff, to come and do what she could.

Charlotte – Aunt Lalla as she was known to me – was regarded as the brilliant member of the family. She had taken a degree in art, and held an exhibition of her paintings in the Guild Hall, Carmarthen, but promise had been destroyed by her meeting with David Bennett, a tall, mild schoolteacher on holiday from England, and they had immediately married and set up house in Cardiff.

Lalla arrived with her husband and their fourteen-year-old son, who proved to be severely handicapped, although his mother, who was dark and intense and spoke in an excited and passionate way, refused to accept that this was the case. Apart from this staggering delusion, I thought she was a clever woman, and that my uncle was a clever man, too. I could not understand how it was that these exceptional people could have a son with a vocabulary limited to about a dozen words, which he pronounced with difficulty. Apart from this lack of communication between us, we got on well enough together. He was tall, strong and active and addicted to very long walks, which I enjoyed, too, so long as they were restricted to quiet country lanes out of view of the town. My Uncle David was a dedicated golfer, accustomed to take his son with him when he went golfing. In this way Dai, also, had become deeply involved in golf. Unable to master the skills the normal game demanded he had invented a version conducted in his imagination with a phantom opponent. He carried a golf club wherever he went, perpetually on the look-out for objects lying in the road – small branches fallen from trees, cigarette packets and the like – to substitute for the ball. My uncle always carried a reserve of empty matchboxes on these outings for use in the case of the failure of other suitable objects to be found.

In my public relationship with the Bennetts I had to proceed with extreme caution. I was accepted on sufferance by the boys of the Pentrepoeth School who at best regarded me as harmless although not overbright, and above all I was anxious not to be associated in any way with eccentric behaviour. It had been a setback – something I was doing my best to live down – to be sent down to the infants' school to be taught Welsh. Now the Bennetts had arrived, and my worry was how my school-fellows would view Aunt Lalla, who was inclined to draw attention to herself, to say nothing of Dai with his over-large head and a tongue that was too large for his mouth, busying himself in the streets with his imaginary golf match.

Aunt Li's unaccountable behaviour in public had been noted and commented upon by my schoolfriends, but here the situation was now well in hand. Whenever we set out on one of our walks I steered clear of the town, and as both our interests lay in the countryside, this was

not difficult. May had arrived and a wonderful collection
of butterflies fluttered about over the marshy fields and
the ponds of Pen-lan. There were white admirals, swal-
low-tails – never reported from South Wales – which I
saw here for the first and last time, fritillaries of all kinds,
and one enormous sombre variety, never identified,
which a local farmer informed us had been blown across
the Atlantic from America, and was occasionally to be
seen at the tops of these western hills. My aunt made up
an osier trap to catch trout in the roadside streams, and
once in a while we caught one. We also trapped a variety
of birds, all of which somehow managed to escape, or
rather – as I suspect now – were secretly released a few
hours after their capture. I always found that I could
speak to Li quite easily, and without hesitation, but there
was no encouragement to do so, as she preferred a
meaningful silence.

Lalla made some progress with Polly and finally got
her to come out of her room. After weeping uninterrupt-
edly for half a day, she suddenly calmed down, ate a
substantial meal, and gathered up the reins of the household once more into her hands, re-establishing a firm,
authoritarian rule.

The proposal on the Bennetts' last Sunday in Carmarthen was for a bus outing, in which I was to be included
– inevitably to Llanstephan. The prospect was a tempting
one indeed, offering not only an excursion to the delights
of the seashore, but an escape from the shades of the
prison house on the gloomiest day of the week. For all
that, it was a proposition to be considered with caution.
It would entail a half-mile walk down to the bus stop at
the Boar's Head Hotel in Lammas Street, and another
risky half-mile to be covered at the end of the return

27

journey. It was a prospect that made me nervous. The alternative was close confinement to the house between morning and evening chapel, with little to do but read, the choice of reading material being Victorian novels that were too old for me, or a manuscript copy of a work by one of my forebears who had kept an eye-witness account at the beginning of the last century of all the numerous public hangings of condemned men from the boughs of the great oaks still standing at Llangunnor, across the river. It was considered irreligious on the Sabbath even to appear in the garden.

In the end I settled for the Llanstephan trip. The sandwiches were made, the empty matchboxes collected and, having given Aunt Polly an undertaking of chapel attendance in Llanstephan, we set out.

We reached the bus stop without incident. There are few people about in the streets in a small Welsh town on a Sunday morning, and I saw no one I knew. Dai, using up energy, cantered along at our side swinging his golf club but abstaining from practising his shots, because my uncle had persuaded him that the finest golfcourse in the world in the form of an endless stretch of golden sands awaited at the end of the trip.

This was a safe time of the year to visit Llanstephan, because it was a good six weeks before the miners and their families would come on the scene at the beginning of August. Much as Lalla disliked and feared them, it seemed possible that she disliked the Williamses even more, and I was grateful that I was not to be exposed once again to the spectacle of Uncle Williams having his food massaged down his throat.

Lalla despised almost everyone outside her immediate family and was angered by the fact that people without artistic talent should spoil the view by their mere presence in a village in which she claimed a kind of proprietorial interest. She and my uncle had lived here for a while after their marriage, and she had been awarded a second prize at the Carmarthen Festival of Arts for her paintings of the sea front, from which all human figures had been excluded. Our family, she said, had had a long association with the place. Some of her memories were dramatic. At low tide a vast and shining sandbank, *Cefyn Setyn* (Silk Back), appeared in the channel. To this, one Christmas Day in her childhood, she remembered two of her uncles had rowed out, taking a bottle of whisky, to shoot duck and to celebrate, but at the end of a festive day they had shot each other, and only one, with a leg blown off, survived. The practice of infanticide, my aunt claimed, had been common here, and she offered to show me where new-born babies had been buried in the back garden of the next-door neighbour of those days.

Llanstephan, at first, was heaven for Dai as he inspected the treasure trove of miscellaneous objects the tide had deposited on the beach, before hitting out at them with his club. Unfortunately the presence of strangers had alerted the inhabitants of the cottages all along the sea front, and they came out to stare and giggle at his antics, and the argument that arose with his imaginary partner.

Soon, to my horror, Uncle Williams, mask pulled well down and ready to deal with unwelcome visitors, appeared in his garden, but after a vague gesture of dismissal went inside again.

From this time on the day began to go to pieces. Dai demanded ginger beer but only barter transactions were permissible in Llanstephan on the Sabbath, and my uncle had nothing suitable to offer in exchange. He had brought a shovel with him to dig up cockles, but as soon as he started to do so he was insulted and threatened by the cockle men, who came running from their shack under the cliff to accuse him of taking the bread out of their mouths. My aunt got her feet wet when the tide came in. We were menaced by an aggressive cow that had strayed down to the beach, and when we presented a dog with the remnants of our stale sandwiches, it went off and returned with the gift of the decayed corpse of a large sea-bird, and could not be driven away. Dai complained that the wet sands were unsuitable for golf, and became quarrelsome and morose, and my aunt struck up a tragic attitude, and said, 'I have sacrificed my life for this.' When the bus left at four, we boarded it with relief.

The return journey was conducted in silence apart from an occasional moan of frustration from Dai, and Lalla, who anxiously studied and responded to the slightest variation in her son's moods, announced that he was unhappy because he had been deprived of his proper walk, so at Llangain, to my consternation, three miles from Carmarthen, she stopped the bus, and we were put down.

From Llangain it was two miles to John's Town and we covered the distance slowly. My uncle got out the matchboxes, and Dai, determined to make up for time lost at Llanstephan, swiped them into hedges from which, often with delay and difficulty they had to be retrieved. At John's Town the first of Carmarthen's houses came into sight, and my nervousness increased as the supply of matchboxes ran out, despite repairs carried out by my uncle to boxes not irreparably shattered by the first stroke of Dai's club. Dai's recurring frustration showed in pleadings and gestures, and my uncle rushed into the newspaper shop at the top of Lammas Street, and persuaded them, on the promise to pay next day, to hand over a whole packet of a dozen boxes of matches. Dai snatched it from his hands, ripped open the packet, tore out a box, threw it on the pavement outside the shop, and demolished it with an unerring drive, scattering the matches in all directions. He crowed and chuckled with delight at having found a new sport, held out his left hand to shake that of his invisible opponent, then addressed himself to the next box of matches. In this way we progressed slowly towards the town's social centre, shifting on Sundays from the business and shopping area of the weekdays down to Lammas Street in the vicinity of the Boar's Head, where people gathered for a chat and a stroll before evening chapel.

The situation here turned out to be even worse than I feared, for not only, and inevitably, were there familiar faces in the crowd, but to my horror Aunt Annie, expecting us on a later bus, was waiting at the bus stop. She wore a feather in her hat, carried a bright parasol, and smiled like a Japanese when we came into sight. I had already discovered that Dai Bennett was the only human being that meant anything in the world to her, and as soon as Dai saw her he rushed forward, waving his club and gabbling with excitement. They fell into each other's arms. Then Dai had something to show her. A ring of curious bystanders had gathered as he put down a matchbox, took up his stance and swung the club. The moment had come for me to sneak away.

The Bennetts went, leaving Polly, it seemed, miraculously renewed, but there were soon troubles in other directions. For a show bird to be at its best when the time came, it had to be given a 'walk', i.e. a separate run, encouraged only by a view of hens, and ideally be permitted to roost at night in the branches of a tree. All these conditions my grandfather provided for his king, although at the expense of security because, having reached the branches of the tree, it was easy enough for the bird to fly down into the garden instead of back into its run. This happened only too often. Aunt Annie, who wore high-heeled, unsuitable boots, rarely went into the garden, and was therefore fairly safe, but whenever Aunt Li and I happened to do so and saw the king skirmishing and parrying through the flower beds, we retreated into the house and stayed there until my grandfather came home in the evening and he and Polly would join forces to get the situation under control. Since the garden beyond the herbaceous borders was a maze of outhouses and chicken runs the time was bound to come when one or another of us was too late in becoming aware that the bird was at large. This eventually happened to Li, and it inflicted a bad wound on her hand before she could escape.

A few days later, happening to look out of his bedroom window shortly after getting up, Grandfather noticed one of the hill farmers' dogs busy with something that looked like a bundle of feathers on the other side of the high garden fence. Going down to investigate, he found the corpse of his king. The bird had been partly eaten, but there was something about the circumstances of this reverse that aroused his suspicions, which were strengthened when the vet he called in was able to tell him that the cause of death had been a crushed skull through a heavy blow on the head. From overheard conversations it was quite clear to me that my grandfather suspected Li of this crime. I do not believe that he ever forgave her.

Polly had a calm month, and Grandfather brightened up after his second-best bird, sent to the Agricultural Hall, took first prize in its class. These were the quiet days of late summer, long enough for evening outings with Aunt Li, fishing in the ponds and chasing butterflies on the top of Pen-lan.

One day I came home from school to hushed voices, excitement and speculations. A plain-clothes policeman had arrived at the house, and he and Grandfather retired to the drawing room. It was later explained to me that at this time the town was suffering from an outbreak of poison-pen letters. The motives and details of this visit were later disclosed in a long meeting between my grandfather, Annie and Li, when some pretext had been made for removing Polly from the scene. The policeman, said my grandfather, who had been most apologetic, polite and pleasant, had shown him a page of one of the letters that were causing the trouble, and asked him if he recognized the handwriting, to which my grandfather had replied, he did not, and the man had then asked his permission to speak to Polly. To this my grandfather had agreed, and he had gone to fetch her. Polly, he said, had been at her best, very calm and reasonable, and accepting with the best possible grace the assurance that this was nothing more than a routine enquiry.

She told the policeman she had never seen the letter before, that she certainly had not written it. She made slighting reference to the cheap, lined notepaper. Grandfather then said that the policeman had asked Polly if she

33

would have any objection to writing down several words. The obvious intention was to compare these with the same words in the letter. Grandfather, objecting, had told her not to do this, but she had done it all the same. He had asked the policeman if someone had made an accusation and, as the policeman replied in an evasive way, it was to be assumed that this was the case. The thing was, as all agreed, that so much time was spent in Carmarthen schools – which I knew to my cost – in the practising of a hand that came as close as possible to copperplate, that all local handwriting was extremely similar. For example, Grandfather said – pointedly, I thought – that he could hardly tell Polly's and Li's handwriting apart.

Next day, or perhaps the day after that, I was amazed to be treated by Aunt Polly with extraordinary kindness. It was a Saturday, with no school. In the morning the jackdaw cake was divided as usual, but before this took place – and it was something that had never happened before – she took me into her room and give me a slice from her share. She then whispered to me to put on my best suit as we were going shopping together. This came as another surprise. The only time she risked going out was when she had had an early-morning fit, leaving her clear for the rest of the day, and I hoped and assumed that this had occurred. We went into several shops where she dealt, and she purchased a few things including a gramophone record I talked her into buying. She chatted in an amiable way to the assistants, cupping her hand to her lips to amplify the sound. An outing for Aunt Polly was a rare treat.

At the chemist's she wanted perfume, and sniffed at several bottles open for testing before she decided on

Jockey Club. I was surprised when she took me into our cousin Morgan's, the butcher's, because there had been a quarrel and the family had withdrawn their business months before. Morgan was there, a burly man, with a face as red as the steak on his chopping block. Aunt Polly bought some meat, shook hands with him, and the quarrel was made up on the spot.

She then told me that she had forgotten to give me a birthday present, so wanted to buy me one now. I was unable to think of anything I wanted, so she took me into the toyshop in Priory Street and bought me a football and a mouth organ. By this time it was about midday, and all I could think of was the possibility that she had not had the morning fit, and she might have one while we were out together.

We reached home without incident, and I breathed again. I was told to take off my best suit and change back into my normal weekday clothes, and Polly removed the hair pieces covering her damaged scalp and washed away the crisp, white mask of make-up, and the bright chequer-board pattern of her cheeks and forehead reappeared.

That afternoon was an exceptionally pleasant one. I kicked the football about the back garden until I was tired, and when I went into the house Polly laid aside the bedspread she was crocheting and put the record on the gramophone which she had been persuaded to buy. It was one I enormously enjoyed, a favourite of the day, said to have been made on the battlefield in the First World War and one of a series that were avidly collected. Aunt Polly's record, 'Our Brave Boys at Vimy Ridge', featured a lead-in of patriotic music; a hymn in this case to Lord Roberts, 'Good Old Bobs of Kandahar', then the sounds of battle, the fixing of bayonets, the enthusiastic babel preceding the charge, a sustained rattle of gunfire punctuated with explosions – to which people listened with their heads stuck into the trumpet – and the faint cries either of triumph or anguish, then 'Good Old Bobs' once again. It was a record I never tired of listening to. The muscles under the mouth the surgeon had given Aunt Polly moved in what I now understood to be a smile of contentment. Although the day was Saturday she was wearing a Sunday dress, and was fragrant with Jockey Club.

The fit, when it took place in the afternoon as I suspected it would, was the shortest on record. Polly got up quietly, went off to the kitchen for her own personal battle, and was back in a matter of minutes. She bore no sign of damage, walked quite steadily, took up her work again, and, after a half-hour or so, was able to speak. She had bought cakes for tea. It may have been the most relaxed day I spent at Wellfield Road.

I was awakened that night by a series of tremendous crashes, the sound of splintering wood, of shouts and of running feet. I got up, fumbled my way down the dark back stairs into the kitchen where a light was on, then slipped through into the hallway to reach the bottom of the front staircase. The bathroom door at the top of the stairs had been smashed open with an axe, left standing against the wall, and pandemonium was going on in the bathroom. I went up the stairs, and Aunt Li in her nightgown, her hair in curlers standing up like a golli-wog's, rushed out of the bathroom to push me away, then dodged back inside again. Following her I saw Aunt Polly, also in her nightgown, who seemed to be stand-ing, very straight and stiff against the wall, held by

Grandfather who was struggling with something attached to her neck, while Annie in the background waved her arms up and down like a frantic bird about to take off. A moment passed before I realized that Polly was attached by the neck to a lamp bracket that had bent double under her weight, so that now she stood on tiptoe. It was a frozen instant in a scene overbrimming with activity, with flying shapes and shadows, and faces frenzied in the candlelight; Annie flapping up and down the bathroom; Grandfather's pyjama trousers falling over his ankles, his deep baying cries and bass sobs; Polly's thin falsetto breaking through with a psalm as soon as the cord was loosened from her throat; the smell of Jockey Club and urine.

Grandfather and Aunt Annie hauled Polly away to her bed and stood guard over her while Li went for the doctor, who at long length arrived and bustled up the stairs carrying a contraption of buckles and straps.

Two days later my mother arrived. During our separation she had changed slowly in my memory, becoming saint-like, calm, aloof and sedate. Now suddenly confronted with her in the flesh, she was a stranger, earthy and vigorous, but almost unrecognizable, and I was disappointed to find that I was less excited and pleased to see her again than I had expected to be, and unhappy with the self-sufficiency that I had developed.

Polly, released from constraint, had dressed and prepared herself most carefully for her reunion with her dearest friend and ally, and I could see that she was her old self once more, ready in her stoical and indomitable fashion, in the way of the hero of *Pilgrim's Progress*, to stand up to the many blows that life would continue to shower upon her. I find it hard to believe that Polly could have written the poison-pen letters. It was not compatible with her character, as I understood it. Nevertheless, even the strain of being under suspicion would have been enough to drive her to her attempted suicide.

Li had sad news for me. It was decided that I should go home with my mother, and we went on our last walk together to the top of Pen-lan. Although I was never able to remember anything else she told me, this I did. 'They're sending me away on holiday,' she said. She clenched her lips until they disappeared, and this, although she had ceased to cry while we were together, showed me that she was unhappy.

'I'm going to another house,' she said. 'A place with a garden. They don't keep cocks.' She brightened up at a thought that had occurred to her. 'They give you tea in the morning before you get up,' she said.

'That will be nice, Auntie,' I told her.

We walked back down the steep and narrow lane together, hand in hand. I was sorry for her. I didn't want either aunt to be sent away, but it seemed unfair that it had to be her, and not Polly.

Part Two

THE OTHER SIDE

Chapter Three

B ACK IN ENFIELD where my parents were, I found
that my father had become a Spiritualist medium.
When my mother unfolded the news she seemed charged
with joy, her eyes fixed as if on the opening of the
heavens to herald the second coming. The Spiritualist
revelation had banished the sorrows of this world, so let
us rejoice. My father, she indicated, was a prophet of the
new awakening. Whereas before I had sometimes
detected disparagement in her tone, now she spoke of
him with pride and respect.

Suddenly the quiet, rather dismal little house tucked
away behind the orchards was full of hushed, soft-footed
activity, and had acquired faint churchy scents. Gentle
smiling people came and went, exuding sympathy and
understanding; all of them extremely kind to me. Just
before my visit to Wales my surviving brother Monty,
aged seventeen, had died suddenly – and to me mysteriously – and now these smiling strangers who came to
our house took me in hand to explain to me that, much
as in my present state of spiritual development I was
unable to see him, he was in no remote heaven, but there
in the house as ever, a permanent, almost tangible
presence with whom I would soon communicate and
who would assure me in his own words that nothing had
changed between us, and that we were together as we
had always been. They congratulated me on my membership of a happy, united family. There had been two
other brothers I had never known. The first also had
sickened and died, also at the age of seventeen, in a

matter of days, and the second, dropped as an infant by a girl who was looking after him, was carried off by meningitis. My other brothers had left their earthly bodies in the cemetery at the top of the Lavender Hill too, but their astral and imperishable bodies were with us, and now that we were on the verge of communi- cation, the last of their sorrows had been overcome.

As I later understood it, Spiritualism was an inevitable reaction to the bereavements of the First World War which, in its harvest of death, had left hardly a family untouched. The established churches provided cold com- fort. Spiritualism made its bid for the allegiance of the bereaved with its proclamation, not that the souls of the dead awaited us in a Paradise the nature of which few could conceive, but that they were still at our sides, as we had known them. They remained eternally young, if young they had been before 'passing on' – grown only in wisdom – or if old, healed by death of the infirmities of age and, while still recognizable, restored to the vitality of youth.

Exposed daily to the reasonings and persuasions of these kindly people it was hard to reject out of hand what they had to tell me. In any case I was a small boy in the second form at Enfield Grammar School, and how could I possibly doubt the findings of such eminent men as Sir Arthur Conan Doyle, or of Sir Oliver Lodge and Sir William Crookes, described to me as two of the greatest scientists of our times, who had accepted and proclaimed the Spiritualist message?

Suddenly my father, a lonely, retiring man, had been thrust into local prominence, for it was around him that local adherents of the sect had gathered. He was a qualified chemist, who had been dismayed to learn after the three years of study preceding qualification, and three more in the research department of a well-known drug firm, that his only hope of earning a reasonable living was to open a chemist's shop. This he did in Southbury Road, Enfield, purely because the rents in this remote and run-down outer suburb were the lowest in the London area, and thereafter conducted a business, which he considered undignified, in a spiritless and lackadaisical manner. This was evidenced by a shop-window display, left undisturbed for many years, consisting of perhaps a hundred books on pharmacology and allied subjects, grouped round a box of Beechams Pills, and a card which said, 'I read all these, to sell this.'

His attitude towards practically all the proprietary medicines and advertised drugs he was forced to sell to pay his rent was one of bitter disillusionment, and he insisted that at best they were ineffective and at worst noxious. Faith, he earnestly believed, could move mountains, and the bodily condition corresponded to that of the mind. Even accidents, he believed, people brought upon themselves, and with the exception of young children, people died because they had had enough of life. When someone brought a prescription to be dispensed, he would skip through the dog Latin and often laugh his scorn, then send the customer away advising him not to allow himself to be poisoned. For those who insisted, despite his pleadings and his contempt, on being dosed, he supplied an 'elixir', containing nothing but garlic flavoured water, and a touch of quinine to impart the bitterness people demanded of anything they imagined likely to do them good. For this harmless but bitter and malodorous nostrum there was an immense demand – and eventually a franchise request from a pharmaceutical chain – and it was only this that kept the wolf from the door. It was the proceeds from the elixir that went to finance the building of the Spiritualist church – the Beacon of Light – in our back garden some years later.

Three years had passed since the last of my parents' losses, and now they faced life with new courage and hope. The Spiritualists had robbed death of its sting, and the grave of its victory, and they had formed this rapidly growing circle to communicate their convictions and their assurances to others, many of whom had suffered equal or worse bereavement.

Some problems arose over the spreading of the faith locally due to the complexities of the English class system. My parents had bought their semi-detached in Forty Hill, two miles from Enfield Town, once a pleasant enough place with a half-dozen Georgian houses occupied by minor gentry and three or four village shops, but latterly overwhelmed by housing development to meet the needs of factories to the east.

Four unplanned terraced streets with great, gaping water-logged holes among them from which the sand to mix with cement had been dug, now replaced the meadows and coppices of the old days. Their occupants, whose breadwinners cycled every day to Enfield lock or were employed on local estates, were working-class, excluded therefore from any of the groupings or gatherings of the lower middle class, to which most Spiritualists belonged, just as they themselves erected a barrier to keep out members of the gypsy minority living in the neighbourhood, or outright farm labourers whose existence was virtually ignored.

Spiritualism, then, had no local mass appeal, and my parents were forced at first to cast their net elsewhere to recruit adherents, many of whom they found among the shop-keeping class, and the office workers of Enfield Town and other outer suburbs of North London. A few middle-class people attended the seances, some of whom had made an apprehensive and shame-faced reconnaissance into this unfamiliar territory, but had then stayed on. One of them was Henri Le Bas, French master at the Grammar School, a man whom it was impossible not to like and respect. He had lost his only son in the war when, as he told my father, German sappers had set off a mine under a strongpoint at Verdun, defended by the boy and fifty comrades, of whom afterwards not a single trace was found. It was Le Bas's sincere belief that eventually, through my father, he would achieve the only thing he asked for in life – to be able to speak to the missing son. His conviction, because I knew and admired him, mattered much more to me than the testimony of distinguished British scientists of whom I knew nothing apart from their fame.

Le Bas and his wife, a little wizened, smiling French-woman with a very red face, were present at the first seance at which, by agreement with the members of the circle, I was invited to take part. It was thought unsuitable that, at thirteen years of age, my first introduction to Spiritualism should be at a seance when my father entered into a state of trance, so this seance was conducted by a visiting clairvoyant, a Mrs Carmen Flint, who proved to be business-like and a little abrupt and who shifted the position of every article of furniture and every object in the room before she settled to preside. Inevitably the seance took place in the gloomy middle room illuminated for this purpose by a single small red lamp, and an atmosphere was established by burning a cone of incense, and playing 'Dare to be a Daniel', and 'Art Thou Weary, Art Thou Languid?' on a musical box which only provided these two hymns.

Mrs Flint, who had been persuaded to journey some miles for this occasion and had been given a high tea, seemed a little critical of the arrangements. In addition to Le Bas and his wife, my mother and me, two members of the regular circle were present, a Mr Thresher who was a local auctioneer, and a Mrs Head, the manageress of the ABC in Lower Edmonton.

Mrs Flint found 'the conditions' poor, due possibly, she thought, to a lack of psychic development of the members of the circle; in my case, as well, to an incomplete aura. She explained, referring to the Le Bas couple, that the inclusion of 'seekers' in a circle as opposed to confirmed believers, while not damaging the vibrations, lessened the power. Nevertheless it was decided to go ahead with the seance and hope for the best. My own feelings at this moment were negative. While it was impossible wholly to resist the constant pressure to believe, I was probably too young in any case to feel much excitement or enthusiasm about what Spiritualism had to offer.

We now seated ourselves at a round table, lifted into the middle of the room, placing our hands on its surface in such a way that each of us made contact with our little fingers with those of our neighbours. Mr Thresher, who spoke in an exceptionally clear and deliberate way, probably as a result of his profession, then said, 'If any of our spirit friends are here with us this evening, perhaps they would indicate their presence in the usual way.' The table immediately rocked once.

'Thank you, friend,' Thresher said, 'for evincing your

desire to communicate with us. Would you please spell out your name?'

The table rocked three times.

'C, probably for Charles,' Thresher said. 'Conceivably Cyril. Would it be Charles?'

This time the table rocked once.

'Charles it is,' Thresher said. 'Now could we have the surname?'

Whereas until now the movements of the table had been very definite, this question met with some hesitation. The rocking became undecided and then stopped. This provoked a firm intervention from Mrs Flint, who had been against the use of the table from the beginning, saying that it used up too much power, and she could feel the conditions worsening. She advised us to put the table away and to sing a hymn to give the spiritual forces time for regeneration. We did this, and sang two verses of 'There's a Land That is Fairer Than Day'.

My father was anxious to convert Le Bas and through him, possibly, other masters at the Grammar School, and now suggested that he should try the planchette, a small board which ran on castors in which an upright pencil was fixed, and which fairly reliably produced messages. Mrs Flint showed herself impatient with this too, claiming that it would only prove an additional source of power loss, as well as distracting from the main purpose of the seance, which was her own demonstration of clairvoyance.

Nevertheless, the planchette and a sheet of paper were fetched. It required two persons to place a hand on it, and I was pleased, even flattered, when Madame Le Bas preferred that her husband should ask me to join him.

'Address the spirit friend or loved one with whom

you wish to communicate,' Thresher instructed, and Le Bas said, 'Jean-Paul, *es-tu là*?'

Immediately the board began to slide about under my hand. This took me by surprise, because I knew that I was not moving it, and I could not believe that Le Bas would do so – at least consciously. The pencil scribbled and wavered over the paper, then stopped, and I found that it had written a single sprawling word, barely recognizable as '*oui*'. Le Bas was trembling when Mrs Flint moved over to inspect this. She nodded in a distant and dissatisfied manner, and then informed us that such diversionary experiments would have to stop forthwith, because otherwise she would be obliged to abandon her demonstration.

Everyone present, with my exception, now joined in begging her to go ahead as planned. She then made us form a semi-circle with our chairs at one end of the room while she stood at the other, wearing a pink eyeshade, and carrying in her left hand a small white fan. Le Bas had been warned to bring some object that had belonged to his son, of whom, we were assured, Mrs Flint knew nothing. He gave her a leather wallet containing a religious medal. Mrs Flint took this, closed her eyes and caressed its surface with thumb and forefinger for a while. Her lips moved silently and she appeared to be on the point of speaking for some minutes before she finally spoke.

'I see a young man,' she said. 'He is trying to reach you from the other side. He has written something above your head. It is the letter J.'

'Yes,' Le Bas said. 'Yes.' His wife was holding his hand, and now he placed his other hand, which had been holding Mrs Head's, over hers.

'Do not break contact with the friend sitting next to you,' Mrs Flint said. 'You will interrupt the flow of power.'

Le Bas joined hands with Mrs Head again. 'The young man is slender, not tall,' said Mrs Flint, 'with brown hair – say light brown. I see him as he was when he passed on. I am taking on his condition, and I feel a pain in the leg. Did he limp?'

Le Bas seemed doubtful. He murmured something to his wife and she shook her head.

'Now the pain has moved to both legs, it has reached all the lower parts of the body. I feel this pain in the wrists, the fingers and the head. The condition I have taken on is connected with the passing.'

She was peering as if through a thick fog, then suddenly she shot out a finger over our heads. 'Now he has appeared again, and I see him very clearly. He is holding up a small object. He is waving it. I believe he is showing us a toothbrush. Does a toothbrush mean anything to you?'

'It does,' Le Bas said. 'My son was very fastidious about his appearance. He cleaned his teeth three times a day. We made a joke of it.'

'Showing you the toothbrush was to prove to you his reality in the astral world, and his love as a son. Now the contact is becoming weaker. I am to tell you he is always with you.'

With this, the seance was at an end. It was regarded as having been a success, and the atmosphere was congratulatory. The Le Bas family were moist-eyed but smiling. Madame Le Bas kissed Mrs Flint on both cheeks and her husband presented her with a bunch of tulips and a brooch. Mrs Flint said that the demonstration had been less than she had hoped for, and listed for my mother a number of ways in which conditions for any future sitting might be improved. She advised her to spend more time in meditation, and recommended a correspondence course in the subject called 'The Power of Thought', to which my mother later subscribed.

Mrs Flint, who had been given an enthusiastic build-up by my mother, disappointed me as a person. I found her manner sharp and officious, and I had been disillusioned at tea by the way she had pounced upon the Welsh rarebit, and the cup-cakes to follow. For all that her portrait of Jean-Paul seemed only explicable by her possession of extraordinary powers.

My father seemed to me to remain strangely aloof in these transactions. He had joined somewhat mechanically in the hymn singing, but beyond polite exchanges had little to say. I sensed a reluctance on his part to become involved on this occasion, or perhaps to be dragged in by my mother. She had asked him to demonstrate the planchette, but he had asked to be excused. I sensed, too, the possibility of an underlying antagonism stemming from a conflict of personalities. 'I am in charge, here,' Mrs Flint had announced in a cautionary way at the beginning of the seance. There was no doubt that she had been informed that my father was a 'direct voice' trance medium, bound therefore to attract more attention than a mere clairvoyant in any such gathering of the faithful. My father, too, was an amateur, she a professional with a regular classified advertisement in the Spiritualist press. Such were the tensions, the trivial jealousies, the thrust for recognition affecting those with a vision of the other world, who communed with the dead and looked into the future, as much as for the rest of us.

Following this first sitting, it seemed that I had qualified, at least on a probationary level, for inclusion in our circle, and my mother began to speak of preparation for the great experience of a direct voice seance, conducted by my father, which several dignitaries of the movement living in various parts of London would be invited to attend. When pressed by my mother to set a date for this event it seemed to me that he was in no hurry.

I saw as much as I could of my father at weekends, or on Wednesday afternoons when he was free from business, and I hurried home from school. He was an excellent companion for a child, because his personality was childlike, and he was strikingly immature in his enthusiasms. In appearance he was my grandfather's son, but was less competent than my grandfather, less ambitious, less attracted to money, power and prestige and the things of this world. Had my grandfather thought of the elixir, he would have contrived a way of inducing every man, woman and child in South Wales to drink it, have built himself a baronial folly, and bought another useless car with the proceeds. Instead, my father put up a chapel in his garden and, in what room was left, set up an aviary in which he kept such exotic birds as would withstand the terrible climate. He also bred, with great success, a rare and extraordinary form of poultry called Polish Fancy, a small black bird having a crest like a snowball of feathers, making it almost impossible for it to see its food. It amused him to hypnotize these birds by stroking them gently then laying them on their sides, where they remained in this position until released by a snap of the fingers.

Although from my standpoint my father's life seemed bleak, even tragic, he was extremely lucky in small ways, and it fascinated me to note that when we sometimes amused ourselves by throwing dice, the law of averages seemed to be suspended in his favour and his score was consistently higher than mine. He invariably won at card games, but what impressed me far more was that when we visited fairs together – which we frequently did in summer – we invariably went home laden with the atrocious china ornaments won off hoop-la stalls. Sometimes the owner of a stall begged him to take his custom elsewhere and I was bathed in his reflected glory.

England, although he enjoyed the cherry orchards through which we wandered together, remained wholly a foreign country to him. After his caning at the Pentrepoeth school, he had lost most of his Welsh, but could never speak English except in a deliberate and premeditated way, like a foreigner, and occasionally, when words or phrases were missing he patched these in with pieces of hastily invented gibberish.

In analysing the difference between the people of Celtic Britain and the rest (the Saxons, as he still insisted on calling them), he concluded that it was largely a matter of the presence or absence of mistletoe in their respective countries. No mistletoe grew in the vicinity of Enfield, but in Carmarthen it abounded. My father arranged for many thousands of berries to be sent to him in the hope of remedying the situation. For some weeks we occupied ourselves sticking these on the branches of trees in our garden, on those of our friends, and then in the public parks, and by next year the plants were growing everywhere, many on trees in which it was believed that mistletoe would not establish itself, and there was an exchange of mystified letters on the subject in the Enfield *Gazette and Observer*.

Our home became the meeting place of people from all over North London having in common an insatiable capacity for belief and a detestation of the sceptic with his blinkered vision and closed mind. They drew together to probe the secrets of death and those of the future, and encouraged each other to look inwards in search of hidden powers they might possess. On a low level of achievement my parents' friends practised such fairground skills as palmistry and phrenology, and told each other's fortunes, inspiring what hope they could with the aid of the crystal ball, tea-leaves, Arabian numerology, pendulums, playing cards, a study of the 'Aura', or even of the flight of birds. All this was crammed somehow or other into a Christian framework, although they were tolerant of intrusion from any other religion. On Sunday evenings the seance was renamed a service, and Mr Thresher, the auctioneer, would read in his reverberant and confident voice a prayer or a passage from the Book of Revelations. Then we would sing 'Lead Kindly Light' before Mrs Head delivered an address, and my father might give a demonstration of clairvoyance which did not particularly impress me, although it was often rapturously received by those singled out in the audience.

After a year or so's correspondence course in psychic unfoldment my mother had progressed to a point when she could conduct a healing session by laying on hands. A feature of the preparation had been two hours' daily meditation in our front room which, with the advice of friends and the gift or loan of oriental bric-à-brac she had turned into something like a temple, reeking of joss sticks, and containing such items as a lingam, the purpose of which she was doubtful, a Tibetan prayer-flag, and a tinkling wind bell imported from Burma by a neighbour who claimed to have been in the Colonial Service. The same widely travelled man assured my mother that the spirits of orientals who had passed on would be more likely to be attracted to my father's seances by the beating of a gong than by the musical box. A fair proportion of the regulars claimed to have easterners such as Hindu ascetics and Buddhist monks as their spirit 'guides', so a pagoda gong was found and installed in a corner of the middle room, and from then on my mother struck this once at the start of a seance, filling the room with soft and solemn vibrations before the musical box tinkled out 'Dare to be a Daniel', and the proceedings got under way.

Very soon, with the advance on the psychic front, the time came when the Sunday congregation could no longer be fitted into the house, and had to be moved out into the garden, while the service was conducted through the kitchen window. The local church at Forty Hill began to feel the effects of the competition, and the congregation on Sunday at evensong dropped to an average of five. My mother, giving free treatment to patients on most evenings, may have hit the medical trade, for a Dr Distin wrote to the paper, complaining as a Christian of those who tampered with forces they did not understand, and defied God's laws by calling up the spirits of the dead.

Dr Distin's letter only served to provide welcome publicity, and the seances increased in frequency, with

ever growing attendance. Pushed forward by my parents
I joined most of them. In the first weeks curiosity helped,
but then my interest began to wane, and it was no more
than a matter of duty, and boredom set in. Twice a week
a clairvoyant would stand up to give tidings from the
Other Side. Their information seemed to me vague and
uninteresting, and above all unimportant.

'Do the initials GHW mean anything to you?'

'They belong to my Aunt Heather.'

'And the name "Rosedale"?'

'That was the house she lived in.'

'She asks if you remember Torquay, and the boat
trip?'

'Yes, I do. Very well. We had a wonderful time.'

Often the evidence offered appeared blurred and
generalized.

'A girl is standing at your side. She has very long,
dark hair.'

'I don't think I know of anyone with hair like that.'

'She passed on many years ago.'

'It could be my sister Mary. She had dark hair.'

'She says to you, "I have unfolded my wings."' (Mrs
Head whispers to the sitter, 'That means she's become
an angel', and the woman smiles with a trace of pride.)

Many of the revelations from the other world were on
the level of messages scribbled in haste on holiday
postcards by writers who could think of nothing much
to say. I soon discovered that the spirits of the dead had
no sense of humour, and there was a terrible flatness, a
lack of enthusiasm in their communications suggestive
of convalescence, fatigue, even boredom. Sometimes
messages from beyond the grave were fragmentary and
meaningless like the random sentences of radio hams,

intent only in testing their equipment. Once when a sitter put the point-blank question, 'What is it like in the Beyond?', he received an answer Hemingway might have given. 'It is good.'

The great and long awaited moment of my brother 'getting through' came when belief was weakening but before all my illusions had collapsed.

'I see a boy, aged about seventeen,' said the medium. 'He is wearing a peaked cap, and a short jacket, and is carrying what appears to be a musical instrument. Will someone claim him?'

It was still hard for me to articulate in the presence of adults, but this was an occasion of such urgency that it was impossible not to speak up, and I forced the words to come. 'It's my brother,' I said. 'He used to play in a band.'

'Have you a message for him?' the medium asked.

'I would like to ask him where he is,' I said.

'He tells you he is in another place. He wishes you and his mother and father not to go to Lavender Hill to look for him. He is not there. There must be no more flowers.'

My disappointment was crushing. My brother, once frank and open, had become guarded and evasive, sounding as I would have imagined like a prisoner answering a visitor's questions in the presence of a warder. Another issue came into this which I had already taken up with my mother. Why should my brother, who had been an excellent musician in life, and whose favourite composer was Bach, now be attracted, as she assured me he would be, by the simple and even sickly melodies of her musical box? Why should our neighbour Mr Olding, who had been on the editorial staff of *The Times*, and a mine of lively information and comment, have nothing more to say of eternity than, 'I read a little sometimes. It's very pleasant here. I sleep on a small bed'?

Many of the spirits too seemed, so far as anything could be learned of their activities, to be engaged in trivial occupations. All Spiritualists – some claimed all human beings – had spirit guides, most of whom, it appeared, had been persons of significance in their life on Earth. Now these once distinguished entities found themselves at the beck and call of earthlings who, for the most part, lived unremarkable existences. My mother's first guide had been a Red Indian – they were very popular in the movement – but now she had moved up to a French lady, once at the court of Louis XVI and Marie Antoinette, who had passed on at the time of the French Revolution in tragic circumstances. Besides monitoring my mother's spiritual evolution she also advised her on household matters, and had been recently responsible for the redecoration of the middle room, which seemed to me to have been carried out in deplorable taste.

My mother had done a little to prepare me for what to expect at my first trance seance with my father, although the reality remained shocking. I was embarrassed, feeling myself in some way personally affected by my father's gross loss of dignity, and longed for the strength of character that would have enabled me to get up and leave the room.

My father sat writhing in his chair as if under torture. His hands were clenched, his eyes closed, his cheeks covered in sweat and tears, and, rolling his head from side to side, he emitted the most blood-chilling sounds. The circle consisted of twelve persons, including Mr and Mrs Le Bas, our hands touching as usual. The light from the red lamp was less than that of a single candle, and I had been warned by my mother of the dreadful consequences at such a time, causing the medium's insanity or even his death, of switching on a strong light or startling him in any other way.

Incense smoke curled from a joss stick, the musical box had tinkled into silence, and my father mouthed and blabbered, watched by the sitters, of which little but expectant faces showed in the lamp–lit gloom. There was spittle on my father's lips and chin, he opened his mouth wide as if half-strangled, and an incoherent gush of words came from his throat: the voices of men, of women and young children, some calm, some shrill, some argumentative; the sound of drunken brawling, a snatch of a sea shanty, then the mixture of voices again, none separable from the other. Later I was to conclude that this was, and probably always had been, the performance of a medium the world over, because many years after this I realized that the almost inhuman sounds made by the medium in the film *Rashomon*, set in medieval Japan, were precisely those produced by my father at this moment.

Something had gone wrong. Although my mother had explained to me that my father was highly esteemed for his gifts, his development was unsatisfactory, as he had no control over the spirits who spoke through him. Hence the chaos at this moment, the great disorderly queue of souls all demanding to be heard, none of them subject to the discipline a developed medium knew how to impose.

Her method of dealing with this crisis was to stand over my father and wave her arms in his face with stern commands, whenever an unacceptable – and often ribald

– voice became audible, of, 'Step out, friend. Please step out.' This took effect, the babel quietened leaving a residue of disconnected words, of sense and nonsense drifting into soft muttering, then silence.

There followed a lucid passage of trite uplift that might have been attributed by the sitters equally to my father himself, or an occupying spirit, but this was soon crowded out by the invading voices, producing from my mother more agitated gestures of exorcism. Once again her arm-wavings produced results and the interlopers were silenced. Then suddenly and with absolute clarity a voice called out, '*Papa! Où êtes-vous?*'

With this outcry the seance achieved its purpose and came to an end. A single audible question had squeezed through a chink of silence in all these unstrung sounds, and this litter of random words. The only comfort it could offer to Le Bas and his wife seemed a cold one. Even if their son had reached them across the barrier of death, he seemed to have come as a wandering spirit, lost, displaced, searching as desperately for them as they for him. This was only the second contact, and my mother assured them that there were better things to come. With the sitting over, my mother resuscitated my father, who returned gasping and groaning to normality. We then tidied up the proceedings with a verse from 'The Sweet By and By' and a polite vote of thanks proposed by Mr Thresher to the spirit friends who had encouraged and assisted us by their presence. Mr and Mrs Le Bas had stolen away into the kitchen where they fell into each other's arms.

For me it was the first of many such experiences. Having at first been persuaded to join in the seances for the sake of the spiritual benefits to be derived from them, my presence was now welcomed and sought after for the new reserve of psychic power I was believed to provide. Mrs Flint, returning to us after a recreative absence of some months, and sniffing at me like a retriever, had carried out a fresh investigation of my aura, which she said, had made astonishing progress. From being dim and flaccid in the previous year, it was glowing and vibrant, to be seen as a violet radiation, particularly marked in the areas of the temples, the stomach and the palms of the hands. This was later confirmed by a visiting 'astra-aural physicist' who arrived with a smoked-glass screen through which he and the members of the circle inspected me in turn, and agreeing that this was so. Like many people steered by the pressure of custom to profess a religion to which in reality they have hardly given a thought, I neither believed nor disbelieved these things. It gave my mother and father great pleasure when I offered lipservice to their convictions, but at heart the best I could manage was indifference, coloured with scepticism. My father made progress in the matter of control, and his direct voice seances were less subject to disturbance, but whatever the voices speaking through him told us, it was nothing of significance, and life beyond the grave remained insubstantial. Slowly the image I had of my brother was beginning to fade from my memory and there was nothing in the few disjointed phrases that reached me from across the void that could recreate anything of him as he had been. I had read somewhere that the ancient Egyptians had done what they had done, carried out their great works and built their enduring monuments in fear of, and in the hope of mitigating, what death might hold for them. It was a fear, I had come to believe, that was wholly justified.

The dramatic change in Mrs Flint's attitude, coupled with the marked interest shown in me by the members of the circle, set me wondering where it could all be leading to. My mother had taken to questioning me in a way that seemed ludicrous, as well as faintly embarrassing. Did I hear voices? Of course, in the same way as anyone else did. She meant inner voices. I never heard them, I told her. If I ever did, I'd let her know. Well, then – visions? To give an example, she mentioned unaccountable lights seen in the darkness. Once again I had to disappoint her. For me the dark remained dark. Did I ever feel unseen presences in a room? I was beginning to feel guilty at letting her down, but I had to admit that I had never had this sensation. Some people could read the thoughts of others. Had I experienced anything like that? I shook my head regretfully. My mother remained undismayed. I was still at an early stage in my psychic development, open too to the disruptive influence of negative forces that were encouraging me to resist. It seemed kinder to agree with her that this was so.

Mrs Head tackled me. 'You are very gifted,' she said.
'I don't see why.'
'We go by the power you bring to a seance. When you join with us the manifestations are so much stronger. We are all helped by your new guide. He has great spiritual force.'

It had been explained to me that I had received a kind of spiritual promotion, following which my first guide, a Methodist minister in a Welsh coal-mining town in this life, who sounded a dull man in our sparse communication through my father, had been replaced by a Tibetan lama.

The lama was imbued with the authority and the incontrovertible wisdom of the East. The interest flattered me and I was gratified for the sake of my parents, because the upgrading advanced their standing among their friends just as if I'd done particularly well in my school examinations. The possibility was slowly emerging that my parents hoped that I would one day become a Spiritualist medium. The pressures and the constant suggestion to which I was submitted made it hard for me to oppose this ambition. Instead, remembering the years that lay ahead before adult decisions would have to be taken, I was content to be carried along by the tide.

Following my experiences in Wellfield Road, Carmarthen, I had adopted a posture of non-commitment like a personal camouflage. I never argued, seldom offered a point of view. Nothing was impossible, but I had no real faith in marvels. When a visiting clairvoyant told me the date on a penny I was carrying in my pocket I felt no special surprise, and my only internal comment was, what does it matter? The house was full of poltergeist sounds that might have excited anyone else's curiosity, but they left me indifferent. Several times of an evening when we were sitting alone in the kitchen there would be a loud rap, seemingly on the face of the clock, which my mother and father, accepting the presence of a 'spirit friend', would cheerfully acknowledge with some welcoming phrase, and at first I was reprimanded for my breach of good manners in failing to do the same. Occasionally, when we went on a visit to friends, we exported the phenomenon with us, and my parents would allude to the sudden interruption from the beyond in a pleasant and proprietorial way, while I was inclined to say, 'Rap, did you say? I didn't hear one.'

It was probably in an attempt to kindle a livelier interest that I was taken to London to witness a demonstration given by a materialization medium, Miss Mildred Frogley, who had once come to our house, and who possessed the rare power, shared by only two other mediums in the country, of reinvesting the spirits of the dead with their human form of old.

Neither my mother, my father, nor any member of their circle had seen a 'materialization' before, and they promised the supreme experience of my life, as they assured me it would be of theirs. For a week before the trip my mother spent most of the time in deep meditation, hoping in this way to conduce to the success of the materialization, even, perhaps – as she admitted – to assist one of our own loved ones to take visible shape.

The small London hall was crowded, full of the soft murmurings of anticipation against a background of sacred music played by a white-haired pianist in tails on a grand piano, with the accompaniment of a lady harpist. After a brief address Miss Mildred Frogley was introduced.

I immediately remembered her, because she had been younger than most of our visitors, and almost pretty, with malformed teeth but a sweet smile, and a soft, kind voice, and above all devoid of the pretentiousness which seemed to affect many of the mediums we had dealings with. I became intensely interested in what was about to happen.

The back of the stage and the boards themselves were covered in a dark material, and apart from the grand piano the only article of furniture it contained was an armchair, to the back of which had been fixed a dim red light, spherical in shape and hardly bigger than an orange. Miss Frogley wore a plain navy blue dress, high at the neck, and with long sleeves. When she sat in the chair the light was two or three metres above her head. She closed her eyes, and her lips moved as if she were saying a prayer. In the ordinary way her teeth seemed to show, but now, with her mouth closed and her head thrown back, she seemed really pretty in a religious way, like the picture of a saint. The lights were switched off, and I could see nothing of her but her face, suspended under the lamp.

Nothing happened for a long time. A soft-voiced choir sang a lullaby, came to its end and began again. Presently, as my eyes got used to the darkness, I could see something moving in sort of stealthy undulation like the umbrella of a jellyfish down close to Miss Frogley's ankles. Her head was rolling from side to side, and her mouth had opened. She was moving her hands about in a rhythmic way, like an oriental dancer, and the jellyfish stuff, which I took to be what the Spiritualists called ectoplasm, was gradually building up and taking shape as what could have been a veiled figure. Then somewhere in the darkness behind us, a torch flashed and Miss Frogley, the ectoplasm trailing from her hands, was illuminated by a sudden beam. She jumped up with a little scream, someone shouted, there were cries of protest and the lights came on. Men broke away from others trying to hold them back and rushed the stage, and the last I saw of Miss Frogley was as she was being half-dragged, half-carried away, dragging a collapsed parachute of ectoplasm which in the strong stage lighting looked remarkably like curtain material.

My father burned the *Daily Mail* next morning within

minutes of its arrival, leaving its tell-tale ashes in the empty grate. The position he and my mother had taken up was that this was just another shocking instance of the malicious interference of an ill-wisher who had not only put a stop to the arduous and difficult processes of materialization, but had placed the medium's life in jeopardy.

Their story failed to impress me. On my way to school I used a penny, constituting one-third of my weekly pocket money, to buy a paper where the headline 'Medium's Hoax Exposed' was spread across an inside page. Miss Frogley, said the paper, denied the allegation that twelve yards of chiffon found on the stage had been concealed in her vagina, which had been operated on to permit the accommodation of so much material. Her unmasking had no effect whatever upon my attitude towards Spiritualism, and I imagine that went for most Spiritualists too, who could take such setbacks in their stride.

I was sorry that my parents should have wasted their money and had a disappointing evening out, but I knew their faith had only been strengthened, if that were possible, by the paper's opprobrium and scorn. Most of all I was sorry for Miss Frogley, whom I still enormously preferred to the unshakeable Mrs Flint; sorry too, that we should not see her again.

Forty Hill had a strangely unfinished look, fostered perhaps by its haphazard sandpits, and could quite well have been a settlement in rural Turkey where building materials were precious. Its landmarks were the Urban

District Council's rubbish dump smouldering incessantly like a pigmy Etna at one end of the village, and the large, but never quite completed parish church at the other.

The Vicar in those days was Canon Carr-Smith who, with his glowing pink cheeks and white beard, looked like an embittered Father Christmas. The Canon had only just taken over the living, which must from his point of view have been a discouraging one. The church, a cut-price Victorian Gothic structure, stood in an untidy thicket all too convenient for the villagers as a public lavatory, and few pews were occupied for a service. In the autocratic days of the present squire's father, farm workers were checked off against his factor's list at the church door, and failure to attend entailed the deduction of two shillings from the week's wages, averaging sixteen shillings a week at the time. As soon as compulsion was removed, the farm workers stayed away and joined the proletarian abstainers of Goat Lane, none of whom had ever set foot inside the church.

A full complement of thirty or so shopkeepers, retired persons and impoverished gentry turned up in force for the Canon's first service, where he was to be judged by a single yardstick; whether or not, as he entered the church, he bowed to the altar. The Canon bowed, and instantly lost half of his small flock. What little popularity he retained ebbed swiftly as a result of his authoritarian manner and the emphatic expression of his dislikes. For example, he detested small boys like myself, whom he described as filthy animals, sometimes waylaying one to bellow in his ear, 'Purge me with hyssop and I shall be clean.' When the Canon found his Sunday evening congregation reduced to five elderly ladies and the permanent staff of a churchwarden, the bell-ringer and the

organist, he was ready to blame the Spiritualist oppo-
sition and preached a sermon entitled 'Oh Ye of Little
Faith', then went to Colonel Sir Henry Ferryman Bowles
of Forty Hall, the lord of the manor, to discuss what if
anything could be done to uproot the dangerous heresy
that had taken root in his parish.

The Colonel was a phenomenon of English rural life
hardly changed since the invention of the open-field
system of agriculture. He had represented Enfield as a
Tory MP longer than anyone could remember – although
he had never made a speech in Parliament – he wielded
huge and uncontested power, paid the lowest wages in
the county, and was understood to possess a harem of
three young, gracious and well-bred girls. Nobody in
the village begrudged him these. It was assumed that the
ruling classes, compelled by custom to eat meat every
day, suffered sexual desires from which the peasantry
were spared by a diet which included meat only once a
week and limited sexual activity to Saturday nights. The
poor applied different moral standards in their judgement
of the rich. They knew only too well from the accounts
of those who served them what went on in the big
houses, but they had a sneaking admiration for their
casual adulteries and their calmly supported cuckoldries.
In Goat Lane spouses remained on the whole faithful
because they had not the time or the energy to do
anything else. Also they had hardly more privacy than
goldfish in their bowls.

About two years before this I had actually met the
Colonel, when I rang the front door bell of the Hall and
asked his permission through the butler to go birdnesting
on his estate. The Colonel came on the scene and
permission was instantly granted. He glanced down at

his watch and said regretfully that he would have come with me but for the fact that he had to chair a meeting of the Primrose League, an association of toilers for the Conservative cause. He seemed delighted to talk to me, relaxed perhaps, as a painful stammerer, in the company of someone who could hardly formulate his words at all. Before he let me go he insisted on taking me to see workmen engaged in digging a trench across his splendid lawn leading to the lake. Down this channel, he assured me, the electricity would flow harmlessly into the water should his house ever be struck by lightning again, as had just happened. It was his own idea, he said, and he could not imagine why nobody seemed to have thought of it before.

Sir Henry was our British village version of a Mafia chieftain, although by comparison Giuseppe Genco Russo, a much larger-scale landowner and head of the Sicilian Mafia whose character and doings I had occasion to study at a later date, was a progressive and socially responsible man, and I cannot imagine that Giuseppe would have recommended – as Sir Henry did, speaking on the bench – the re-introduction of man-traps to put an end to poaching. Both men rewarded their friends and dealt with their enemies after their own manner. The main difference between them in their respective feudal environments was that Giuseppe was companionable and relatively democratic. If a peasant came up to him in the dejected square of his home town, Mussomeli, and bent to kiss his ring, Giuseppe would embrace the man over whom he exercised power of life and death, and invite him to have a drink. Sir Henry – although not for me – remained aloof and God-like, isolated from such contacts by his underlings. Sir Henry owned the houses his workers lived in, and they were entirely dependent upon him for work. If any of them quarrelled they would go up to the Hall together and, just as Giuseppe did, Sir Henry would settle the dispute on the spot, in the way, short-circuiting the lawyers, that such disputes had been dealt with since the Norman Conquest. If a man displeased him – as for example in the case of a tenant who put up an election poster for the Liberal candidate – Sir Henry's factor paid him a visit, not armed in Sicilian style with a sawn-off shotgun but in the English fashion of the period with the no less deadly threat of destitution. Ninety-five per cent of the electors of Forty Hill, few of them believing in the true secrecy of the ballot, cast their votes for Sir Henry, and his supporters were invited annually to a lavish entertainment at the Hall, with swings, roundabouts and coconut shies for their children in the grounds. Liberal and Labour voters, besides being certain of defeat, were debarred from these pleasures and other small inducements, such as sick-bed visits from the charitable ladies of Sir Henry's Primrose League, with which loyalty was rewarded.

As my family owned their own house in a tiny enclave of independence called The Freehold, a call from Sir Henry's factor to investigate the facts of Spiritualism would have been unsuitable. Instead my mother received a visit from a Miss Phoebe Tupperton, a young relation of Sir Henry's whose branch of the family had fallen upon hard times, and who had come to live with her mother in one of his houses.

Miss Tupperton was one of the three young ladies forming, as it was supposed in the village, Sir Henry's harem and who, by gossip conveyed through servants at the Hall, shared his company with each other on a one-month-in-three system. She was tall, willowy and beautiful, with the famous English upper-class clear complexion, based on plain but nutritious food, plenty of exercise and a damp climate. She appeared a member of a different race from the village girls who lived on suet puddings and chips, thus clogging their cells with starch, and in consequence had murky skins and heavy, brooding expressions like young feminine versions of Beethoven. This ethereal presence in the village caused some excitement among the village youth, who formed a club to exchange gossip and personal fantasies about her, and thus stimulate each other to acts of indecency.

The visit to my mother took place without warning, and therefore at an unpropitious moment. My mother dared not risk damage to the favourable vibrations gradually built up in the front room set aside for meditation, and the middle room was piled with Spiritualist paraphernalia of all descriptions, so Miss Tupperton was seated, gracious and smiling, at the end of the kitchen table, as far as possible from the work area, and slowly the inevitable odour of cooking vegetables was suppressed by that of Coty.

I was just home from school when this encounter took place. For the first time I was within a matter of feet of the woman I suspected of being the most beautiful in the world, and I was intoxicated, almost faint, after inhaling the assorted fragrances of her body spreading through the atmosphere of our kitchen, whether negative or polluted. I longed for her to become a Spiritualist.

What must it be like, I wondered, for this splendid and delicate creature, accustomed as she was to the palatial settings of the Hall, to find herself in a room with steamed-up windows, decorated by a framed advertisement for Wright's Coal Tar Soap, a stuffed rat in a case having a fifth paw growing from the side of a thigh, and a plaster angel on the mantelpiece clasping a tiny box which I knew to contain the cured thumb of one of the crew of the Zeppelin shot down in flames in the year 1916 at Cuffley, two miles away.

I scuttled about, pushing out of sight such unappetizing sights as the dog's bowl with the turkey's feet it had not been able to finish. There was nothing to be done about the mouse-nibbled chair, which was sacrosanct since a visiting medium had reported seeing the ghost of James IV of Scotland seated on it the year before. Miss Tupperton appeared not to notice these things. Small silver bells chimed in her voice as she asked my mother if it was true that she was a spiritual healer, and my mother readily agreed that she was.

She had read some criticism of her activities by a local medical man in the *Gazette and Observer*, Miss Tupperton said, who had even suggested that what she was doing might be illegal. My mother told her that she had seen the letter too, but that according to advice she had received from the association to which she belonged she was doing nothing wrong. She laid no claim to medical knowledge, gave no medical advice, and charged nothing for her services, which were wholly concerned with the treatment of the psyche, or if Miss Tupperton preferred the word, the mind.

In making her point my mother's tone was conciliatory and affable. She told me later that she found Miss Tupperton exceedingly charming, and quite devoid of upper-class affectation of a kind that seemed often to produce an asphyxiating effect on people struggling for a foothold on the lower rungs of society.

'Could you explain just how this is done?' Miss
Tupperton asked winningly, and my mother explained
that by communing with the infinite she was able to
switch on something that felt like a current coursing
through her, which then, as a healing force, flowed out
on contact with a human body through her hands.

'And you place your hands on the affected bodily
part?' Miss Tupperton asked.

'Where possible,' my mother said. 'Or in the case of
the internal organs, as near as I can get to them. Healers
who have reached a higher degree of development than
myself are able to heal at a distance. Even by post.'

Miss Tupperton shook her head in sweet wonder,
scattering soft lights through her hair. 'Would you show
me your hands?' she asked.

My mother wiped her hands, which were permanently
damp from the sink. They were almost as large as a
man's, with stubby fingers, reddened and coarse from
work. The lines which interest students of palmistry had
become grooves in the soggy flesh of the palms; there
were roughnesses left by ancient chilblains over the
knuckles; and the fingernails were broad and flat, slightly
corrugated, cracked in places, and flaked with archipela-
goes of white spots of a kind said to derive from a
calcium deficiency.

Miss Tupperton gazed down at them with the deepest
interest, and possibly amazement. She caressed my
mother's splayed-out fingertips with her own, which
were as smooth and as delicately tapering as those of a
porcelain Chinese goddess of mercy which had been
recently brought from Hong Kong and added to my
mother's collection by a grateful patient she had cured of
long-standing arthritis in the knees. 'How wonderful it

THE OTHER SIDE

must be to have found such a mission,' Miss Tupperton said, and my mother agreed in her rather flat, downright manner.

'What do the people who come to you tend to suffer from?'

'Well, headaches,' my mother said. 'Headaches they can't get rid of.'

'Only headaches?'

'Backaches, too. Bad legs, varicose vein trouble. Fallen arches. A lot of people suffer with the kidneys these days. Half of it's in the mind.'

'Do you ever treat them for stomach troubles?' Miss Tupperton asked.

'Once in a while, but two pennyworth of castor oil usually does the trick. It's the people who are out of tune with the psychic forces that I can help. I give them a fresh start along the right path. After that they manage for themselves.'

'The healing process,' Miss Tupperton said. 'Is this something an outsider like me is allowed to see?'

'There's nothing secret or mysterious about it,' my mother said. 'It's no different from first aid. I work without bandages and splints, that's all. We hold a simple service on Sunday evenings, and anyone who cares to can join in. After that those who require healing stay on, and I do what I can for them.' Something occurred to her. 'Is there any way in which I can be of help to you?'

'Not personally,' Miss Tupperton said. She tinkled brief laughter. 'Let's say not at this moment, thank goodness. I'm terribly interested in what you do, but I wasn't thinking of myself.'

'It doesn't matter who comes to me in search of help,' my mother said. 'All are welcome, irrespective of their

73

beliefs, and no appointment is required. Some Sundays I
may deal with a dozen requests for healing. Sometimes
nobody comes. I'm always there if called upon, and you
don't have to sit in a waiting room. There's nothing
miraculous in what I do. I'm dealing with a body in a
state of rebellion against the psyche, and I try to put a
stop to that rebellion.'

Miss Tupperton shook her head in wonderment. What
a great day it would be for me, I thought, if only my
mother could make a Spiritualist of her.

'Come along if you can,' my mother told her. 'I can't
promise you any great surprises, but I think you'll find it
a happy experience.'

Miss Tupperton said she would very much like to
come, and thought she might be able to.

The seance preceding the service and the healing on this
particular Sunday night was a very special one. It was to
be conducted by a celebrated medium, brought at some
cost from Sydenham, whose speciality was the employment of a trumpet through which the spirits made direct
communication, speaking therefore quite independently
of aid provided by the human vocal cords, and in voices
recognizable to those who had known them before
passing on.

There was a touch of hard-edged professionalism
about these proceedings of which Mrs Carmen Flint
would have heartily approved. The medium, a dark,
stern-faced young man arrived with a middle-aged Indian
lady assistant with a red spot painted on her forehead,
and a portmanteau full of equipment. The medium and
his assistant scampered through the downstairs rooms,

checking them for their vibrations and astrological align-
ment, lighting incense cones and making sure that when
the lights were turned off not a chink of daylight could
be seen through the curtains. The use of my mother's
musical box and her gong were spurned, instead of
which the lady assistant plucked the strings of what
might have been an Indian zither for a few moments,
before the lights were turned out, and the seance began.

Instantly the room was filled with the sounds of
shuffling, bustling movement; there were soft winged
bats in the darkness above us and a strong breeze as if
from an electric fan stirred my hair. A muffled mega-
phone hooting began in the darkness several feet above
my head, then, linked to a sound of the kind a balloon
makes when suddenly deflated, blew itself away round
the invisible cornices.

The bats flapped back, there was a sound – reverently
received by the sitters, no doubt – of an artificially
prolonged fart, a gush of gibberish, some insane tittering,
a catcall, the drone of a preacher in an unknown
language, then a few lucid sentences on some insignificant topic. Just before the lights went on, something like
slobber splashed copiously across my cheek and lips,
and a moment later the other sitters gathered to congratulate me as a recipient of materialized spittle from the
beyond.

The supreme moment of surprise and delight followed
when one of the sitters, putting his hand into his jacket
pocket, discovered something unexpected and brought it
out, holding a small spherical object, in appearance like a
badly-made marble, upon which mystic signs had been
painted. This was an 'apport', also from the other world,
and a moment later there were cries of astonished

pleasure as more apports turned up in pockets and handbags. Communication with the other side had been less than satisfactory, the medium explained, through various adverse circumstances which he listed, but he hoped that the apports would help to compensate for that. He was assured that they would.

For me this was a wretched performance, and I was immensely grateful that my mother had held back from persuading Miss Tupperton to be present.

The laying-on of hands took place, as it often did on a fine summer's evening, in the garden. A number of chairs had been grouped in a cleared space in front of a greenhouse full of pot plants on which my father was endeavouring to grow mistletoe, and here the patients awaited my mother's ministrations.

There were seven of them, all women, and Dr Distin had given them up. They were all imprisoned in the long humdrum years called middle age, which here occupied the half of a lifetime. Their bodies had lost shape, were over-fat or distorted into crippled angularities. They suffered from stiffness of the joints, swollen knees, pains that rejected diagnosis, skin ulcers, bed-wetting and bad dreams, and, although they often wore expressions of shallow satisfaction, despair masquerading under as many forms as the death which waited so many years ahead cast its long shadow upon them.

My mother had learned that in some of the more stubborn cases the purely spiritual processes of the laying-on of hands could be bolstered by at least a pretence of manipulation, about which at this stage she knew nothing, although she had begun to study this also by correspondence. The illustration to the first lesson, to deal with fibrositis of the neck, had shown something like a simple ju-jitsu hold to be followed by a sharp tug, and on this occasion the method was used for the first time. Other bodily parts that had resisted the power of thought were kneaded and pounded in accordance with instructions, and in all cases my mother was rewarded by claims of instant relief.

The medium and his assistant, who had packed away their gear, stood looking on with supercilious smiles until the time came to leave to catch their bus. They had been asked by the excited members of the seance for an explanation of the mystic signs on their apports, but this they were unable to give, saying only that they were of unusual interest as materializations from the third astral level.

It was a fitting end to a successful evening, although with all the members of the congregation going off home, the musical box at last silenced and the last incense cone burned to a tiny crater of ash, my mother was a little perturbed and disappointed that Miss Tupperton should not have put in the promised appearance.

Then, with a squeaking of brakes, a rattle and a cough, Sir Henry's Lanchester limousine drew up. The chauffeur jumped down to open the passenger's door, and Miss Tupperton stepped down just as the last of the departing patients hobbled past. She came into the garden, full of apologies. The car, she said, had absolutely refused to start. My mother had hoped and even expected that she would have been accompanied by a friend in need of treatment, and later explained to me that she had held in reserve part of her spiritual resources to deal with this possibility. But Miss Tupperton was alone, apart from the chauffeur carrying a receptacle like a large hamper basket. This he put down and opened to disclose a French

I CAME, I SAW

poodle lying on a soiled and malodorous cloth. 'The most terrible diarrhoea,' Miss Tupperton explained. 'The poor pet's been like this now for more than a week. I'm utterly shattered and the vet's quite useless. I felt sure you'd help me if you could.'

Chapter Four

M Y FATHER NEVER ceased to be stunned by the credulity of others, although he lacked self-criticism in this matter. Suddenly there was a fad for yeast and people were spending up to a quarter of their incomes on the yeast tablets they crammed themselves with. It was the epoch of Dr Simpson's Iodine Locket, worn openly or in secret by millions of English men and women. More extraordinary even was the addiction to the use of the Wonder Worker. This was a small spade-shaped Bakelite contraption designed for insertion in the rectum, intended originally as a cure for haemorrhoids but later accepted for its talismanic properties in the treatment of all human ills. Innumerable intelligent people, including the cream of local society such as the Bowleses, Orr-Lewis—who had survived the *Titanic* disaster – the fearful virago Lady Meux – once a Gaiety Girl – probably General French who had presided over the massacres of Ypres, possibly even Miss Tupperton herself, were walking the streets and the country lanes of England with these things stuck up their bottoms. Their gullibility, my father said, passed all comprehension. Yet he himself seemed to me avid for belief, and went to endless lengths in support of the Spiritualist position in his search for occurrences that might be presented as contravening the accepted laws of nature.

Photography appeared to him to offer scope in this direction, and he argued that the silver emulsion of a film or plate was sensitive not only to visible light but to allied radiations undetected by the human eye. He bought a postcard-size Kodak camera, and went round the house clicking the shutter endlessly, particularly in the meditation room in the vicinity of the Chinese figurine, the prayer flag, the lingam and a small Indian dancing idol with ten arms. All of this was to no purpose, and nothing ever came out.

Someone gave him a photographic text-book, from which he learned about stops and exposures. He changed to a Zeiss with a big lens and loaded it with high-speed Illingworth plates. Using a stand and making time-exposures, he got reasonable pictures of the furniture and of those of his friends who could hold themselves still for fifteen seconds, but nothing appeared in the pictures other than what the eyes saw. This he put down to lack of technical skill. The Spiritualist press published photographs full of misty apparitions and ectoplasmic messes coalescing into human form. He corresponded with the photographers and set to work again, fortified with new theories. The problem was, he learned from the experts, that spirits were as much on the move in the ordinary way as the inhabitants of our world. Therefore flashlight shots offered the best hope of success. It was also valuable to make contact with a spirit in advance, explain what was required and fix a time and place for the photography, thus ensuring the co-operation of the spirit friends. This seemed to him and the other members of the circle perfectly reasonable.

Several circle members had Red Indian guides, and these had a reputation for dependability. The senior Red Indian was attached to Mrs Head: a shaman of the Blackfoot tribe named Thunder Star, who in a feat of intense mental concentration had caused a small tributary of the Missouri River to run backwards, before passing on in about 1830. When Mrs Head, using my father as intermediary, had put this problem to him, explaining the photographic processes involved, he had readily agreed to assist, promising to put aside all his other duties to be present on the next Sunday evening seance.

When the time came, the mouse-bitten chair in which Thunder Star would pose was carried into the middle room, my father set up his camera, opened the lens and exploded a small heap of magnesium powder on a tray. The flash was like looking into a cold sun. Membranes of layered smoke lifted gently to the ceiling. Mr Thresher thanked Thunder Star on behalf of the members of the circle for his co-operation and, since this chair was deemed to have been vacated, it was removed and the seance proceeded as usual.

Later that evening, the dishes and chemicals came out and we developed the plate, and as soon as it was dry next day, a print was made. Examining it, my father's excitement was immense. It was starkly lit, as it was bound to be, with all the faces crowded into it white-washed by the flash, and familiar objects surfacing from onyx seas of shadow. But the derelict chair was not quite empty, for at the level of the head a tight nebulae of stars shafted rays in all directions. This my father pronounced to be a halo, although of the head that should have supported it there was no sign. The picture produced a sensation among circle members and per-suaded two or three waverers to join the movement. A print, accompanied by a full description of all the circum-stances in which the photograph was taken and a sentence or two about the terrestrial existence of the shaman Thunder Star, was sent to *The Two Worlds*, who returned a letter worded with guarded enthusiasm.

Mentioning the phenomenon to the man from whom he had bought the camera, and whom he hoped to convert, my father found himself brushed aside. The man looked at the print without any evidence of surprise. His opinion was that the unusual effect, as he termed it, had been produced by nothing more mysterious than the reflection of the flash striking the surface of the lens. That, although my father indignantly refuted the explanation, was the end of the photography.

Enfield's most interesting native, and its only celebrity, was Sir Henry's younger brother, Augustus Bowles, who happened to live quite nearby at Myddelton House, Bull's Cross. The Bowleses were descended from Sir Hugh Myddelton, a man of protean achievement, jeweller, banker, engineer, poet, interloper on the Spanish Main, begetter on his first wife alone of a total of sixteen children, and deviser of the herculean enterprise by which water was brought from the artesian wells of Hertfordshire to relieve the plague-stricken London of the seventeenth century. By my time, whatever the spirit or impulse had been that had raised this family to wealth and prominence, it was fast fading, although Augustus Bowles may have retained a particle of his ancestor's genius, for he was a good painter and one of the most famous of English gardeners, who had had many plants named after him and had written standard works on botanical subjects. Unlike his rather foolish brother, he was a deeply thinking man, philosophically committed to the existing order of things, and he had once persuaded Stanley Baldwin, with whom he was on terms of intimate friendship, to come along and address selected villagers on some national occasion. Mr Baldwin had quoted to us (as if we needed to be reminded), 'the rich man in his castle, the poor man at his gate, God made them great or humble, and ordered their estate'. In the village Mr Bowles fulfilled the perfect image of the squire, doing good works, holding the church as well as he could together, but above all interesting himself in the religious education of the boys for whom he conducted weekly confirmation classes in his house.

Every boy in the village, without exception and including myself, attended these classes, purely because of the irresistible benefits they entailed, although I cannot remember a single one who after confirmation bothered any more with the Church. A series of ten classes were held and, as we saw it, it was worth putting up with the boredom of nine of them for the top-rate entertainment offered by the tenth, on the subject of sex. In this class Mr Bowles discussed the facts of life with extreme frankness, and we had learned from boys attending the classes of previous years of an interesting demonstration he could be encouraged to give if faced by what he believed to be total incomprehension. For this purpose he kept ready two antique French dolls, and when at our last class there were cries from us of, 'He doesn't understand, sir. Show him your jig-a-jig,' Mr Bowles unlocked and opened a drawer under his birds' egg cabinet and took these out. In the rather solemn and awestruck tone he normally used for reading the lesson in church, he drew our attention to the manner in which they were joined together. After that, a match was put to the combustion chamber of a tiny steam engine fuelled by cotton wool soaked in methylated spirits, to which the dolls were connected, and soon the tiny hips started to bounce, first slowly, then frantically as the engine warmed up, till finally with an ecstatic squeak of steam through a valve it was all over. A brief prayer in which we all joined followed, and our preparation for life was at an end. None of us realized at this time that Mr Bowles was a dedicated homosexual.

He was also a man who saw deep into the minds of boys, offering in return for their companionship the run of his magnificent garden, fishing in the section of the New River running through it, a game of billiards at any time in his sports pavilion, and a Bank Holiday entertainment three times a year, with organized games, more fishing with rods and tackle provided, and a lavish tea. In accordance with some ancient feudal custom the servants were sent away for this occasion and we were served by smiling members of the aristocracy themselves, who interested themselves for an hour in our lives and pressed us to stuff ourselves with cake.

Mr Bowles was happy on these occasions to show us, in person, the grand collections by which he expressed the typical countryman's love of nature. He had beautifully arranged and labelled cabinets filled with many thousands of birds' eggs which, in the case of particularly rare species, he still collected. In other cabinets were displayed some five thousand British butterflies and moths, sometimes including a hundred or so specimens of the same kind, showing slight colour variations. These included the even then celebrated Large Blue, and Mr Bowles told us, excited by the reminiscence, that he had gone to a place near Royston, where the last of them were, and helped in this extreme rarity's extinction.

More stimulating still was Mr Bowles' museum, housed in part of the stable buildings, containing an elephant's skull, innumerable fossils, and a wonderful collection of stuffed birds. Mr Bowles employed his own taxidermist, the possessor of remarkable imagination and taste, who did not simply stuff birds, but 'set them up', in naturalistic and convincing attitudes, furnishing the large cases in which they were displayed with objects such as stones and artfully counterfeited grasses, twigs and foliage in reproduction of the subject's natural environment.

Mr Bowles, who himself did not care to shoot, had shown ingenuity and perseverance in establishing his collection. His method was to distribute coloured illustrations of rare birds to all the gamekeepers in the area with a list of bounties payable, based on the bird's scarcity. In this way he had secured, as he put it, great rarities, including a bittern, a hen harrier, and the only great spotted woodpecker recorded in this country, all of them shown in the sprightly postures of feeding, of courtship, or aggression. The taxidermist's masterpiece was a family of long-eared owls, the last chick having actually been assisted to hatch out before inclusion in a still-life composition which the young all clamoured for their share of a vole in which the male bird, wings outstretched, was shown holding in its beak.

We were free to wander at will over the Bowles land, which shared a special kind of stagnant beauty with that of the great neighbouring estates. This had once been part of a royal chase, in the making of which so many homesteads and hamlets had disappeared. What remained was a vista of parkland sparsely planted with oaks and elms, and a small wood here and there where once the red deer hunted by the King and his nobles could take shelter and reproduce their species. The deer had been able to look after themselves, but the pheasants that replaced them could not, and their rearing for the gun demanded the elimination of half the native forms of wild life. Nowadays the woods were full of little gallows on which the gamekeepers displayed their ghastly trophies.

The sportsmen had got rid of the fauna, and Victorian planthunters had completed the gentle monotony of the scene. Mr Bowles could remember from his childhood the royal ferns, the orchids and the lilies of the valley that grew here before they had been uprooted to end their days in Victorian conservatories. Of these not a sign remained. This was a place, too, without a past. There must have been heroes, prophets, saints, here too as there had been in Wales, but if so no memory of them remained. In Forty Hill, Bull's Cross and Whitewebbs, we faced the matter-of-fact nothingness of present times from which the imagination offered no escape. Here we were watched by no unseen presences. Who could have imagined Arthur or the enchanter Merlin walking amongst these trees, or Druids working their magic in these fields?

Mr Bowles was always available to us, always pleased to be called on. We were debarred entrance by the front door of Myddelton House, but he was usually to be found sitting at the window of his study at the back, or else on the seat of the adjoining lavatory, which displayed two-thirds of his body to the garden. A whistle would bring him to the back entrance to let the caller in.

He painted wild flowers for reproduction in his books, often taking several days over a single crocus. He would freely, as if talking to another artist, discuss his work, but apart from that the talk was usually on mending the fences of character. His theory was that all of us boys suffered from a 'besetting sin', and having established what it was, he would hammer away at it continually. Although most of us felt that there was nothing much wrong with us as we were, a wickedness had to be concocted to satisfy Mr Bowles. From the way the conversation went it was clear that he was on the look-out for admissions of lust, but failing all else he was ready to settle for gluttony or sloth. We played our part in a straight-faced way in this charade, but it struck us, nevertheless, as absurd that a boy who had to get up at five every morning to do a paper round for which he was paid one shilling and six pence a week should be obliged to accuse himself of being lazy, and that others who suffered the ignominy of being fed 'on the parish' at the soup kitchen in Lavender Road School should confess to being gluttons. We would have agreed in a respectful and uncritical manner that the rich as we saw them were slothful, lustful, wrathful, covetous and gluttonous, but the sins Mr Bowles warned us against were in the main beyond our reach.

Mr Bowles was convinced that religion of almost any brand – including even Spiritualism – was good for the poor, but was not at all sure that spiritual healing, as practised by my mother, could provide any real benefit. He saw it as tending to short-circuit the reformatory process of sickness when associated with a reasonable amount of pain. What, after all, would become of the quality of fortitude if pain did not exist? Nevertheless, he was much intrigued by the story, which had gone the rounds, of Miss Tupperton and her dog, and asked for whatever further details of the case I could get. These I promised to provide.

It turned out that, confronted in the end with Miss Tupperton's tearful beseechings to heal the animal of its diarrhoea by a discharge of her spiritual currents, my mother had stalled by telling her that she would have to consult with members of her circle, now twelve in number, before reaching a decision. Thus Spiritualists had never been able to define the territories of their belief, nor make up their minds on a number of fundamental principles. In this case a dispute immediately arose as to whether or not animals had souls, and it was argued that if they had not, spiritual healing was neither appropriate nor would be beneficial. For decades now innumerable seekers after the truth had plied the spirits with their questions, yet the beyond remained seen as through a glass darkly. Did the birds sing there? Did the flowers bloom in spring? Should there be no more cakes and ale? Was love still thwarted? Could it be, according to a large body of Spiritualist opinion, that those who passed on were not even freed from the processes of ageing – however benign – and if youthful skin was wrinkled in the end, and hairs turned white, did not a second death await them on the other side?

Those who were attached to animals were in the majority in Forty Hill, and they could not imagine a future life in which they would be separated from their horses, their dogs, their cats. But all the voices of the other world speaking through such as my father seemed unable to decide – or even to have failed to notice – whether they were present or not. The arguments that went on through the movement were reflected in the conflicting opinions of my mother's circle. My mother believed that domestic animals, 'put into the world to serve men', were immortal, but that all the rest lived and died and that was the end of them. She was opposed by Mrs Thresher and several supporters who argued that you had to draw the line somewhere. If dogs, why not rats? Why not jellyfish? Why not tapeworms? Why not the most primitive of all forms of life, manifesting itself in a single cell? Long and earnest discussions took place, but in the end my mother was victorious, agreement was reached and pets were confirmed in their possession of souls. Miss Tupperton was invited to bring her dog back for treatment, which was successful, for in due course the diarrhoea cleared up.

Two years later I visited Myddelton House for what proved to be the last time. I found an enormous green Bentley standing outside the front entrance. It belonged to a nephew Mr Bowles did not particularly like, and I had reason to suspect that as soon as he had heard the bellow of its exhaust in the drive he would have slipped away to hide, either in the museum or the garden. In the end I found him in his summer house painting a fritillaria dug up on some Greek island. The summer house – his favourite place of refuge – was built over a little lake upon which floated the great enamelled shapes of water lilies of many colours. The banks had been planted with Japanese irises and a Chinese thicket of bamboo and thorns, to provide cover for the birds which flashed their wings and sung among them continually. Once in a while, Mr Bowles said, some rarity – and he had mentioned a Cetti's warbler – would be attracted to this seductive environment and encouraged to nest there. When this happened, he would send for a marksman to secure the bird or birds, and his taxidermist would create another masterpiece, in the case of the Cetti's warbler perched on a reed, a dragonfly in its bill, over the nest: an aquatic tableau completed with feathery rushes, waxen flowers, and green painted glass that never quite counterfeited water.

He looked up from his work, and for a moment I thought he hadn't recognized me, but then he waved. I noticed that he was using a magnifying glass held in his left hand, while he painted with the right, and remembered that back in the days of the confirmation class his sight had seemed to me to be weak.

I may have been the only one of his pupils who displayed interest in his garden, and he was eager to show me his latest example of the triumph of ingenuity over environment. This was a small orange tree, imported from Spain, its roots still embedded in a hundredweight of Spanish soil, which after much experimentation with mulching, fertilizers and liquid feeds, but without the aid of artificial heat, had produced a single, small greenish fruit. Although, like so many rich men, Mr Bowles believed himself to be poor and wore his brother's cast-off clothes, he had spent a considerable sum to build a walled enclosure round this tree, fitted on the inside with adjustable mirrors which had to be constantly varied in their angle to the sun to reflect its maximum light. It was a bad time for the visit, for on entering the enclosure, the first thing we saw was the single orange lying on the ground, where some small boy had thrown it in disgust after biting into its bitter flesh. Mr Bowles showed stoicism over this reverse, the latest of many acts of vandalism from which he had suffered. In the last week alone, the cloth on the billiard table had been ripped, and the display case with a tableau of Long Eared Owls smashed and their stuffed newly-hatched chicks scattered about the floor. It was a small price to pay, he seemed to think, for the satisfaction it gave him to watch over the young and guide them into the right paths at the time when they were most open to influence.

We walked on. One of the members of this year's confirmation class was cutting his initials in the trunk of a tree from Patagonia, and others chased each other across beds in which rare plants grew that had to be fussed over by the gardeners like sickly children. Mr Bowles followed them with his failing eyes, intoxicated with the aroma of early adolescence – so soon to fade. His one sorrow was that none of them could be relied upon to become regular church-goers, and would almost certainly desert the faith as I had done. His theory was that boring sermons lay at the bottom of the trouble. Mr Bowles' father, who had been patron of the living, had refused to allow sermons to be preached at all, and in his days every pew had been full. I knew only too well why, but it had nothing to do with sermons.

He asked how many people attended my mother's church – managing to infuse the word with a civilized tolerance that concealed his contempt – and I told him up to two hundred in fine weather.

'And do you really think she cured that wretched dog of diarrhoea?' he asked, and I said I thought it would have got better in any case.

'She's reputed to be very successful with her treatment, however unorthodox it may seem.'

'Half the people who go to her only imagine they're ill, sir.'

'So it's faith, then. A case of pick up thy bed, thy faith hath made thee whole.'

'That's all she claims for it,' I told him.

'Did you know your father makes up wonderful medicines?' he asked, and I told him I helped with the bottling at weekends.

'Interesting to know what they contain.'

'Nothing very much,' I said. 'Water and flavouring mostly.'

'A case of faith again.'

'Yes, sir.'

'I wish you hadn't told me that,' Mr Bowles said. 'I've been taking that elixir of his for years.'

Our path led us to the bank of the New River, the great canal cut by Mr Bowles' ancestor, Sir Hugh Myddelton, to bring well-water to London, upon which the family's fortunes had been established. Several boys were fishing. One of them, at a distance from the rest, was dressed in a grotesque fashion. Mr Bowles explained that this scare-crow result followed a campaign by the Mothers' Union to persuade necessitous mothers to attempt, at least, to make their boys clothing in addition to dresses they normally made for their daughters. This boy, like several other members of the class, had been sent to mix with his friends wearing a cap and jacket produced in the home, and they had turned their backs on him. All the Mothers' Union had succeeded in doing was to create social pariahs.

While this sad business was under discussion we suddenly heard the sound of ringing, jubilant voices, recognized with alarm by Mr Bowles as those of his nephew and the girl he had brought with him, who were clearly coming in our direction. He hastily grabbed me and we ducked into some bushes remaining hidden until the couple passed. From the glimpse I caught of them he was as handsome and dashing as I knew he would be, and she as beautiful, the pair of them differing not so much from natives of Enfield in their beauty and their dignity, but by the way in which they spoke, and for all who might be listening to their intimacies to hear. The fact was that Mr Bowles' village boys had no existence for them. They probably did not even register their presence. They were so splendid, but why had God given them the Earth?

When they were out of sight – although the gay lilting voices went on and on – Mr Bowles and I came out from behind the bushes and began our walk back, and soon the summer house was in sight. Around us the birds kept up their chorus. A shower came and went, bringing down a little sodden blossom and pelting the surface of the lake with the heavy summer raindrops the dragonflies so effortlessly avoided. The smoke of burning sap from the gardener's fire tickled the membranes of my nose, a dog barked, a fish splashed, the swifts dived on us with their thin, delirious screeching. Even the rich could possess no finer moment than this.

Mr Bowles took up his brush and his magnifying glass again. 'My eyes are going fast,' he said.

'Can't the doctors do anything for you, sir?'

'I've seen the man at Moorfields and he's given me up.' He laughed. 'Your mother's my only hope now. Perhaps I should see her.'

I nodded, showing apparently slight enthusiasm.

'You seem so sceptical,' he said. 'Why don't you say something encouraging?'

'I know she'd be happy to see you,' I said, 'and there's nothing to be lost in seeing her, but if it's the faith that counts, I suppose it depends more on you than upon her.'

Chapter Five

B Y THE TIME I left Enfield Grammar School the ice-age following the great American slump had set in. At best a grammar school education, however sound, offered few more exciting prospects at the end of the day than employment in a high street bank, and the world crisis and its dole queues had put even this beyond my reach. In common with most of my friends I had to turn my hand to whatever came my way. The experience of those years fostered resilience – possibly even, of necessity, a sense of adventure.

Some of my schoolfriends who had hoped to sit at office desks found themselves earning their bread in less conventional and often less sedentary ways. One, unable to continue his accountancy studies, was appointed assistant rat-catcher to the council, and later set up on his own and did well. A second who suffered from some sexual obsession became a professional partner at the Tottenham Palais de Dance, enabled in this way to kill both the financial and sexual birds with one stone. A third made journeys to Spain and returned laden with cheap Toledan crucifixes which he advertised in the Catholic press as blessed by the Bishop of Salamanca. For a while I did less well, continuing to bottle the elixir for which I earned about thirty shillings a week.

Questions of prestige were closely limited to those of economic necessity in the matter of finding employment. Enfield possessed some of the largest apple and cherry orchards in that part of England, and there was cash to be had when the season for their picking arrived. In the case of the apples it was easier to concentrate on the windfalls, but the prestige job – picking from the trees – entailed the manipulation of heavy ladders, and the very small risk of a fall, and although there was slightly less money in it, it was what everybody wanted to do.

The part-time employment to be found in the cherry orchards was not only in picking the fruit, but in scaring away the thousands of blackbirds and thrushes that would come winging in for the feast, particularly in the early morning hours. It conferred prestige to be engaged by the farm to shoot these with a twelve-bore – a bird's corpse had to be produced for every cartridge expended – but social annihilation to enrol oneself among the group that patrolled the orchards in the early hours beating on drums. The most demeaning employment of all, taken by one of my ex-school friends, involved him in washing up for a Soho restaurant, and placing himself, dressed as a clown, at the entrance to display the menu provided for the lunch-time and evening meals.

With the expiry of childhood, Enfield had become a dull place. Almost from one year to another Mr Bowles had become old and blind, and I no longer took refuge at Myddelton House. The alluring Miss Tupperton was carried away by a dashing Major Pinkies, who had dropped in to the Hall one day to visit his old commanding officer and had not hesitated to plunder him in this way. Her place was now taken by a pretty and muscular young nurse, called in to help with Sir Henry's gout. My parents had come to the realistic conclusion that whatever dormant psychic gifts I might have possessed, I had little to offer the Spiritualist movement, and there was no hope whatever of my following in my father's footsteps.

Nevertheless, membership of their church continually increased.

I lived in a place, as it seemed to me, where nothing happened. Once Enfield had been a large and attractive village at the end of an escape route from London, travelling down which it took a coach and pair an hour and a half to reach unspoiled country in which a succession of monarchs had taken time off to go hunting. It had an interesting school built in the reign of Mary Tudor, a fine church, several outstanding pubs, and the grandest and oldest cedar tree in the land, planted in about 1670 by Dr Ridewood, headmaster of the Grammar School, who brought the seeds from the Lebanon. This spread its stupendous umbrella of the deepest green foliage over the heart of the town until it was finally demolished to make room for a departmental store.

The magnification of an ancient village such as Enfield into a modern town is always a calamity. No sooner had the venerable cedar gone than a Mr Sidney Bernstein built his super-cinema, called the Rialto, in the old market place. The Rialto was modelled, as we were told, on the Roxy in New York, with an organ having 2,800 pipes and thirty-five miles of wires, and only lesser in the facilities it offered than the original in providing no built-in medical operating theatre. Few people in Enfield were sure of the origin of the word Rialto and some confusion arose when the first film, *The Power of the Borgias*, was shown, over unfamiliar names. Mr Bernstein, we learned, overwhelmed by the splendour of a bridge in Venice, had been ready with the supreme accolade. 'Know something?' he said to his retinue. 'I'm going to put this on the map. I'm going to name my cinema after it.' But the muddle in Enfield continued. Even the local newspaper got itself into a mix-up, or perhaps suffered a Freudian slip, speaking in its eulogistic review of Sidney Borgia, the cinema owner, and retitling the film *The Power of the Bernsteins*.

The competition in the opening week of *The Power of the Borgias* – advertised in Enfield by a parade camel having a pronounced limp – was *The Great San Francisco Fire* (second time round) on offer at the town's original, sad flea pit, the Queen's, and a private showing of *Mustapha's Donkey* in a windowless cell at the back of the Oddfellows' Hall. This latter may have been the first pornographic movie ever made. A higher percentage of Enfield males had seen it several times, and it was so grainy and so ravaged by age and use that it was hardly possible to distinguish the donkey in the star role from the human actors it featured.

I saw *The Power of the Borgias* with an old schoolmate, Alexander Hagen, who had been good at maths and had set his sights on becoming an airship designer, then jettisoning the idea owing to the state of the world, and philosophically accepting employment at the sewage farm in Ponders End. A ritual Saturday night meal followed at Mrs England's Dining Rooms in the passage at the back of the station, where the tables were screened in such a way that patrons did not risk loss of face by being seen there, scuffling their feet in the sawdust. We began to ask ourselves if in fact we really existed or whether what we took to be life could not be a complex illusion, an endless, low-quality dream. These threadbare surroundings in which we sat hunched over a scrubbed table, our backs to the light, came very close to being nothing. Perhaps we too were nothing, had come from nothing, were journeying through nothing, towards a distant goal of nothingness. Enfield was nothing, the Rialto cinema nothing to the accompaniment of organ music, the Queen's nothing with fleas. We had come here to confront a supper of nothing, boiled, fried or scrambled, with or without chips, to be followed by custard if desired at no extra charge. After this it was back home to nothing, or down the town to pick up a couple of girls at the bottom of Church Street, and engage them in a lively conversation about nothing plus sex, or just nothing.

Christ stopped at Eboli, but he would have found people there who still had the spirit to sing and dance, and Mr Bowles mentioned once that on the Greek island where he went to dig up plants the impoverished peasantry got away with fifty days of what was supposed to be the working year and used them up on parties, pilgrimages and processions. What had happened to us? Why had the lives of Sir Henry's serfs, and the workers at the Lock, been reduced to survival without distractions? Why had communal activities in the surroundings in which I was born come down to a couple of hours over a pint of sour ale in The Goat?

No wonder we took refuge in make-belief, dealt in pretence and self-pretence, and half-believed the personal myths of our own creation. No wonder our pudgy-faced local beauties started life as Ethel, Gladys or Florence but ended as Esmée, Phoebe and Diane and inflicted upon themselves their soulless accents.

Hagen had been assumed from his name to be a Jew, whose people had been carried in the stream of emigrants out of the East End, through Bethnal Green, Hackney, Clapton, Tottenham and Upper and Lower Edmonton, along the road taken by John Gilpin on his ride, until the great urban mess finally expired in the grim streets of Enfield Wash, Enfield Lock and Freezy Water where, discouraged from further advances by the disconsolate greenery of the countryside, the emigration had come to a halt. After a stretch at the sewage farm, he had walked out and set up as a wedding photographer. In this he did well, made money quickly and, while not going so far as to change his name, showed a preference for being addressed as Alexander rather than Alex, and asked his friends to pronounce the A in Hagen 'ah' not 'ay'. Up to this point none of us had known much about him, nor visited his house. Now he let drop the information that he was half-German, and that his father had been German ambassador to Liberia where he had met Alex's English mother, who was engaged in missionary work. They had separated after his mother's return to this country.

Hagen was a great watcher and imitator. He watched the men he hoped to mould himself upon, but of necessity from afar, so that his imitation never quite convinced. The tie was right but the voice was wrong. When he spoke, an echo of Central Europe lingered on which he said was Bavarian, but it only went down with girls who had never heard an Englishman of the ruling classes speak. Intelligent as he was, he would never raise himself to half the stature of Mr Bowles' spirited nephew who had been born under the wings of victory. Hagen, like the rest of us, was too cautious, too premeditated, too afraid at bottom of his own shadow. He made money easily, but for all the calculated swagger that went with it, and the arrogant tilt of the homburg hat, he gave the impression of listening to the noises of the pogrom in the next street.

For a while I was in partnership with him in the wedding photography, which called for little technical and less artistic skill. The wedding guests lined up like trained dogs, put on their boozy, foolish smiles, you clicked the shutter, and that was the end of it. They expected to look unnatural and they did. Seeing himself as the organizer, Alex abstained from involvement in physical labour of any kind, which he would have regarded as an inefficient use of his time, so I developed the films and made the prints, working under primitive conditions in the kitchen after my parents had gone to bed. My father never failed to inspect these pictures of the bride and bridegroom at the church door, and the family groups ranged with their inane grins in order of height, and occasionally he would draw attention to a small defect, usually caused by fogging, in the hope that this might be a blurred countenance from the spirit world, squeezed in forlornly among the all too solid flesh of Ponders End, or Palmer's Green.

Part Three

THE CORVAJAS

Chapter Six

WEDDING PHOTOGRAPHY was sporadic and seasonal in its revenues, leaving time to be put to other commercial uses. Hagen bought lost property at trade auctions conducted by the railways at their various depots. Sometimes we carried out a combined operation, as we did in a lot comprising 360 umbrellas of various kinds, eventually trebling our money on their resale. My fortunes took a temporary upswing when I bought for £6 at one such auction a racing motor cycle which had been abandoned somewhere abroad, and brought back to England after its rider had been killed in an attack on a speed record. I rode this in the novice class in several dirt track races at Harringay and the White City, coming last in every race but one, when two of the four contestants crashed. In spite of this poor record of achievement the organizers would always accept my entry and pay me the valuable sum of £5 in starting money, in the belief that it did no harm to the gate to feature a rider who could be relied upon to fall off in three races out of four. It was a great reverse when after a month or so the machine's engine exploded and I was forced back for a short time into dependence upon the elixir.

Slowly mercantile operations began to take over. It was to be seen that a living was to be had for such as us, debarred from creative endeavour, by keeping a close watch on auctions of the ordinary kind, in which an often bewildering miscellany of goods were put up for sale. At these, low prices were the general rule, and when from time to time an article of value came under the hammer it could usually be bought cheaply and rapidly resold at a profit in an auction of the better kind. This could be an exciting and even romantic business. Experts who spent a lifetime in manoeuvrings of this kind, having dedicated years to the science of market values, could expect once in a while to pick up spectacular treasures cleared from attics that found their way to the auction room. We knew our limitations and confined ourselves to goods requiring little or no expertise, gathered loosely under the heading 'scientific articles' which might include anything connected with photography, microscopes, barometers, sextants, surgical instruments, and when the occasional artificial limb turned up at a sale, or in one case a box of pickled anatomical specimens, we knew that Stevens of Covent Garden were the outlet for them, and they too were taken in our net.

This trade was a nomadic one, involving endless journeyings into the remote suburbs, north, south, east and west. It became necessary to set up our headquarters near the centre of London, so we rented the first floor of a house in Woodberry Down, near Finsbury Park. This was a Victorian mansion built in prison style, probably under the influence of the nearby Holloway Gaol, with an attractive view of a reservoir from its back windows.

Woodberry Down, we soon discovered, had been colonized by Russians escaping the severities of the Stalinist regime, particularly at the time of the liquidation of the kulaks, and this tree-lined, rather somnolent street harboured a number of the kulaks or their children who had managed to get away. They were tribal people, Ingushes, Chechens and Kazakhs, who made no concessions to their present environment, dressing and largely behaving, it was to be supposed, as they and their parents had done back in Kazan or Tashkent.

Several families had joined forces to take a long lease on a house a few yards down the road, had installed English stoves and converted them so as to be able to sleep on top of them in Russian style in winter, and had pitched their black tents in the enormous Victorian rooms. The men, we were told, always slept fully dressed ready for an attack, but the women stripped naked and rolled themselves in bear skins. They drank *pivo*, a home-brewed Russian beer laced with methylated spirits, smoked yellow cigarettes with Cyrillic lettering on them, spent their money on fireworks, and kept the street awake with their all-night parties at which they let off rockets, beat tambourines, danced and wept.

Hagen became fascinated by the Russians after an encounter we had with one of them called Aron. We were driving down the street within days of moving in when Aron, wearing a roughly-tied black turban, the tails of his long coat swinging, and amulets hanging from his wrists, stepped out into the roadway to stop our car, merely to ask the time. He invited himself into our flat, looked it over, and said, 'you must give this place personality.' He advised us as to how this was to be done, and he and his friends painted the floor red, covered the walls with tin foil and stuck blue stars and crescents over them. When the work was over we held a party, and the Russians brought their beer, their methylated spirits and their tambourines, ready to dance the night away. Two of them were princes, but Aron freely admitted that they were from Caucasus where every valley had its prince. What we failed to realize was that some of our friends were Muslims – although there were Christians and Jews as well – and the date suggested by them for our party happened to be the feast of Mouloud, celebrating the birth of the prophet – an occasion for rejoicing. Some time after midnight and a short halt for prayer, the fireworks were let off and, under the direction of one of the princes, the Russians made a raft from our furniture, poured petrol over it, carried it down to the water, and set it alight. It made an awe-inspiring spectacle in the demure setting of inner-suburban London, and the Russians cheered and wept at the beauty of it. The party ended with the pointless arrival of the fire brigade, who were followed by the police. Hagen and I were on a three months' tenancy, and when this expired it was no surprise to us that it was not renewed.

While looking round for fresh accommodation I returned to Forty Hill, where any changes that had taken place were for the worse.

My father, who suffered from boredom, was going through a bad patch, sometimes causing him to groan aloud, and my mother was tired after a visit to Carmarthen where she had gone in response to my grandfather's pleadings to do what she could to get Polly through a current crisis.

Forty Hill, and with it much of North Enfield, was moreover on the verge of a great calamity, for the great and beautiful orchards among which I had spent most of my childhood were about to be cut down and replaced by housing estates.

Against the long-term prospect of gloom, my mother

had a single recent triumph to report. A woman called Mrs Edwardes from the superior residential area of Enfield known as The Ridgeway, who had been vacillating, undecided, on the fringe of my mother's movement for at least a year, had been finally persuaded to join together with several of her friends, following a macabre experience to which she had been subjected. The tragedy of this poor woman – whom I had once met – was that over some fifteen years she had given birth to no less than ten still-born children. After the loss a short time previously of the last of these, and some final hesitation and misgivings, she had agreed to be present at a seance to be arranged purely with the object of attempting to communicate with the spirits of her unfortunate offspring. Some problems arose over differences of opinion among the circle members as to whether the still-born had souls or not. Right-wing extremists contended that a child who had never drawn breath did not, while the liberals held the view that even a foetus in an early stage of development did – although no one could draw a line as to whether the promise of eternity was present within hours, days or weeks after conception.

The seance for Mrs Edwardes called for a major organizational effort, and was attended by invitation by persons known to possess exceptional psychic endowment from outside the area. I remembered that my mother had even tried to encourage me to attend to contribute to the formidable barrage of astral force that was being prepared. The occasion, she said, was a huge success. My father had been supported by a professional medium, and at least five of Mrs Edwardes' still-born babies had given evidence of their presence, ranging from the infant mewing of the last of her children who had so nearly come into the world to the strong and confident greeting of her (now) teenage son.

At this point I was ready with the questions that made my mother impatient with me. Until what age would the Edwardes family continue to grow on the other side? Until the ideal age – the best possible age – she thought, but she could not suggest what that age might be. And at that age they would remain throughout eternity? Yes, she thought, a little doubtfully, they would. Throughout eternity.

The success of the seance for Mrs Edwardes had been due, my mother believed, in part to the astral power provided by several members of a group of local 'seekers' calling themselves the Sons (or Daughters) of Osiris. Their movement – very closely allied to Spiritualism – had taken its inception following the publication of a book called *The Voice of Osiris, the Book of the Truth*. The people of Enfield, few of whom bothered much with books, were buying it by the hundred in the belief that it had been written through a medium by the Egyptian god Osiris, personification of the power of good and the sunlight, and that the revelations it contained held the key to the transformation of unsatisfactory lives. It was printed on paper with a faintly perfumed smell, and illustrated with softly shaded pencil drawings of posturing dehumanized humans and a menagerie of sacred animals: cats, dogs, falcons, ibises, owls. Scattered through the pages were the symbols of ancient Egypt held in a web of cosmic rays, and great vacant eyes stared back at us from faces emptied of all expression by divine insight.

It was my mother's ambition eventually to absorb the

children of Osiris into her church. A problem remained. Her following described themselves as Christian Spiritualists. Could the adorers of an ancient Egyptian deity be at the same time classified as Christians? The fact was that Spiritualism fostered open-mindedness in the matter of dogma, and I had no doubt that a way would be found of reconciling even such hugely dissimilar faiths.

Another of my friends compelled by the times to pursue an unusual economic strategy was Arthur Baron, who, working at first from a small garage in Bookham, Surrey, trained himself to become a skilled mechanic and then an engineer. He specialized in buying up wrecked cars of the better kind – always cheap and, if there had been a fatality, very cheap. With patience, skill and devotion, and frequently a trivial outlay of money, these could sometimes be restored to near-pristine condition.

My first car was from this stable, although this was one that had not been crashed. It was a 'straight-eight' Bugatti, the property of a rich Indian, who had altered its appearance in many ways. In doing so he had made it too fanciful and, needing garage space for new purchases, had cleaned it out for any price he could get, without argument, to the first buyer he could find.

This car immediately disproved a theory of mine that the thirst for pretence was the hallmark of the English lower middle class, for this rich and probably powerful man, living in a palatial Wimbledon house, had ordered a special body built in Paris for his car – in the shape of a boat, or as nearly as this could be achieved. There had been little to be done about the front, but the rear end had been furnished with a polished wooden deck, enclosed by a low brass rail, and with fittings of the kind seen on yachts. There were also four small portholes. The Indian liked the poetic association of the word sunbeam, so he had removed Ettore Bugatti's tiny elliptical trademark from the top of the radiator and replaced it – this was the process applied to all his cars – with that of the Sunbeam Motor Company, and an adaptation had been made to the radiator cap to accommodate an image of the Hindu's elephant god, Ganesh. An ivory plaque covering most of the instruments on the dashboard showed a pair of lovers in lascivious oriental intertwinings.

It was a car to cause pained eyebrows to be raised anywhere in the neighbourhood of St James's, but was received with astonished admiration in the outer suburbs, and seen by such as Alexander it was a human version of gaudy attraction hung by the bower bird in its lair to entice the female of the species within range.

Alexander's involvement with the dangerous Russians of Woodberry Down had been prolonged by the fact that he had fallen in love with one of them and was therefore concerned at this time with the need to show himself off to the best advantage. She was a Jewess, pretty and amazingly fair, the daughter of the Grand Rabbi of Astrakhan. Making a shallow dive into the history of his own people, Alexander had learned of the existence of an originally non-Jewish people, the Khazars, who had been converted to Judaism in the Middle Ages – hence the Rabbi's daughter's Grecian rather than Semitic features. The Rabbi, her father, had remained behind in Astrakhan, but the rest of the family had been in England for some years and Zahra had been sent to school in Highgate. She showed neither surprise nor emotion of any kind when Hagen told her he loved her, merely saying that she would have to speak to her mother and her brother about it.

A family conference took place, after which Alexander was invited for an interview, not only by the mother and brother but also by a local rabbi whose advice they had taken and who questioned him searchingly on his family background, his prospects, but above all on his religious beliefs. In all three areas Alexander was on dangerous ground. He had never been inside a synagogue, and little remained about him that was Jewish but the faint and slowly disappearing accent. The rabbi watched him with troubled eyes as Alexander tried to explain and excuse the religious liberalism of the community to which he belonged.

Zahra's family asked for time to consider the matter. In the meanwhile further meetings with the girl were not ruled out, but the stipulation was made that one of her friends must be present.

The picnic party in the Bugatti was inevitable, and the car was useful in its way, too, as it turned out, because the minor shared hardship generated by such excursions helped wonderfully to break the ice, and spice the encounter with mild uncertainties and adventure.

It was Sunday, the first of May, a steely and near-arctic day, with a black tapestry of cloud over London under which the buildings of the city were as white as old bones. Zahra had been spending the weekend in Bloomsbury with a friend who was of Sicilian origin with whom she had been on a course in English life and culture designed by London University for the benefit of visiting foreigners. Having removed the erotic ivory plaque from the dashboard, we arrived at the meeting place, the old Euston arch, just as a few small snowflakes began to fall. This involved us, as soon as the girls arrived, with the predicament of erecting the hood which, when not in use, was stowed away in the boot. This the girls, working with us and their hands like ours blue with cold, entered into in the spirit of fun.

Both girls were exceedingly vivacious. Zahra was more beautiful than her friend, but Ernestina, who reminded me of Carmen Miranda and sported a good deal of jewellery unsuited to the climate, had more to say. Our intention had been to drive out for lunch to a little place on the river near Richmond, but a small difficulty arose over Zahra and kosher food, and she had come provided with sandwiches. The girls had heard exciting reports about Epping Forest, and were eager to see it, so we went there instead.

More sandwiches were bought at the Robin Hood pub near Chingford, after which we parked just off the road by the side of a small, slatternly mere. Both girls, neither of whom had left London during the time they had lived in England, were enchanted by their surroundings. Ducks copulated with noisy and incessant ardour in the shallow water among the half-submerged oil drums and the bicycle wheels. The wind had snatched the snow-flakes away, but now the landscape was fleeced with rain. Once in a while, as we munched our sandwiches and shook the water from our sleeves, a little derelict sun-shine burst through a rent in the clouds to produce a sombre and fleeting illumination among the trees which Ernestina found 'Turneresque'. Although she knew nothing of England beyond what she had read in books, she had formed an attachment for the country and its people based largely on Dickens and fallacy, and was ready to excuse anything. We discussed the class system which she saw as evidence of the dynamic democracy of our institutions. In Spain, where she had been educated, there was no democracy, and only two classes, the rich and the poor. Surely we were better off? The English could do no wrong. I dressed badly and knew it, but what I realized as a personal shortcoming, an incurable untidiness, she almost certainly saw as commendable humility.

The matter of love came up, although treated in a somewhat academic fashion. The fair Zahra, who had ceased to nibble her last sandwich, turned her soft, trusting eyes upon us and spoke of Jewish idealism and the five-year betrothal preceding marriage in Astrakhan, where such idealism was practised in its purest form. Ernestine shocked her by assuring her that all married men in Sicily who could afford to do so, kept mistresses.

'What happens if they're found out?' someone asked. Ernestina lifted a hand, clasping an invisible pistol to her forehead, crooked her forefinger as if pressing a trigger, clicked her tongue and giggled (she had a most infectious laugh).

'They get shot,' she said.

'You don't mean that.'

'I do,' she said. 'If they are so foolish as to be caught, what good are they to anyone? Far better out of the way.'

'And do the wives go to prison?'

'Of course not. These are family affairs. They're hushed up.'

'Would you shoot your husband?' I asked.

'No,' she said, 'but I won't marry a Sicilian. Just to be on the safe side.'

Alexander was giving his set display of the worldly wisdom of the man about town, but I felt that it failed to impress, largely because it was not understood. Whenever the opportunity arose, Zahra fixed him with her soft eyes and plied him with a question. Soon I began to realize that Alexander was being subjected to a renewal of the rabbi's interrogation, a subtle affair of small, artless queries through which all the facets of his character were under test. He was encouraged to talk on, and he did and Zahra watched him, probing and sounding. Despite the swagger of the Russian group as a whole, I saw her as cautious and calculating. In all probability we all wore disguises for this occasion, but Alexander, so carefully dressed for the part, was least convincing. There was little indication of the hard centre almost certainly concealed beneath Zahra's confiding personality. I caught at her thoughts:

Handsome, yes, but penniless. An adventurer who will receive no inheritances. My father has a sense of humour, but never where I am concerned. How would he take this? Is it possible to imagine this man awaiting me as I am led in procession to the chappah? If he has no money, how can he offer the mishrim of gold coins, and the sharab in silver drinking vessels? Could he, even for this one occasion, play a single note on the r'beg or the toba? Oi, what complications! Could he take the traditional kobeiba of mince meat and cracked rice from its salver, shape it skilfully, using forefinger and thumb alone, into perfectly round kefta to feed both me and himself before our assembled friends, without covering us all with shame? Assuredly not. Would he respect the mikvah and learn in reasonable time to chant the prayers for the saba'a? It is improbable. As an Ashkenazi, spoiled with the fat living of the degenerate West, could he be persuaded to live on unleavened bread and dates during the fasts? No.

Chapter Seven

UNLIKE ZAHRA Ernestina was clearly not a walker in the old ways. She was full of what probably sounded to her revolutionary utterances, one being that in no circumstances would she marry an Italian, and on second thoughts she would do her best not to marry at all, although this did not rule out the possibility of living with a suitable male – above all one who was not her parents' choice. She also said that she despised religion, and more than religion itself the educated Latins of her acquaintance who paid lip-service to a faith they regarded as intellectually inadmissible. Sicilians, she said, were the worst of the lot, the insincere tag-end of a society in decay. She contrasted them with the English of the books she had read and the lectures she had attended, by comparison so devoid of deviousness, so upright in all their dealings, so bound by their word.

One of her theories – and it was one held by so many continentals – was that the weather had made them what they were. Ernestina had lived in hot climates and studied their enervating effect upon those who had to support them. Here the cold and the rain protected you from the siesta and kept you on your toes. Now the picnic over, she turned down a suggestion from Alexander that we should give up and go home, and urged further exploration of the sodden landscapes of Essex.

Another meeting was arranged for the next Saturday evening, but my instinct warned me that Zahra would not appear, and she did not. Instead Ernestina was there on time outside Euston Station, bearing a brief note from her to say that she had a cold. Reading through its sparse lines Alexander was inclined to the belief that he had seen the last of her. Meanwhile it was clear that Ernestina expected to be taken out, and the awkward prospect of a threesome was settled by his withdrawal.

Ernestina and I then walked down Tottenham Court Road and settled for dinner at the Corner House. St Giles' Circus might have been Xanadu as far as either of us was concerned, and little did we know that the audience played to by Lionel Falkman and his Apaches was composed in the main of intelligent *au pair* girls, and that such Lyons establishments were beneath the notice of native Saturday night pleasure-seekers from Finchley and Golders Green. Lionel in his embroidered Balkan blouse made the routine round with his fiddle and we were pleased and a little surprised when he halted to play a few bars at our table. Ernestina had nothing but enthusiasm for her surroundings, for the elegance and restraint of the decor, the immaculate table linen, the sheen of the cutlery, the decorum of the clientèle, the democratic consideration with which customers summoned a waiter with an unobtrusive gesture instead of hissing or clapping their hands, the dignity with which he took the order, the wholesome simplicity of the food he brought and the noble indifference with which he collected a tip without so much as a glance at it. A suspicion grew that this was the first time she had been alone with a male escort, although there was grudging reference to an admirer who called at her house from time to time to hold her hand in a deferential fashion and recite Spanish lyrical poetry, which she thought was pretty poor stuff.

There was something she found distinctly Parisian

about the atmosphere and style of the Corner House, although it lacked the familiar grubbiness of an equivalent establishment in Paris. She had seen something of the great cities of Europe, and described and compared them with vivacity. Here was cosmopolitanism indeed. After Santander in North Spain she had been sent to be educated at Beauvais, then back to the University of Madrid. She was fluent in five languages and prepared to quote and discuss Proust, Dante and Cervantes in the originals. All I could offer by way of linguistic accomplishment was a half-dozen sentences in Welsh, drilled into me in the infants' school of the Pentrepoeth, and in the sphere of literature a nodding and uncritical acquaintance with Arnold Bennett and H. G. Wells. In spite of these cultural shortcomings and the fact that my travels had carried me no further than the soggy villages of South Wales, we found a good deal to say to each other.

After several more outings Ernestina peremptorily decided that the time had come for me to meet her parents. I was given no advance warning of this and therefore no time to prepare for the experience, which proved overwhelmingly strange. I was shown into a large room in the family house at 4 Gordon Street, Bloomsbury, which was lit as powerfully as if for a stage presentation. A strong overhead light in a chandelier was supported by a complex of lamps behind frosted panels at each corner of the ceiling. Pieces of period furniture had been placed here and there on a small prairie of magenta carpet, and my attention was captured by a gilded door, its panels incised with an abstract geometrical design. This was the setting for the surrealistic happenings of a Buñuel film to come. I became aware of my crumpled suit of inferior cloth, of trousers that were too short and sleeves too long, of untended fingernails and creaking shoes, of the untidy parcel of books I was carrying and the badly-folded evening paper stuck into my jacket pocket. 'My father is very informal,' Ernestina assured me. 'He is easy to get on with, and you will like him. He will not understand your English, and you will not understand his Italian, but that doesn't matter.'

A moment later the gilt door swung open and a short, corpulent man entered the room. He was dressed in a dark suit of conservative cut which he might have been wearing for the first time. His eyes were black and protruding, and his black hair was brushed close to his scalp and no expression showed in his face as he came towards us, taking short, shuffling steps. We shook hands, he gave me a quick, mechanical smile, and said something incomprehensible in a language which I presumed to be Italian in a cracked, grating voice that managed in some way to be pleasant. 'Daddy is welcoming you to our house,' Ernestina said. 'He asks you to make yourself at home.' I bowed and, stricken momentarily with my old speechlessness, produced a faint, inarticulate gargling, before seating myself, still gripping my frayed parcel, on the edge of a small golden throne. Thus begun my long acquaintance with Ernesto Giovanni Batista Corvaja, a singular man.

At this point my attention was distracted from his somewhat hypnotic stare by the entrance of his wife, Maria Corvaja, a short, smiling over-elaborately dressed woman who, to my enormous relief, turned out to speak excellent English. We sat facing each other and a maid brought wine in cut glasses that added their iota of scintillation to the sheen and the glitter of the surroundings. All the interiors of my life until this moment had possessed their nooks and their crannies, places where untidy parcels could be stuffed out of sight, the alcoves and the recesses of rustic architecture which promised concealment in emergency. Here we sat together transfixed by protocol in our cube of pitiless light, from which there was no escape.

Madame Corvaja poured out routine affabilities, criticized Stalin and praised the *Marriage of Figaro* being performed in London at that time. But it was clear that the real business of the moment was with Ernesto, from whom I was divided by a linguistic chaos. Sometimes, I judged by the rise in his tone of voice and his eyebrows that I was being questioned, and I was obliged to reply by mumbling almost anything that came into my head. I was irresistibly reminded of a waxwork grouping at Madame Tussaud's, to which a miraculous animation had been added.

Eventually the presentation was at an end. Following instructions I bent over Madame Corvaja's hand and brushed it with my lips, Ernesto gave me a limp hand, and renewed his perfunctory smile and the parents withdrew. I was told that in leaving the room Ernesto had said to his wife, '*Machè? È un cenciauolo?*' ('Has she brought a rag-picker home?') for which, when his comment was repeated to his daughter, he received a severe reprimand.

A month or two later, to the huge surprise of those who knew us, we were married. It was to be a marriage with a difference, a bold experiment undertaken with open eyes, a step in a new direction. Society – in this case represented by Ernestina's father and mother – would demand a signed legal paper, and they should have it.

Thereafter concessions would stop. We agreed that a working partnership between a man and a woman could be a valuable arrangement, but there were to be no ties or sanctions. Ernestina would keep her own name, and we declared ourselves free to come and go as we pleased, and to part – if it ever came to that – without claim on each other. Needless to say, we were both earnest students of the doctrines of Bertrand Russell, and much as we agreed with his views on the subject of free love, we proposed to go a step further. This, we agreed, was not a love match. Romantic love was dismissed at best as an invention of Victorian novelists, at worst as a psychotic interlude. It was an arrangement inconceivable in any period outside the Thirties when revaluation of social customs could take extreme forms, and it was destined not to work as well as we had hoped it would. Later, in retrospect, I was more and more inclined to see the union as a way designed by Ernestina of freeing herself from the claustrophobia of family relationships, and from a Latin tradition she was at that time set upon renouncing – perhaps at any cost.

Inevitably all the circumstances attendant upon the ceremony were perfunctory and austere. Vows were exchanged in a quick embarrassed mumble in the prosaic setting of the Henrietta Street register office, the witnesses being Alexander and a current Hindu mistress, said to be heiress to a Bombay garment-making fortune, who suffered from a streaming cold. Following the ceremony the Woolworth's ring was thrown in the nearest dustbin, after which the ticklish problem presented itself of breaking the news to the Corvajas.

*

We found Ernesto and his wife under the blazing lights of the drawing room of Number 4, Gordon Street, neither of them having received the slightest warning of what was about to happen to them. Ernestina delivered a short take-it-or-leave-it speech, and as Ernesto listened, a grey patina seemed to spread across his cheeks. In silence he drew a hand across his face and the shadow was gone, and a defeated looseness of the jowls was drawn tight.

'Show me the paper,' he said in Italian, and Ernestina took the marriage certificate from her handbag and gave it to him. He read it very slowly, his eyes moving from side to side as he followed the lines of print, halted by so many unfamiliar words before plodding on. He examined the stamp and the signatures, nodding in the end his stunned conviction. At his back Madame Corvaja, a bloodless smile carved in her face, had been turned to a pillar of salt.

'*Non è uno scherzo, Papa,*' Ernestina assured him, eyes sparkling with a kind of triumph. I began to understand how firmly she was in command of the situation, and how in some way this was for her a moment of victory in her relationship with her father.

Suddenly Ernesto shook his head – as if to free himself from a web clinging to his face. He straightened and smiled at me, a little wolfishly, I thought. What I was witnessing was a classic example of the stoic Sicilian reaction to irretrievable calamity, known in their enigmatic island as 'swallowing the claws of the toad'. As if he had remembered an essential part of a religious ceremony, he next stepped forward a little stiffly, and took me into his embrace, stretching to his full height to squeeze his cheeks against mine and kiss the lobe of each ear. For a moment he rummaged through his stock of English for the proper words. 'I will give you my blood,' he then said.

Madame Corvaja, released from her spell, had rushed from the room and was now back with a maid, carrying a tray with champagne.

I moved on a temporary basis into the Corvajas' house, being instantly and wholly accepted as a member of the family. The situation is a familiar Mediterranean one where, by the survival of an ancient custom, it is normal for a husband to live – often for some years – with his in-laws before setting up a separate household, although the reverse is less frequently encountered. The tensions inherent in such an arrangement in the Anglo-Saxon world are rarely present in such cases, and the English stereotype of the overbearing mother-in-law is absent. Almost overnight I was absorbed into the traditional Latin family. Being a Sicilian household this 'Latin-ness', whatever its advantages and disadvantages, was exaggerated, seeming to call upon the individual member to surrender a little of his separate identity in exchange for the solidarity and protection of the tightly-knit family group. Despite this highly traditional background, the senior Corvajas faced each new situation as it arose in an alien land with an extraordinary openness of mind, and whatever astonishment they may have felt when Ernestina announced to them that we should be occupying separate rooms, nothing of this showed in the quasi-oriental composure of their faces.

Neither of the senior Corvajas ever permitted themselves a criticism of me, except on the single occasion when, as we were about to visit a restaurant together, Ernesto suggested that I should smarten up my appearance. To this, as if inspired by an afterthought, he added, ' – and always strive to develop character.'

Rootlessness and isolation were prime factors in our being married. I was isolated and Ernestina was even more so, isolation in her case being largely a product of the excessive cosmopolitanism of her upbringing. The Corvajas were a family of Spanish origin who had settled in Sicily in the seventeenth century while it still remained attached to the Spanish Kingdom, and it was perhaps to retain some link with the ancestral country that Ernestina had been sent to complete her education in Spain. It had been first Sicily, then the United States, followed by Spain, France and England. Thus she had never lived long enough in any country to soak up the prejudices and adopt the standpoints by which a personality is to some extent defined. She, like her parents, was devoid of class-consciousness, religious belief, and patriotism. There was not even an anchorage for her in a true native tongue which, even for a polyglot, is the vehicle for thought, because she spoke English, Spanish, Italian and French with equal fluency, and I am sure that there were times when she was not sure which language she was speaking. She was in urgent need of a tradition, a sense of history, allegiances, attitudes and a firm point of view, and I was the last person to be of any assistance to her in the attainment of any of these things.

Imprisoned within the intensely parochial life of the outer suburbs, the working day surrendered to sales patter for yeast tablets and the fraudulent elixir, the glum pick-ups in Church Street, Enfield and Hilly Fields Park, the teeth-baring bonhomie of the saloon bar of the George and Dragon, and the Saturday night hop at the Oddfellows' Hall, I had lifted up my eyes to the expansive horizons of the cosmopolitan world. But the situation in which I found myself was not quite that. In their way – and with good reason, as I was to find – the Corvajas joined me in the search for escape, although we pursued always fugitive ends in markedly different ways.

There were four in the Corvaja family, including a teenage son, Eugene, who went to a London school, and was becoming rapidly and fairly painlessly Anglicized. How far this process had gone can be gauged from his reaction to a family ceremony which had taken place a few years before. A number of Ernesto's friends had called at the house, and Eugene had been instructed to remove his trousers and climb on a table to permit his penis to be examined, to ritual cries of astonishment and delight. This would have been of no importance to a Sicilian boy steeped in the local tradition, but, infected as he was by this time with Anglo-Saxon prudery and reserve, it was an incident Eugene remembered with some embarrassment.

My mother-in-law, Maria, conducted the usual household tasks aided by a pair of young Welsh girls imported from some wretched mining village in Wales, who suffered the normal degree of exploitation that was the lot of so many of the daughters of that martyred country. What time that was left over from her severe and exacting surveillance of their work she would devote to the making of unsuitable shepherdesses' dresses, or the reading of literary classics in several languages. The possession of a near-photographic memory – this she had passed on to her daughter – enabled her to read at great speed and to devour books at a rate of never less than one a day.

Ernesto might have been regarded by an outsider as

the most interesting member of the family. His ancestor, Prince Corvaja, had bought his princedom (one of 147) from the Spanish crown for 2,000 scudi, and built the small but exquisite Corvaja Palace in Taormina, now a national monument. Some of the new princes and dukes who had had to scrape together the money to pay for their titles remained poor for the rest of their lives, others became some of the richest men in Europe. The Corvajas did well out of sulphur, scooped up by child slaves in the most fiendish of all mines, crawling through tunnels that were too narrow to admit an adult. These were the facts of history and his family's past which Ernesto declined to discuss. Withdrawn in manner as he was, and dressed always as if attending at an important funeral, he was obsessed by an appearance of gaiety, with brilliance and light. The decorated gilt panels on the doors of his drawing room were his own work, and their Arabian motifs and geometric abstraction were repeated throughout the house. Having finished with the doors he began work on the ceilings, painting them with cheerful and indulgent scenes of fat-limbed *putti* bouncing on haloed clouds, his personal inspiration reinforced by Michelangelo's oeuvre in the Sistine Chapel, of which he possessed an excellent set of hand-painted illustrations.

Strong light shone everywhere in the Corvajas' house. They eschewed shadows and the dark. There was no unlit corner, no spookiness under the stairs, no heavily-draped curtains behind which an intruder could lurk. Every cupboard, when opened, was flooded with refulgence from high-powered lamps. Occasionally, when it seemed to Ernesto that a total of several thousand candle-power offered insufficient illumination, a spotlight of the kind used on a film set would be switched on as soon as a visitor appeared in the doorway. Sometimes Ernesto, described in his passport as a diamond dealer, would take a fine lawn handkerchief from his pocket in which, in professional style, he sometimes carried his diamonds. Placing a square of black cloth on the table immediately beneath the chandelier he would pour the diamonds from the handkerchief which, as they fell, made a faintly watery sound, the hiss and crackle of a high, thin waterfall tumbling off a distant cliff. I had no evidence of his ever buying or selling a single diamond, but this was an operation from which he clearly derived much aesthetic satisfaction.

The central feature of life in the Corvaja household was the evening meal. By day the house was a quiet one. Ernesto was normally engaged in a struggle with problems of perspective in ceiling-painting in one of the upper rooms. Maria would be gulping down snatches of Stendhal in brief interludes from the vigilance maintained over the work of her Welsh drudges. Eugene was at school and Ernestina had just taken employment with the firm of Lever Brothers where she worked on the translation of confidential documents into a number of languages under security conditions resembling those of a military establishment.

In the evening the family came together for the dinner ritual, conducted in a scene of the greatest animation. In their contacts with outsiders the Corvajas were quiet and undemonstrative, and although I have no way of knowing that this was the case, it was my theory that they sought release from the restraints they imposed upon themselves each day in what may have been a traditional

Sicilian way. Breakfast and lunch were regarded as unimportant, and consumed rapidly and in near silence, but the evening meal was elaborate and lengthy, eaten in the usual glare of lights, and to music – always excerpts from the operas of Verdi or Puccini, to which the elder Corvajas were passionately devoted – played on a first-rate gramophone turned up to an almost unendurable pitch.

Ernesto imported his own wine from Sicily, a lusty, full-bodied vintage with an alcoholic content causing it to be bracketed with sherry for the purpose of the payment of duty. The wine was imported in casks and siphoned with a rubber tube into innumerable bottles – a task which occupied many hours. By the time it was over, Ernesto's normally cadaverous complexion was suffused by the vinous flush caused by unavoidable swallowing over a long period of tiny amounts of wine. Under this unsuspected intoxication his normal reserve dropped on one occasion, and I was astonished to hear him talking of Palermo of the far past, shaking his head at the folly of which the young of his day had been capable. One day he had been driving with a friend in the Parco della Favorita, and the coachman, boasting of his skill with the whip, had pointed to a cat by the roadside and said to them, 'If I can kill it with a single blow, will you eat it?' The bet was taken, and the coachman killed the cat, and Ernesto and his friend descended from the carriage and set about preparing the meal. Branches for firewood were taken from convenient bushes, someone was sent for a pot, for olive oil and tomato sauce, and the stew was prepared and eaten on the spot. 'It was impossible to welsh on the bet,' Ernesto said. 'A man of honour cannot go back on his word.'

The park was a place where up-and-coming young males went to prove themselves, sometimes in a desperate fashion. Another acquaintance of Ernesto's, seeking to 'make his bones', as the Sicilians put it, provoked an encounter with a prestigious rival, and received a knife thrust delivered with such practised skill that he was virtually disembowelled, without however the actual severance of an intestine (Ernesto, who may have been joking, said that such thrusts were practised on pigs or sheep). It was a moment, as the victor wiped his knife on his immaculate handkerchief, bowed smilingly and withdrew, which called for cool-headed action, and this the wounded *piciotto* took. Gathering his entrails with no signs of dismay, let alone panic, into his hat, he stopped a passing fiacre, got in, and had himself driven to hospital. In a couple of months he was out again and back in the park, settling to wait for weeks, months, if necessary years, for the opportunity to settle accounts. 'He showed great presence of mind,' Ernesto said.

After two or three glasses of Ernesto's powerful wine an extraordinary change came over the members of the family. As if by agreement they began to argue with each other, arguments leading to quarrels of a violence I had never experienced before, with members of the family screaming to make themselves heard over the powerful operatic bellowing of Caruso or Tito Gobbi. Whenever this happened the terror-stricken cats shot under the table, and the fairly tame kestrel, equally startled, took off from the reproduction Donatello's David on which it normally perched, to flap in a distraught fashion round the room before coming to rest again on David's head upon which it would invariably release a copious dropping.

These nightly disputes arose over the most trivial causes, differences of opinion as to the highest building in New York, or the number of children given birth to by Queen Victoria. They were accompanied by terrible oaths in various languages, Eugene having recently been able to increase the repertoire of family invective by listing all the swear-words in English he had picked up in school.

Suddenly, at a moment when I felt sure that real violence, even tragedy was not to be averted, the storm was past, and reason and urbanity reigned again. Ernesto would settle himself, benign and contemplative, with a small brandy, Maria might pat her temples with *eau de Cologne*, while Eugene would avail himself of the moment of reconciliation to take off 'Your Tiny Hand is Frozen', and replace it inconspicuously with the new Duke Ellington.

The two most vociferous disputants were always Ernestina and her father, and despite the almost purely ritual character of these daily rows I began to suspect beneath the familiar histrionics the reality of a latent antagonism. It was some months before Ernestina admitted that so far as she was concerned this was the case.

The story was that shortly before being packed off to school in Spain, a nanny had been brought into the house to look after her brother and herself, a pretty girl about whom her mother had instantly had her doubts. Ostensibly the girl was the daughter of an old friend Ernesto wanted to help out, but, employing a private detective, Maria soon discovered that she had been Ernesto's mistress for some time before he had conceived the daring but ill-starred plan for making her person more readily available by smuggling her into the family home. With extraordinary professional competence the detective had been able to discover Ernesto's password by which he obtained access to his safe deposit in Chancery Lane, from which a number of letters were recovered full of amatory material of the most explicit character. What I was not told, but learned from a gossiping in-law much later, was that Maria waited for Ernesto just inside the front door when he returned home that evening and shot him at close range with the ridiculous little .22 pearl-handled revolver she still carried in her handbag when I first knew her. The occasion was dramatic but the damage slight, for the bullet, aimed at the heart, stuck in the gristle under the collar bone. Ernesto took a taxi round to the doctor who readily extracted the slug, and was back within the hour, by which time Maria had doused the nanny with the contents of a slop-pail kept ready for the moment and thrown her into the street. A fulsome reconciliation followed, and life at Gordon Street went on as if nothing had happened.

It remained a mystery to me that, while the relationship between husband and wife had settled to an obviously affectionate one, Ernestina should have decided to take up a cause her mother no longer had the slightest desire to defend. I could only suspect the existence of obscure psychological factors of which Ernestina herself may have been unconscious. Up to this time the relationship between father and daughter seemed to have been an exceptionally close one. Ernesto had made sure that his eldest child should have – as he saw it – the best of everything, while up to and through her adolescence she made it quite clear that he had occupied the centre of the stage of her life. Each saw the other as a paragon. Everyone complimented Ernesto on the possession of a beautiful and talented daughter, on her great store of precocious knowledge, her charm and her wit. She in turn constantly witnessed the deference shown her father by visitors to the house from Europe and the United States, how they bowed themselves into his presence and, if from Sicily, frequently pressed his hand to their lips. Now, suddenly, womanhood had taken her unawares, demoting an immortal father to common humanity, exposing his innumerable fallibilities, and she was guilt-ridden and resentful that her love for him should have failed. So this sordid little passage salvaged from the past had come to her aid. It was impossible to say to him, 'I no longer love you.' Far easier, 'You betrayed my mother.'

The watershed, as it seemed to me, in the relationship between my father-in-law and my wife, was reached as a result of the episode of the emerald ring, although this too, I suspected, was no more than an excuse to open up a campaign on a new front, when the quarrel over the fake nanny had begun to flag.

Ernesto had bought his daughter several valuable necklaces, a diamond-encrusted wristwatch, a spectacular diamond and sapphire ring, and for her seventeenth birthday he had made the journey to Santander to present her with a plain gold ring in which was set a large emerald.

She was proud of the journey, undertaken with some effort at that time, as well as the ring itself. 'He was three days on the train,' she said. 'All that way to be with me on my birthday. I was the envy of the whole school. The diamond ring is more valuable, but I don't like it so much.' She would slip off the emerald ring, twist it under a lamp and laugh with pleasure, or hold it against a background of a silk scarf, or her dress, so that the emerald tempered the colour of the silk with its secret viridescent flash. Spanish was the language reserved for the praise of the emerald: '*Ay qué bonito! Mira los colores. Es exquisito. No te parece?*'

But one day Ernestina's suspicions about the ring seem to have been aroused. She took it to a Bond Street jeweller, under the pretence of offering it for sale, and he put a glass in his eye, examined the back of the stone, shook his head and handed it back. Briefly he told her that the emerald was a 'chip' cut from a larger gem and that, possessing a flat base, was of far less value than a perfect stone shaped as a rhombohedron.

Possibly by Ernestina's design I was present when the inevitable confrontation took place.

'Did you know the emerald was a chip?' Ernestina asked, deadly calm in her manner.

Ernesto said, 'You were a young girl. Only an expert can tell the difference. It was an expensive ring.'

'You deceived me,' Ernestina said. She took the ring from her finger, walked to the window and threw it into the street. Now she had discovered a personal grudge with which to reinforce vicarious injury.

The formal visit by the Corvajas to my parents in Enfield took place shortly before the opening of the breach. Ernestina and I had been to Enfield on many occasions, but by the time the Corvajas had brought themselves to the pitch of journeying to the outer suburbs a coldness had developed between Ernestina and my mother, the fault lying largely with my mother. Ernestina got on well enough with my father, who was warm in manner, more adaptable, and could even be gallant, but my mother exhibited all the traditional defects of an Anglo-Saxon – or in this case, Welsh – mother-in-law, and it was clear to all of us that Ernestina would never be received by her as a daughter, however much Ernesto and Maria Corvaja treated me as a son.

The Corvajas rarely left their house except to visit the opera or once in a while for some celebratory meal, eaten in an upstairs private room in Gennaro's restaurant in Frith Street. The journey to Enfield involved them in much forethought and planning. Sicilians are the most urban of people, with an affection for bricks and mortar and the consoling familiarities of the home. Largely this is a response to an environment which has compelled people to draw close together for protection, in a country with no isolated houses, no villages and no town so small that it could not muster a defence force in an emergency to fight off an attack by an armed band. As late as the period immediately following the last war there were some twenty of these at large, spreading terror through the countryside.

In the Corvaja household one minded one's own business and asked no questions. So engrained is this traditional Sicilian reserve that I was sometimes inclined to the theory that normal human curiosity, as we understand it, did not exist among them. Sometimes however, grudgingly, reluctantly, sensitive facts could no longer be suppressed, and what began to look like more and more extraordinary security measures controlling the family's movement had to be explained. Ernesto, Maria explained, had to be on his guard from a visitor from America who might visit London with the intention of killing him. Hence the ineffective pistol carried in her handbag. Hence the imposing snub-nosed (and loaded) revolver in the top drawer of Ernesto's desk. She added one further piece of information: that Ernesto had narrowly escaped death in an ambush a few days before they had taken the first ship out of New York, his hat on this occasion having been blown off his head. On these matters Ernesto himself preferred to add no comment.

The visit to Enfield must have seemed to the Corvajas as novel and strange as a traveller's first experience of the Amazon rain forest. They knew nothing of England outside a square mile of London's West End, and the ten-mile drive in the old Bugatti through some of Europe's seediest suburbs came as an eye-opener to them. Maria, a kindly and compassionate woman, although imbued with a 'let them eat cake' attitude where the poor were concerned, could not understand how people could consent to live in Tottenham and Edmonton, and why there were no taxis about. Forty Hill, Enfield, bewildered the Corvajas for other reasons. Apart from the rusty planes growing in Gordon Square, Ernesto had seen few trees since the old days of the Parco della Favorita in Palermo. Now, suddenly, he found himself deep in flowering cherry orchards, reacting to them with a curiosity not wholly free from suspicion. Sicilians had good reason to distrust wooded places, so much so that precautionary deforestation had left a single sizeable reserve of woods in the whole country, the Ficuzza, which still gave shelter, I was informed, to numerous outlaws.

Our small house must have astonished them too, in its terrible vulnerability. We trudged together up the garden path, and it occurred to me that this might have been the first time in twenty or thirty years that the Corvajas had walked on anything but lush carpets and city pavements.

The unfamiliar presence and scent of foreigners set all the local dogs barking, and Ernesto nodded his approval of their outcry. It was good to have reliable watchdogs about the place.

The meeting, from the very beginning, showed signs of being a great success, and the Corvajas, who had probably prepared themselves to crunch on the claws of more toads, were clearly delighted to find that my father and mother were normal human beings, eccentric perhaps in their choice of living accommodation, but no more than that, certainly harmless and reasonably intelligent in a cold-blooded English way. Ernestina, who was exceedingly vivacious when pleased, made a successful effort to be kind to my mother, and my father nodded instant agreement when I asked him to switch off the musical box tinkling 'Guide Me Oh Thou Great Redeemer' in the background.

After the brilliant emptiness of life at Gordon Street, our modest house, the garden and the surrounding orchards seemed to the Corvajas encrusted with small wonders, which they investigated with the delight of children collecting offerings left by the sea on a sandy beach. The exotic birds in my father's garden aviary entranced them, and Ernesto wondered if he could not build something similar into one of his bathrooms. My father amazed them with the present of a pot plant which had been in some way cajoled into becoming host to mistletoe. Best of all for them were the weird-looking Polish Fancy chickens that lurched about the place half-blinded by their feathered crests, and Ernesto took the name of the last remaining supplier, determined to buy some to relieve the squalor of his back garden. Although both my father and Ernesto could only normally be understood by members of their own family, it was quite extraordinary the degree of communication they established, although my father admitted later that it had proved a disappointment to find that his dog Latin did not help.

Maria, grossly over-painted, frilled and flounced, danced from plant to plant in the garden, insisting that everything she found growing there was edible if cooked with the right herbs. For once the sun shone, the trees held their umbrellas of blossom over us, hundreds of blackbirds were in full song. A spotty local girl on the arm of her lover arrived to deliver a pot of cream, and Maria said it reminded her of a scene from *Cavalleria Rusticana*. What could be a greater tribute to Forty Hill, Enfield, on a May morning than that it should be seen so closely to imitate the opera? Life, displayed here in so many small facets of delight, must have presented a moment of joy of the kind the Corvajas had not known for years.

The Corvajas had brought with them the ritual gift of *panetone*, the bread of love from pagan times, exchanged by all Italians on feast days, and in particular at Christmas. When removed from its festive wrappings of blue and gold paper, what remains is in fact stale bread dressed up to look like cake, but my parents munched it with a civilized pretence of relish. Ernesto had also brought a bottle of Gancia along to wash the stuff down with, and this was opened up. My father had his fair share of Welsh hypocrisy where alcohol was concerned, and normally let himself be seen only drinking Wincarnis, which he claimed – despite his contempt for medicines – that he took for health reasons. He had to be persuaded that Gancia was its Italian equivalent before he consented to take a glass – although this was soon followed by a second.

It was inevitable that my mother, refusing to be guided by me, should have gone to her friends for advice as to what her foreign guests would like to eat. The general agreement was that where Italians were concerned one could not go wrong with spaghetti, and this view received further support from the strong body of vegetarians in the movement, who declared this to be a vegetarian dish. When informed at the last moment that this was what was proposed, my heart sank, for spaghetti like panetone is ritual food, bearing as prepared in the average English home little resemblance in appearance, substance or flavour to the Italian original. The Corvajas, moreover, were tremendous gourmets. Maria was an exponent of the refined north Italian cuisine in which a strong French influence is to be detected, while Ernesto's preference was for typical Sicilian dishes. These suggested the survival of a Moorish tradition, and whenever an excuse could be found the meat they contained was spiced with such ingredients as ginger, cumin, coriander, cardamoms and saffron to which might be added various kinds of chillies, and above all an abundance of garlic. The Corvajas rarely bothered with spaghetti, but when they did it was cooked with rare expertise, and finicky attention to detail.

My mother led me away to inspect the dish in course of preparation. I found it to be a coarse version of macaroni, the only form of pasta to be had locally, a rank of thick-walled, rubbery tubes simmering in cream in a dish under a layer of tomato sauce squeezed from a tube. My mother worked from a cookery book which suggested a cooking time of thirty minutes, but she was allowing forty minutes to be on the safe side. By this time I foresaw that the macaroni would be reduced to a pulp.

In due course we were seated at table and the guests were invited to serve themselves from the ochreous mess sizzling in the dish. Gastronomic disaster was confronted by the Corvajas in the same adventurous spirit with which the other incidents of their day in the country had been faced. The Gancia was now at an end, but my father produced a bottle of Wincarnis, of which, for his health's sake when the rest had been served, he permitted himself a half-glass.

Despite everything, and largely due to the Corvaja enthusiasm and resilience, things were going remarkably well. Ernestina had put on the best possible front with my mother, and insisted on helping out with small domestic tasks, and now they frequently exchanged sickly smiles. Watching my father closely however, I detected certain familiar and worrying symptoms. They were picked up by my mother too, who began to wave her hands about vigorously as if to dissipate a cloud of smoke. Ernesto and his wife paid not the slightest attention to this behaviour which they probably assumed to be part of a traditional welcoming ceremony in a British household.

I knew only too well now what was about to happen. After a decade of mediumship my father had never developed predictability or controllability. At his best his performance probably surpassed that of the average professional medium, but these whatever their limitations, accomplished what was asked of them in a subdued and orderly fashion, and with as much regard for the niceties of time and place as, say, an insurance broker. My father had never achieved anything approaching this bland professionalism, and there was something haphazard and all too spontaneous about what he had to offer. A group which had gathered for a seance might sit for hours on end in a fog of incense, to chant Sankey and Moody and set the musical box endlessly tinkling, and absolutely nothing would happen. Father dealt in the unexpected. It was a painful fact that at no other time could he call up the souls of the dead with greater ease than at the table set for Sunday lunch, with possibly a couple of relatives present, when without the slightest encouragement or preamble and before the guests had had time to dip their spoons into their soup, he would unleash his apocalyptic torrent.

These experiences, to which I never became hardened, caused me paralysing embarrassment. The first time at the age of twelve or thirteen, when trapped in such an ordeal, I scrambled under the table and remained there until it was all over, and later I got out of the room as fast as ever I could, on picking up the first warning sign. But now, knowing what was coming, there was no escape. My mother's gesticulations of exorcism would clearly fail, and the stern commands with which she ordered the hovering spirit not to intrude upon our lunch party would also, as I could see, have no effect. My father closed his eyes, and began a soft, preliminary braying, the knife and fork fell from his hands, and he began to writhe and sweat.

All these goings-on appeared to escape the Corvajas' notice, as they continued to tackle their macaroni with imperturbability. Ernestina, who had been warned by me that such things could happen, looked down and dickered with the mess on her plate. My father, ceasing to writhe, had now begun to babble softly, and this was a danger sign. My mother, realizing that the thing was out of control, had given up and was murmuring a prayer, eyes closed. I gripped the edges of my chair, ready for the worst, while the unshakeable Corvajas continued their mastication.

There was a moment of electric silence, then a child's voice spoke. 'Mamma, mamma, mamma.' It was impossible to continue with the farce of pretending to eat. We exchanged bewildered, stricken looks. My embarrassment bordered on panic. I longed to get up and dash from the room.

'Mamma,' the voice said again. 'Mamma.' It was thin, and unearthly and troubled, and I felt Maria at my side go tense.

'Yes, darling. Darling, I'm here. This is mamma.'

Now I was confronted with the second shocking aspect of this situation. Maria Corvaja, a self-proclaimed atheist, had been taken by surprise by belief.

'Mamma, oh mamma.'

'I'm here, darling. I'm listening,' Maria cried out. 'Where are you? Talk to me.'

'Oh Mamma, mamma, mamma.'

The thin, whining little voice had become progressively weaker, and now it trailed off into silence. It was all over. My father opened his eyes, blinking, still far away from us, and my mother was ready with a sponge and cold water with which she sponged his forehead. Then we all got up and went into the garden, where Maria affirmed her conviction that the voice was that of her second child, who had died some ten years before. For me the voice could have been that of any young child, but it remained a puzzle and always would, how it could have been produced by the vocal cords of a man of sixty. I had no way of knowing whether my father had ever heard of the existence of this second daughter.

The visit had two lasting effects on the Corvajas' lives. Maria became a clandestine spiritualist, although to me her furtive incursions into that uncharted and illusory territory in which my parents had so long wandered in search of their lost one, suggested little more than the exchange of resignation for heartache.

An unimportant development was that Ernesto now became even more of an animal-lover than he had been, adding to the dog, the cats, and the tame hawk so often encountered in Italian families, a brood of chickens in which he delighted, and which for him typified the delights of the rustic scene. Since Polish Fancies and other freakish breeds of the kind recommended by my father could not be procured at short notice, my mother-in-law went to the pet shop in Tottenham Court Road, bought a dozen week-old Rhode Island Reds, plus a sizeable coop, and installed this in their bedroom – a large semi-basement chamber in which an almost complete absence of daylight was compensated for, in Corvaja style, by a huge excess of electrical voltage.

The chicks' stay in the coop was short. During the daylight they had the run of the room, fouling the Bokhara carpet to their hearts' content, and at night they slept in the matrimonial bed. Both Corvajas took an interest in their diet. They were fed the best Italian food, chopped mortadella, Parma ham, and rice flavoured with garlic and saffron, plus occasional cannibalistic treats of chicken flesh cooked in various complex styles. The result from this remarkable start in life was that they all developed extreme cases of rickets, staggering through the basement rooms, balanced on their wing tips, upon grossly bent and distorted legs, although otherwise in good shape and possessed of exceptional sexual energy. Like all other mild eccentricities abounding in the Corvaja household, the poultry-keeping mania was accepted by Ernestina and her brother with extreme phlegm.

All in all the trip to Enfield could be counted a success. The Corvajas and my parents had taken a liking to each other, and Ernestina now did her best to conquer her dislike for my mother, and to make allowances for her absurdly over-possessive attitude towards her only son. There followed regular visits by my parents to Gordon Street, where they were entertained – in the preferred English way, as the Corvajas believed – invariably with the accompaniment of hot crumpets and strong tea.

Chapter Eight

WITHIN A FEW weeks of the Enfield visit a summons came to Wales, and this filled me with huge misgivings. I had paid two duty visits in Carmarthen since the disastrous eighteen months spent there in child-hood, noting – although Li lived at home once more – a change for the worse in my grandfather and my aunts. Now it was my turn to be involved in family affairs of the kind I would have wished to avoid.

About two years previously my grandfather, who had continued to sell tea until the age of eighty-six, passed away in his sleep. When the will was read my father learned that he had been disinherited – something for which he was well prepared, and which in no way surprised him. There were more grievous consequences for his brother, my Uncle John, who had worked for the old man all his life. The business had passed on to him, but the transfer had been tied up in such a way that most of the profits had to be paid to the aunts. John, under-standably, took to the bottle, died within the year, and his widow Aunt Margaret was obliged to sell her Car-marthen house and move into one of the picturesque, if slightly sinister cottages on the beach front at Llanste-phan. A low price for a quick sale was accepted for the business in King Street, and most of the money raised went to the aunts.

Following an unsatisfactory, even mystifying corre-spondence with solicitors and my Aunt Polly, a diplo-matic visit to Wales on my father's part was called for, to see what, if anything, could be done to rescue Margaret from the penury into which she had been plunged. At this point my father informed me that he was tired of life, and that nothing would induce him to leave Enfield again. The diplomatic visit then fell to my lot. My problem now was that Ernestina was determined to accompany me.

'You don't realize what you're letting yourself in for,' I said.

'It's no good trying to talk me out of it. I wouldn't miss it for anything.'

'What you have to remember is you're not dealing with ordinary, civilized people. They'll probably tell you to go away.'

'Well, if they do, I will.'

'Or even throw something at you.'

She giggled. 'Not even relations of yours could be as uncivilized as that.'

'All right then, but don't say I haven't warned you.'

There were two aspects to this particular quandary. The first was the traumatic effect the madhouse in Wellfield Road might have on our relationship. The second was that Ernestina's unaccommodating personality might endanger any hope of a negotiated settlement with these elderly and unbalanced ladies, consumed as they were with suspicion and paranoia, and inevitably detesters of foreigners of every kind.

A central legend of the Celtic people is that of the Lady of the Lake: the union between a human being and a fairy who endows her human husband with all manner of material and spiritual benefits, but who leaves him when he objects to her irrational behaviour. There were times in our association when I was reminded of the legend. The fairy at Myddfai startled the human beings among whom she lived by exaggerated displays of feeling, and this sometimes happened with Ernestina too. She had a quick sense of humour which was easily stimulated, and would fall into paroxysms of laughter over some episode that most English people would not have found particularly funny. When listening, on the other hand, to an ex-convict describing in Hyde Park what it was like to suffer the cat-o'-nine-tails, she burst into vociferous weeping. Her rare fury was demonstrated by the occasion of the emerald ring.

I was convinced that it would not be a good idea at all to take Ernestina with me to Carmarthen, but she refused to be left behind. 'It sounds quite an adventure,' she said. 'I'm going to enjoy it.'

We drove to Wales, and stayed at the Ivy Bush Hotel in Carmarthen, where I called on a number of distant relatives and made enquiries as to the situation at Wellfield Road. They were able to tell me little. The aunts had become recluses, no longer seen outside the house, which was dirty and neglected-looking and badly in need of a coat of paint.

Carmarthen too had changed for me, grown smaller, seedier, drained of all the magic it had had for me, even as a captive, when a child. There had been so many freedoms no one had been able to shut out: the little bright snails, pink, yellow and blue, that had come over the walls in their hundreds to deliver themselves into my eager collector's hands; the cackle of the knowing jackdaws awaiting their cake; the song of the linnets and the goldfinches I trapped; even the freedom expressed in the smell of the country town itself, spreading through all the lanes and entering every window, which was of ferns, and milk and freshly wetted earth. Above all I remembered with nostalgia the great freedom of escape with Aunt Li to the summit of Pen-lan, followed as we trudged up into the mists by the chiming every quarter-hour of the bells of St Peter's church, which became thinner and sweeter until they were gone, and I heard nothing more but our footfalls and Aunt Li's sighs.

Having spied out the land as best I could, there was no point in putting off the evil hour and we found ourselves at the door of the house in Wellfield Road, which was much smaller and greyer than I remembered, set in a garden that had become a tangled thicket in which brambles predominated. A square of cardboard covered a hole in one of the grubby windows, and the jackdaws nudging and jostling each other peered down at us from the roof. One thing remained in all this change and decay that was almost startlingly well cared for. This was the lawn, as immaculate as ever, and at that moment a grey little wraith of a woman, who I understood could be none other than my Aunt Li, was mowing it with an astonishing, almost frenzied vigour. Spotting us she stopped for a moment to treat us to a hostile glare before starting off again.

I rang the bell and the door opened instantly, and a firm, spruce, smiling man was there, hand outstretched. He introduced himself as Emrys Davies, a Baptist minister, who knew all about us and our projected visit. 'Your letter was passed on to me,' he said. He had put less important things aside to be able to welcome us in a proper fashion. Miss Warren Lewis, he said – referring in this way with formal respect to my Aunt Polly – had not been herself for the past few days.

We were conducted into her presence by someone who clearly had the run of the house. She sat, very small, shrivelled and shapeless, in a large rustic chair at the head of the scrubbed table and, bending down to kiss her cheek, it seemed to me that the squares and oblongs of grafted skin were even more clearly outlined than before. Small, writhing shapes like those left by worms showed on the areas they left uncovered. Her eyes moved and she made a faint sound like a *tchk* of exasperation, but there was no way of knowing whether she recognized me.

All the ugly, functional kitchen objects were in their places as I remembered them, and a trick of memory brought back the faint bloody reek of pigs' intestines in a tin bath awaiting their transformation into chitterlings. The Reverend stood behind her, bland as a Buddha, like a man displaying a well-grown vegetable at a show of garden produce.

'Auntie,' I said. 'Auntie, we've come to see you. How are you, Auntie? It's been a long time.'

The stripes of tissue that served for lips parted, to release a faint, scratchy whisper.

The Reverend Davies translated this. 'Very happy indeed she is that you and your new wife have come here to see her,' he said.

The faint throaty sound went on. At one point Aunt Polly nodded her head in emphasis of whatever she had to say, showing a scarred and polished scalp that was now quite bald.

'A long and arduous journey from London as we all know,' the Reverend Davies went on. 'Nice it is to be showing such consideration for your aunts. Better it might have been to postpone your visit for one week, as

Miss Lewis has just embarked upon a new treatment for her condition, which recently has shown signs of deterioration. After lunch I always insist on a short nap, which is important to conserve her strength. Your Aunt Elizabeth asks to be excused for one moment until she has completed her task in the garden. But your Aunt Anne will be waiting for you in the breakfast room when you are ready.'

'She'll frighten you out of your wits,' I warned Ernestina. 'She can't stop laughing, and you'll probably find she's dressed up as a pirate.'

The scene that met our eyes in the breakfast room was quite otherwise. Annie sat on the floor, barefoot and dressed in a grubby shift. The hair hung like grey seaweed over her eyes, and the laughter had dried up. She was absorbed in painting a tiny face which had inherited her vacant smile on an acorn, which would when finished be added to a small pile already painted in this way, and there was no sign that she was aware of our presence. This, the Reverend Davies later explained, was a therapeutic task she had learned in a 'home' where she had been confined for some time, and where Li, preceding her, had been kept busy endlessly mowing lawns. So this was the end of Grandfather's once cherished and protected family, and of the little empire founded on spoiled tea that had brought him the Model T Ford, the house with teak doors, the deaconhood of his chapel, the French mistress, the touch of a king's fingers.

'Mr Lewis, bach,' the Reverend Davies' musical voice sounded over my shoulder. 'Come you, Mr Lewis bach, and Mrs Lewis. Time now to partake of something to refresh the body. You don't mind in the kitchen? Miss

Lewis is happier there. This is my little kingdom, she sometimes says.'

He had slipped away while we had been occupied with Aunt Annie, and now, as if by magic, places had been set at the table, with napkins folded intricately and thrust into glasses. The Reverend lifted a chicken in a casserole from the oven. 'Head cook and bottle-washer I am today,' he said, cheerily. 'All I'll be needing now is a chef's hat.' He picked up a small brass bell and dingled it, and Annie shuffled into the room carrying a bowl like an oriental beggar, and he sawed delicately at the chicken's breast to cut off two slices of meat, which he dropped into the bowl before shooing her away. There was no sign of Li but we could hear the irrepressible click and natter of the mower as she trudged backwards and forwards over the lawn.

'Come now, Miss Lewis. Time for a little nourishment, isn't it?' The Reverend Davies had taken up a position behind the chair on which Polly sat like a freshly unwrapped mummy, her features blurred from the old injuries and the tiny, black, motionless eyes veiled in a pinkish webbing which the body had provided in an effort to replace the lost lids. He had placed a fork in the small, clawed-up right hand and with it he helped her to skewer a morsel of chicken and lift it to her mouth. 'Miss Lewis, fach, eat you now,' he said, cajoling her in the comfortable country style. 'Necessary it is to refresh the body, as the soul.' He snatched a beautifully folded napkin from a glass, unfolded it and dabbed at the corners of her lips.

When it was all over, Ernestina and I took refuge in the drawing room, shabby and smeared now with the grime of years, where the parrot cage of old still stood, and the crack-throated piano had been left open to bare its yellowed teeth, and the ancient clocks, mysteriously kept wound, still disputed the hour of the day.

'Well, what do you think of it all?' I asked Ernestina and she shook her head.

I told her in a quick mutter that I'd summed Davies up by voice and manner as a one-time hell-raiser who'd won the battle for the Lord in the hills where sin meant unnatural conduct with animals before moving down to Carmarthen where the devil set up heavier targets.

A moment later, the Reverend joined us again, more breezy and self-confident and a little less bland in these fusty surroundings than he had been in the kitchen.

'Mr Lewis, far be it from me to wish to pry, but I would like to ask you if you will be visiting your Aunt Margaret in Llanstephan on this occasion?'

'I expect to see a number of my relations. As many as I can. Why do you ask?'

'Will you have heard that there has been a split between the two branches of the family?'

'Yes,' I said. 'I've heard that.'

'Mr David Warren Lewis was a member of my congregation for some years,' said the Reverend Davies and, studying his face again, I realized that he was probably twenty years older than I had taken him to be, a man comforted by certainties that had kept him young. 'The Miss Lewises are among my most cherished friends. I can hardly express my admiration for the courage with which they have faced certain afflictions.'

'They're very brave,' I said.

'It is my sincere hope that this quarrel that has arisen can be kept within bounds. A pity it would be to upset the delicate process of conciliation.'

'Mr Davies,' I said, 'I shall take the opportunity to see a solicitor while I'm here but I hadn't heard there'd been any conciliation. As I've been told this was a take-it-or-leave-it situation. And seeing the state my aunts appear to be in I don't see that they're capable of taking such a decision – or any other decision, for that matter – for themselves.'

'They're not, Mr Lewis, bach. That's the fact of it. They are obliged to lean upon their friends.'

'Including you.'

'Well naturally, as their pastor, including me.'

'Mr Davies, what are you trying to say? I can't see quite where all this is leading to. What do you expect me to do?'

'Well, since you put it that way, my advice would be to refrain from raising false hopes in Mrs Margaret Lewis's bosom. That is what I'm saying to you.'

'And you think I'm likely to do that?'

'Everything is possible. I know Mrs Margaret Lewis well. She's a very persuasive lady. To be absolutely frank, I would like to reach an agreement with you. Some very small concession might be possible. I can't promise it. If Mrs Lewis renounces any claims, I'm saying.'

'Much as I appreciate your kindness and your assistance, Mr Davies, this is a matter arising between my aunts. The most I can do is give them my advice. You talk about reaching an agreement with me; but I don't see where you come into it?'

Smiling and unruffled as ever, he reached in his pocket, took out a paper and handed it to me. Without reading it, I knew that it was a power of attorney.

Turning our backs on the depressing situation at

Wellfield Road, we drove to Llanstephan to consult with
my Aunt Margaret – always my favourite relative – a
glowing, pink-cheeked woman who had had the misfor-
tune to marry into the Lewises, and thereafter waste her
sweetness on the desert air. She had been a pretty girl
apprenticed to a master baker in Lammas Street when
my Uncle John had first spotted her. Such essential
occupations as bakery, with its sacramental undertones,
conferred little prestige in Carmarthen as elsewhere by
comparison with parasitic employment, and the scornful
nickname Maggie the Bun stuck to her for the rest of her
life. When I had lived in Wellfield Road as a child I had
sometimes been allowed, as a concession, to visit my
warm and hospitable Aunt Margaret in her own home,
but she was clearly never welcome in my grandfather's
house. In terms of all the human qualities, particularly of
dignity, she was enormously superior to my uncle, and
it was a shame that she had been forced by a pregnancy
to marry him.

In Llanstephan they no longer stoned holiday-making
miners, and ten years had gone since Mr Williams had
put up his placard for the last time warning Sunday
visitors to keep holy the Sabbath day, but a tight rein
was still kept on religious belief, the social life of the
village being firmly bound up with the chapel which
took a hard-line fundamentalist approach in matters of
faith.

Ernestina had fallen silent after Wellfield Road, but
her spirits revived at the edge of this salty wilderness.
Madonna lilies spread their faint, sweet deathliness in
every garden. It had rained earlier and now the sound
arose everywhere around us of the flinty chuckle of
pebbles moved by water in the bright rivulets on the

beach. These were the scents and the sounds, and for the eye there was nothing but the healing vision of the great smooth hump of the Silk Back over the water, and in it one last blackened spar of the old wreck, like a finger crooked at eternity. No one here could drag themselves clear from the past. In a nearby cottage curtains were lifted by unseen hands, then let fall, and presently two tall thin women in black, wearing flat wide-brimmed hats of the generation before, came out and began to walk very slowly and in step away from us, as if at the head of an invisible procession. A man with a donkey cart selling cockles and illegally netted sewin had turned the corner. Not a bad place for a widow to retire to, one would have said, after the drab terrace house in Carmarthen.

'Pretty it is, yes indeed,' my aunt agreed with enthusiasm. We sat in her trellised rose arbour, sipping the slightly salted Lewis tea. Wearied of beauty, she had placed herself with her back to the great seascape. 'But there's a sameness, isn't it?' she said. She was a philosophic old lady, never a one to complain, and now she faced the reality that there was faint hope of a civilized arrangement with her sisters-in-law or their advisers with profound resignation.

The problem that troubled her was the encroaching shadow of loneliness. Since she was likely to spend her remaining days in the village, acceptance into the local community was essential, and to do this she would have to become a member and a regular attender of a chapel where services were conducted in Welsh. This, as a townswoman, she spoke in a defective fashion, and was therefore placed at a great disadvantage. The minister had listened sympathetically and proposed a kind of associate membership during a period when she would be expected to learn some biblical texts and essential responses in classical Welsh. On the Sunday when this formal induction into the chapel and the life of the community was to take place, Aunt Margaret, full of hope and enthusiasm, had risen early, collected a large bunch of flowers, put them into a vase, and taken them to the chapel, to be interrupted as she was about to place them at the foot of the pulpit by the minister who rushed in, arms thrown out and shrieking in horror. 'Paganiad, Mrs Lewis, fach. Paganiad.'

Aunt Margaret's paganism would have to be publicly acknowledged and repented in an act of contrition to be spoken in Welsh. It was a proposal that daunted her, but she could expect to be cold-shouldered by the village until she had gone through with it. The inhumanity of her treatment by her sisters-in-law and their legal and spiritual advisers was the least of her problems.

Chapter Nine

THERE WAS SOMETHING in the atmosphere that forbade all reference to our recent experience on the drive back to London, although the conversation was lively enough upon other topics. I suspected with Ernestina that this was an occasion as with a young child when calamity is dismissed without comment. A little to my surprise she seemed anxious to get home. The journey to Wales was to have been part of a larger sight-seeing excursion. She had seen nothing of the country, and I suggested we might make a good start with Bath. But the projected side-trip seemed to have been forgotten. England was failing to live up to her expectations and, if not the English, almost certainly the Welsh too.

This small misadventure had happened at a time when Ernestina gave the impression of wishing to move further and further out of her father's orbit, and as a first step we had left London and rented a cottage in a wood at Iver in Buckinghamshire. It was the property of a noblewoman we never met who had filled it with majestic, decrepit beds, with imperial eagles embroidered on their silk counterpanes, and with drinking vessels of all shapes and colours, more than fifty varieties of them, designed to contain every known alcoholic liquor. Here we had lived in the deep shade of the pines for some weeks before Ernestina decided that the countryside no longer held any attraction for her and we found ourselves back in Gordon Street once more.

The day after our return from Wales Ernestina went through what I was now beginning to recognize as a recurrent phase. She was a girl who needed to laugh, and there were times when she would commit herself to an orgy of laughter, provoked in any way she could find. She had found that the easiest way out was to visit one or more of the so-called news cinemas that had recently opened in London to provide a short programme of news-reels interspersed with cartoons and knockabout comedy items. The first day back in London was spent in entertainments of this kind to which I did not accompany her. Apart from that she settled to reread old favourites from a collection of humorous writings she possessed, including much of Wodehouse, Jerome K. Jerome, and a prized hoard of excellent comic papers sent to her from America. After two days of this treatment she had quite recovered from whatever it was she had suffered, her giggles subsided and she could cope with the normal solemnity of the world.

Now suddenly she announced that she had given up the idea of living anywhere in England, and made the suggestion that we should emigrate to Spain, where she had spent the happiest times of her life. It was an idea that seemed attractive enough to me if only a way could be found of making a living there. In the early summer of 1936 we made a trip by car to Spain to investigate the possibility of such a move.

We drove to Seville and stayed there with the Estradas, friends of Ernestina, a young couple who lived in a tiny Moorish palace with an unimposing entrance next to a shoeshop in the celebrated Calle Sierpes – thus named from the serpentine fashion in which it twists through the heart of the old town. We found the city in a state of turmoil, and were told and could read for ourselves in the newspapers that the rest of the country was no better off. What we had no way of knowing was that the outbreak of the Civil War lay only a few weeks ahead.

Like most of Spain's upper and middle classes of their day the Estradas were staunch fascists. It would have been hard to imagine a man milder in appearance and manner than young Juan Estrada, but he was a landowner in an area where the peasantry lived in the harshest conditions in Europe, employed as seasonal labourers on vast estates for extremely low wages. The newspapers reported almost daily cases of peasants dying of starvation in nearby villages, and some three years before the police had carried out a massacre in the village of Casas Viejas where the peasantry had attempted to occupy uncultivated land.

On the first evening of our stay with them the Estradas took us for dinner to a fashionable restaurant some three miles out of town, an ancient coaching inn of great charm in a setting of featureless prairies of ripening wheat. On each of the tables placed in the shade of the vines a small pile of copper coins had been placed. Peasants – largely women and children – emaciated and in rags, lurked by a hedge surrounding the restaurant, and from time to time one of them would make a cautious advance to a table and, at a signal from a diner, pick up one of the coins – a half-peseta piece known as a *perro chico*. At intervals one of the restaurant staff would run out screaming abuse to slash at the beggars with a whip and drive them off. Within minutes they were back again and the mute submissive collection of these coins of minuscule value went on, virtually unnoticed by the diners, as before.

Juan Estrada very quietly and calmly explained to us that the time had come to put these people in their place.

He and a number of friends, all of them landowners and all excellent riders, had formed a band – well, almost a private army, he said – and in a matter possibly of days they would make the rounds of the villages and deal with the Reds in their own fashion. One of our fellow guests was a *rejoneador* who had been spearing bulls in the ring in Seville only the Sunday before, and laughingly he referred to this as valuable practice.

It was an environment in which Ernestina and I found ourselves out of our depths. Next day we started off on our way back, making for France. We took the direct route through Cáceres and Salamanca, to avoid Madrid, but just short of Plasencia we were stopped by a police roadblock and directed, with no reason given, to a diversion through the small town of Ciudad Rodrigo. The Sierra de Gata had to be crossed. It was the Europe of the Dark Ages, ghostly and skin-and-bone poor, with weasels sunning themselves in the dirt road, macabre trees, and once in a while a grey, wall-eyed shack with no glass in the windows and the slates sliding off the roof. For hours on end there were no signs of human presence.

Ciudad Rodrigo, grimed, sullen and silent, was closed up from end to end, doors bolted and windows shuttered. There was no one to ask the way, and when we stopped to study a road sign we heard the sound of shots terribly close and resonant in the narrow canyons of the streets. At the far end of the town we found the main hard-surfaced road to Salamanca, but a few miles further on two carts barred the road, and men carrying firearms of all descriptions came out from behind them. They had the underdog's face of the Spanish countryside, fleshless, displaying all the details of the skull, and they would have been interchangeable with the wretched peasants begging for ha'pence at the smart restaurant outside Seville, but for the dignity conferred by hunting rifles and fowling pieces.

They were quite happy to explain, almost in a childish way, what was going on, and to provide acceptable reasons for their interference with traffic. They pointed proudly to their red armbands, explaining that they were *milicianos del pueblo*, and that their village had been under attack by a fascist band which they had beaten off, leaving one dead. An unshaven, wild-eyed man, looking like a bandit but describing himself as the schoolmaster, had pushed to the front, and began a short pedantic lecture on the political situation, before being cut short by a heavy burst of firing from the far end of the village. At this we all lay down in the road behind the carts for perhaps ten minutes, after which, following the example of the *milicianos*, we began to crawl on hands and knees for the shelter of the nearest houses. We found ourselves in a small, dark, earthen-floored room with a mother and her two small children under the table and, resisting an impulse to join them, remained standing with our backs to the wall as far as possible from the small window, for about an hour, while sporadic firing went on – some from the roof above.

After that the schoolmaster was back, happy and excited by some new triumph. A mopping-up operation – he savoured the expression affectionately – and we would be obliged to go back to Ciudad Rodrigo to spend the night. The inn was for people who brought their sheep with them, he said, but at the other end of the scale, the Parador Nacional was highly to be recommended, and as this was closed for the emergency he proposed to go there with us and open it up.

A stop was made on the way to pick up a cook. The schoolmaster hammered on the great feudal door, and the caretaker let us in. He was happy to welcome us, he said. There was a hint of a suggestion by the cook, in her recommendation to us not to worry if we found there was too much to eat, as she had a large family at home who would help out.

In the morning the schoolmaster joined us for breakfast, so changed in his appearance as to be almost unrecognizable. He had had a close shave and was wearing a clean shirt, buttoned at the neck, and polished shoes, and the wild eyes of the night before were calm and confident. The gun slung over his shoulder seemed out of place in the sumptuous and orderly environment. He caressed it like a child before propping it against the leg of the enormous table and sitting down.

'Were you disturbed during the night?' he asked.

'I thought I heard shooting.'

'You did,' he said. 'The last of it. Now we are at peace again.' He gestured in a regal manner at the dark, grandiose furniture, the paintings, the tapestry. 'All this belongs to the people,' he said. 'Stay as long as you like, and tell them to send the bill to me.'

The cook, beaming and nodding, came in bearing a lordly dish on which tiny eggs with bright red yolks that might have been laid by a thrush floated in greenish olive oil. A separate platter held rashers of black mountain ham. It was clear that she had served English guests before, and understood their breakfast requirements. She was followed by the caretaker who opened shutters and windows, and we listened reassured to the slow exchange of neighbourly pleasantries, and the chiming of a bell.

'In Italy and Germany the fascists overthrew the people,' the schoolmaster said. 'What they did not understand was it could never happen here. When they struck we were ready for them. It was all over in a few hours. From now on you can go where you like, and no one will bother you.'

Four days later we were back in England, and a week later the Civil War broke out. The whole province of Salamanca was instantly occupied by Nationalist rebel troops, and there were few towns such as Ciudad Rodrigo where massacres did not take place; it is virtually certain that the schoolmaster would have been killed in one of these.

Chapter Ten

EARLY IN JUNE it was the Corvajas' custom to pack up and move to Ostend where they stayed for the three months' gambling season at the Casino, so that by the time we were back in England they had already left. Ernesto gambled every day, but gave us no account of his operations, nor did he welcome the presence of any member of his family when he was at the tables.

This year we were invited to stay a week with them. In conformity with Ernesto's dislike of flamboyancy in any form we found that they had installed themselves in a second-class hotel in a side street, where they had arranged for us to be put up. We took our meals in restaurants of the family kind, with the proprietress keeping severe watch in something like a telephone booth and with elderly waiters suffering from scurf, with copious grease-stains on their jackets. Ernesto, in fear of being despised by such as these, always overtipped, but then studied their faces anxiously to assure himself that they were satisfied.

The routine after dinner was that the couple would go off to the Casino together and Ernesto would stand by and watch Maria lose her small daily limit on rouge et noir, after which she would take a taxi back to the hotel. Thereafter, for her husband the business of the evening began in earnest. One evening there was an urgent telephone call from someone speaking broken English with a French accent, whose voice I recognized as that of a regular visitor at Gordon Street. Neither Ernesto nor Maria could be found, so the man left a message to say that his car had broken down, and he would not be at work at the usual time. Maria came in first and let the cat out of the bag. 'Oh, that must be Georges,' she said. 'The head croupier.' It is only to be supposed that Ernesto and Georges were involved in what is now known as a sting.

Ernesto never admitted to having won at the tables. At most he would say, 'I made my expenses.' Back in London when the season was at an end I would watch for signs of an increase in affluence, but there was none. There was no way of knowing with the Corvajas, remembering their traditional avoidance of conspicuous consumption. Maria went on wearing the same absurd dresses it seemed to me she had always worn, and the same old valuable but dowdy jewellery, and there was no scope in Ernesto's simple existence to indicate a change in fortune. In reality life offered them all they asked for without whatever extras Ernesto's forays at the Casino might have provided. Only one thing was denied to them – freedom of movement – for outside these annual trips to Ostend they had lived for so many years in what amounted to close confinement in London.

Life with the Corvajas had the effect in time of stifling natural curiosity. In a way the family members seemed to be reaching out with tentacles to anchor themselves to each other, and were ant-like and corporate in their activities. Yet with this it was clear that personal privacy was closely guarded, and no one was allowed to look into the Corvaja mind. Like the Arabs, the Sicilians seemed absorbed in current affairs. Just as in Arabic, there is no future tense in the Sicilian dialect, and in discussion I found that there was little taste or talent for reminiscence. These attitudes, I suspected, resulted from

the training of a sad history. Sicilians are avid for the
physical company of others, probably inspired by that
ancient and universal saying that there is safety in numbers. Yet when they are together – in the case of the
Corvajas apart from the ritual of the evening quarrel –
they easily fall into silence. I have never forgotten the
experience some years later of standing after nightfall in
the main street of the small Mafia-ridden town of Các-
camo, and watching the groups of males trudging endlessly up and down, each group carefully maintaining its
distance within a dozen or so yards of the next, while no
one spoke.

Suddenly, just after the return from Ostend, Ernesto
asked me to do him a favour, and what was proposed –
much to his discomfiture – could not be accomplished
without a revealing discussion of the problems involved.
He was obliged to begin at the beginning, cautiously and
grudgingly, and sketch in the details of his early life. Up
to this moment I had heard of little more than the
ambush in New York, and a few garish anecdotes of his
days as a young blood in Palermo. He now told me that
while in his twenties in Catania he had been charged with
a major crime, had escaped from prison and – through
the influence of an uncle, the Prior of one of the religious
orders – had been smuggled away to America. Later I
was to discover the existence of a family legend that he
had been carried aboard the ship bearing him to the New
World in a coffin in which the necessary air-holes had
been drilled. A further admission was that in New York
he had become a member of the Unione Siciliana, an
organization by his description formed to look after poor
Sicilian immigrants who suffered intense exploitation in
the States. To use his own words, 'My people were

under attack and I felt it my duty to do what I could to protect them.' For the first time I learned that he had studied law at the University of Berne, the suggestion being that he had served what is seen by outsiders as a somewhat sinister association in a largely advisory capacity. In New York he seemed to have lived in some style in an apartment stuffed with antique furniture, and not having by that time developed their appreciation of music, he and Maria spent their leisure hours together filling scrap-books with 'artistic pictures' cut from American magazines.

What must have been a pleasant and possibly exciting existence came to an abrupt end when Ernesto fell into the ambush as he was stepping down from a cab outside his apartment. The survival rate of those exposed to such an experience is negligible. Two machine-gun bullets carried his hat away, but he lived, and two days later he and his wife, leaving all their possessions, including their treasured scrap-books, took the boat for Europe. They chose England because, after the expiry of the original arrest warrant, Ernesto was placed under an order of permanent banishment from Italy.

Now, after the years of exile and the patient but possibly reluctant devotion to craftsmanship in the home, relieved only by the all too brief annual escape to Ostend, a way had been opened for the return to Italy. It all depended on the backing, if this could be secured, of a powerful fascist hierarch, Count Aldo Giordano, who lived in Milan. An approach had been made and negotiations that showed promise entered upon by one of Ernesto's Sicilian contacts. Then suddenly, when the affair seemed to be in the balance, all communication with this man had ceased, and all Ernesto could suppose was that he had fallen foul of the law. At this time I was interested in the possibility of importing used Italian sports cars into England, and had mentioned that I might make a quick trip over there to see what was to be had. Ernesto hoped that it would be possible for me to do this without delay and at the same time carry a message for him to Giordano in Milan.

I agreed and, before I left for Italy, Ernesto treated me to what I came to recognize as the set lecture kept in readiness by any Sicilian to try to explain away the sorrows of his country. For a thousand years Sicily had been under the heel of a succession of a dozen or so foreign governments, from that of the Arabs to United Italy with its capital in Rome. Each of these, in the ends of the efficient extraction of booty, had made its own laws to be added to the legalistic muddle left by its predecessors. In the end there were tens of thousands of enactments, most of them quite ununderstandable to the layman, and many of which contradicted each other. Since the law as it stood failed to protect the citizen, it had to be every man for himself and, under the polite and civilized exterior that was all the foreign visitor saw of Sicily, the reality was one of survival through sheer personal strength, political connections, through skill in forming defensive alliances, and the power of the bribe. Ernesto believed that the best any man could hope for was to be able to look after his family and his friends. In the depths of this harangue I suspected a lurking plea of extenuating circumstances. I never came to know what was the crime for which he had been obliged to flee the country.

*

Count Aldo Giordano was glutted with fascist honours and awards. He was one of the youngest of the motley crew who had tagged after Mussolini in 'the march on Rome', was officially designated a *squadrista*, having been inscribed in the early fascist squads, and had been decorated with the government's highest award, the *Sciarpa Littorio*. He was probably the only Italian who regularly wore a bowler hat, and when he came to pick me up at my hotel in Milan and take me to lunch, he had one of these with its inevitable associate, a furled umbrella, resting on the seat beside him of the open black Alfa Romeo he was driving.

We lunched in a roof-top restaurant under the laced profile of the Cathedral of Milan. There were soldiers everywhere, many in splendid uniforms and wearing plumed Alpine caps. These were for Italy the intoxicating days following the conquest of Abyssinia, and a revolt in the Tripolitanian colony had just fizzled out after its leaders had been captured and thrown from aeroplanes. It was hard to think of the Count as a participant in the aggressive policies of the fascist state. He was small-boned and fragile-looking and a little monkish in his dark, heavyweight English suit. He spoke good English learned from a Scottish nanny, with a thin, bleating voice, and mentioned that his family were descended from the Longobards, ninth-century invaders of Italy who wore long beards, but were said to have exceptionally small penises – a disadvantage, he added with a dry smile, that had rectified itself with the passage of centuries.

The count said that he was interested in money and, having read in my presence Ernesto's letter, he asked me if he were rich, to which my reply was, probably, but there was no way of knowing. He mentioned that he was in the import-export business, trading in such diverse goods and commodities as goat skins, ostrich feathers, bilingual talking dolls, Hornby train sets, and camel flesh which, minced up with appropriate herbs and served with pasta of various kinds, formed an important part of the rations of the colonial troops. His many possessions included a balloon, a mountain of china clay, and a finger-bone – one of many small relics gnawed under the pretext of a reverent kiss – from the embalmed body of St Francis Xavier, on display at the Church of the Bom Jesus in Goa. His wife, said this small, rather bird-like man, was an ex-Miss Italy. He sipped his Pellegrini contemplatively and added that his sexual needs were well attended to, as he kept a brace of mistresses as well.

When I mentioned an interest in Italian cars the Count was instantly interested and sympathetic. Italians in general like to make themselves useful where they can. As a matter of course – of national tradition – the Count would have helped me when he could, establishing a small balance of favour here and there, some which he would cash in, and others he would not. If calculation came into this at all, it may have been that it would have been useful to get off on the right foot with Ernesto in whatever dealings he might have with him. Whatever the motive, he immediately found me an Alfa Romeo that had won a 24-hour race at Le Mans, which I bought at an absurdly low price and drove back to England a few days later. When I eventually resold it, it was out of necessity and with great reluctance, at a large profit.

Two weeks after the encounter in Milan, Giordano arrived in England, bringing the beauty queen wife with him, who – while a little jaded perhaps after the fifteen years that had passed since the crown had been placed on her head – was certainly one of the most charming women I had ever met.

An Italian-style banquet, in the tremendous refulgence of Ernesto's dining room, took place, during which the Count told Ernesto all about the ramifications of his business empire, the Longobards with their small penises, the two Doges of Venice in his later family history, his recent dinner with Marshal Badoglio and his audience with the diminutive but intelligent King Vittorio Emmanuele, who had probably listened to his outpourings, as did Ernesto at this moment, with an occasional sickly grin and a nod of the head. It was hard to believe that these two men, one so passionately absorbed in the vanity of prestige and the vanity of material possessions, the other so devoid of such considerations, could be the product of the same nation.

Giordano stayed three days in London, spending part of each evening with his wife watching all-in wrestling at Blackfriars. The sport, recently introduced, was enjoying something of a vogue, although it was banned in Italy as a degenerate spectacle that clearly awoke some of the spirit that the Count must have shown in his old days as a *squadrista* for, on the occasion I accompanied them, he leaped to his feet galvanized with excitement, shouting curses and threats at one of the wrestlers, and finally took off one of his shoes and threw it at him. This was not returned, but what did it matter? he said. He had brought a dozen pairs with him; and possessed sixty in all.

The wife, Celestina, had a suggestion to put to Ernestina which seemed startling in England in those days. When Italians of their class and age-group went on holiday, she said, they were always on the look-out for a possible exchange of mates, not necessarily because they were *libidinosi* but because a holiday was not a holiday without all the new vistas and experiences that were to be had. Whether or not you were inclined to promiscuity, said Celestina, you embraced an unknown body, just as you took the waters (which might even taste dreadful) or went for long health-giving walks. What did Ernestina think of the idea? Reporting back to me, Ernestina said that as a person of avant-garde ideas she had felt a loss of inner face in having to turn the offer down. 'But just imagine Aldo Giordano. . . .'

Whatever the object of the Count's visit had been, it was, at least in large part, successful, for within a few days of the Giordanos' departure we saw Ernesto and Maria off on the train to Rome. They returned from what sounded like an almost triumphant visit to all the old haunts of Ernesto's youth to a state of near chaos at home.

Maria's brother, Franco, a man Ernesto could never abide, with his indiscreet wife Florence had moved into the house while the Corvajas had been away, and as ever disaster had followed on their heels. With Maria's outstanding exception, the Darbellays sounded an ill-starred race. The males of the family were depressives who turned easily to the bottle, and one of Franco's younger brothers had recently committed suicide with some difficulty, by drowning himself in a three-foot-deep fountain in the centre of Berne in broad daylight.

Franco, too, was a depressive, weak, ineffective and defeated, who suffered the additional disadvantage of having a sickly, complaining wife, suffering among other ailments from an irreparable prolapse of the womb, causing her frequently to drop whatever she was doing and wander off, taking a hand-mirror, to the lavatory to check whether her cervix was visible.

At normal times, with Ernesto's cold and disapproving eye upon him, Franco vegetated calmly enough, a background presence hardly noticed in the house by the other members of the family, but left to himself – since Florence spent much of her time in bed – he was liable to be seized and transfigured by mischievous and destructive energy.

The Corvajas returned to a double row of milk bottles on the front doorstep, finger-painted graffiti in black boot polish on the gild doors, Florence's uterine ring in disinfectant in an antique Chinese bowl on a sideboard, a faint smell of vinous vomit that penetrated to every corner of the house, and Franco asleep in a firmament of broken glass on a once superb Aubusson carpet now irretrievably stained with the dark wine of Sicily.

Next day it was explained to Franco that he would have to go into hospital for treatment. This he accepted without demur, dressing himself with extreme care when the time came, with a new shirt, a dark well-knotted tie, and a smear of brilliantine on the tightly curled fair hair that was only beginning to turn grey. There followed a firm parting handshake for everyone, and Maria took him to the French Hospital in Charing Cross Road, where she waited until he was in bed, embraced him and then went off. Walking out into Shaftesbury Avenue she saw a small, excited crowd that had gathered on the pavement nearby. People were running. Looking up, she saw one of the hospital windows was open, with faces at it, and that part of the balcony had broken away. Even before she had pushed through to the front of the crowd, she knew that it would be Franco. He was dead.

A few days later I was called by my mother to Enfield to reason with my father. He had ceased to dispense his elixir, sold his pharmacy, and now, reasonably, feeling the life drain from him, appealed, like Simeon, to God to be allowed to depart in peace. My mother, a woman of hard and resolute fibre, but on unsure ground where my father was concerned, must have suspected that God might hear him, and my mission was to appeal to my father to change his mind.

It was too late, he said. He had devoted fifteen years as a Spiritualist medium to proclaiming and providing proof of the survival of the human personality beyond the grave, with little desire to investigate its quality and attraction. Yet even this infinitely shadowy territory, to which the Spiritualists had done no more than add a dimension of triviality, seemed preferable to him than continued existence on earth as an old man confined with his memories among the vanishing cherry orchards of Forty Hill.

It was too late, he explained, and with a kind of quiet triumph he took my hand and placed it over a swelling in his stomach. This, he said, was cancer. The only thing that gave him any pleasure now was the sight of flowers in bloom. Winter was upon us. He might survive, he thought, until next spring, but then he would surely die. He felt no pain of any kind.

Although he refused at first to see a doctor, one was fetched. Next day he was taken to hospital. The day after he was operated upon, and that same night he died in a most tranquil fashion.

*

175

My father's death was followed in quick succession by the deaths of two of my aunts, Annie fading rapidly from some unknown cause, and Polly, inevitably, of multiple burns after falling in the fire in the nursing home where she had been placed by the Reverend Emrys Davies, who had decided that it was no longer safe to leave her without proper supervision in the house. Surprises were to follow, as I learned through my cousin Dai Owen, who lived within a hundred yards of the house in Wellfield Road and, attuned to all the currents of gossip in this town where a part of religion was to know one's neighbour's business, was well placed to keep track of what went on.

Everyone in Carmarthen had assumed that the Baptist minister would inherit the two aunts' worldly possessions, but to the general astonishment this proved not to be the case, for all Annie's and Polly's property passed to Li. The Reverend had obtained power of attorney in the two senior aunts' case, but mysteriously enough, Li had held out. The emergency had suddenly uncovered in this confused and vulnerable little old neurotic a core of lucidity and determination. Like a Threspotian goat-herd called by oracle to be priestess, Li was transformed. The minister was shown the door. Li straightened herself, dressed in new clothes to appear in the streets of Carmarthen and paid a visit to her solicitor where, according to confidential information supplied by the clerk, she showed a clear grasp of the situation in which she found herself. Her next call was on a firm of builders and decorators whom she employed to smarten up the house before it went on the market. Li cleared the dismal thickets in the garden, packed off the furniture to the King's Street salerooms, and ordered a holocaust of the books, including a collection of every issue of the *Christian Herald* since its first publication, and – alas – the painstaking eye-witness record of all the public hangings at Llangunnor which as a child I had so longed to possess. In some way Dai Owen had learned that Li – whom I found it hard to believe had ever put pen to paper – had kept in touch with her sister living in exile in Canada, sent there after the birth of an illegitimate child to marry a settler who advertised for a bride. The sister was long since dead, but her son now invited Li to come to Canada to live with his family, and to Canada in a matter of weeks Li departed, to be seen and heard of no more.

In Forty Hill the Spiritualists, deprived of my father, managed to carry on much as before, employing visiting mediums in his stead. My mother's fame as a healer continued to spread, and a custom had sprung up, based on a tradition established at Lourdes, of leaving behind, after a successful visit to her, the appliances and vessels of orthodox medicine for which the patient no longer had any need. These trophies festooned the equivalent of the vestry in my mother's church, the Beacon of Light. My mother's cures were not of a spectacular kind, so there were no discarded crutches, but there were a pair of reinforced boots employed for weak ankles which had strengthened under the healing touch, a brace of trusses, several iodine lockets, and even a Wonder Worker, and many empty bottles that had held once indispensable medicaments – Dr Collis Browne's Chlorodine, Parr's Sovereign Expectorant, Ashton and Parsons' Phosforine, and the like – that were no longer required.

Chapter Eleven

MUCH OF 1938 was spent in travelling, journeys financed by occasional windfalls from my incursions into the world of trade, added to a little money Ernestina had of her own. A peregrination took us through Central Europe into the Balkans, through Rumania and Bulgaria to the Black Sea, and back through Yugoslavia and Hungary. It was done on the cheap in an elderly Ford V8 costing £31, bought expressly for the journey and thrown away at the end. Discarding comfort, we chose the seediest of accommodation, and when no inn existed in a village when we decided to stay the night, there was never a problem about finding a room in a peasant's home. In this way our outlay was hardly greater than if we had stayed at home.

That spring I had met Ladislas Farago, a Hungarian Jew, and the author of a successful book, *Abyssinia on the Eve*. Many years later Farago was to create the Bormann legend, publishing a book that purported to describe his meeting in South America with Martin Bormann, Hitler's vanished deputy. This was said to have netted him a million pounds. It was a minor spoof and of slight importance. What was of disastrous consequence for the American people was that Farago should have become one of President Nixon's evil geniuses and an inspirer of his policy in Vietnam. Ladislas, who was considerably older than myself, was the possessor of irresistible charm, fatally allied with the power to carry conviction in all his utterances. I found him in those days also a kind man and it was hard to believe that he could have perpetrated the cruel deceptions (for he knew and cared nothing for the Far East) by which the sufferings of the war were prolonged.

I listened to Ladislas' pronouncements as to an oracle, accepting without question all he told me. His new project was a journey to the North Yemen, about which he would write a book for which his publishers had already paid an enormous advance. He suggested that I should go with him to take the photographs, and I instantly agreed, being at all times, both before and since, the ready prey of any Pied Piper.

In those days the North Yemen remained a *terra incognita* to Europeans, previously visited by two or possibly three Englishmen, and Ladislas painted pictures of the marvels it contained. It was ruled over by an all-powerful despot, the Imam Yahya, who daily administered the ferocious Koranic justice seated under a tree at the gates of his palace, and entrance to the country could only be granted by him in person after application through his envoy in Aden. The application had to be sent by sea – carried in a dhow – to the port of Hodeida, thereafter by despatch rider to Sana'a, the Imam's mountain capital. It took up to two months to receive a reply.

In the event we spent seven weeks in Aden and the enormous area of the Protectorate – much of it, with its medieval desert cities and their mud skyscrapers, of great fascination – before word arrived through Imam's emissary that we might travel to Yemen, but only as far as Hodeida, where we should receive further instructions.

We bought a chestful of Maria Theresa silver thalers, the only currency acceptable in the Yemen, provisions for a week and boarded the first dhow bound for the Red

Sea. Every aspect of the voyage was attended by uncertainty, and at the back of the mind there was always the nagging statistic that ten per cent per annum of such ships depart on voyages from which they never return. The captain, establishing his viewpoint with the remark that only God could be sure of anything, said that according to the winds, it could take anything between three days and three weeks to reach Hodeida, and warned us that he would not sail on Fridays and holy days. He insisted that we should accompany him if at any time he decided to interrupt the voyage to take part in some local pilgrimage. Having carried all our gear aboard and settled where we could find space to await the hoisting of the single lateen sail, we found ourselves suddenly, with all the rest of the passengers, ordered ashore again. A canoe coming alongside had brought an invitation to the captain, and all who voyaged on the ship, to attend a wedding in the family of an old friend from the Hadramaut to the east of Southern Arabia, now settled in Aden. 'You must go with us, too,' the captain said to us. 'Now you are my brothers. We shall eat together, and then we shall dance until dawn. Tomorrow it is my intention to set sail, and if not tomorrow, the day after that.'

There was nothing for it. We disembarked and were conducted to a great tent that had been put up on the town's outskirts, there at an all-male party – the bride and her friends being elsewhere – to feast and dance the night away. The food was varied and exquisite, but above all strange: great saffron-flavoured lucky dips of rice and meat to be searched with the fingers, camel's-hump fat, lamb's testicles, delectable innards in batter, lurid fish from the coral reefs, locusts *en brochette*, great bustards as big as turkeys baked in clay, skewered ortolans. All-pervasive was the suggestive aroma of *ras el hanut*, compounded of dried rose-buds, pepper and Spanish fly, supposedly aphrodisiac, and certain if consumed to excess to provoke severe irritation of the urinary tract. After the inflammatory food, plenty of good healthy exercise, leaping and cavorting to fife and drum, while a flying fugleman brandishing a stick rushed up and down the lines of the dancers to whack out at the evil spirits attracted to such festivities, with an occasional shout of triumph whenever he managed to flatten one that had settled with predatory interest upon some part of a guest's anatomy. Prudently such parties ended, as this one did, with communal chewing of large quantities of *qat* leaves containing a mild narcotic which instantly quenched the fires lit by the *ras el hanut*, exorcized improper visions, and turned the mind to spiritual themes.

At daybreak we went down to the dhow, and with this demonstration of the righteousness of patience the voyage began, and in this spirit of tolerance and resignation it continued. There were thirty-two passengers on this small ship, Arabs of every condition plus a trio of Yemeni Jews, and for the purpose of this journey we were all to become members of a united family. In a moment of emergency when the main sail was torn to shreds in a brief squall, able-bodied males gave a hand to the crew. When we were becalmed for days on end and food began to run short, there was a voluntary distribution of private provisions, shared out in the most scrupulous fashion, although sometimes with difficulty, for how in compliance with this desert protocol did we set about the division of a fruit into thirty-two pieces?

Nothing could have been more gracious, more diverting or more generous than the company with whom we travelled on the dhow; and the considerable drawbacks to the voyage, unsuspected when we set out from Aden, would have been brushed aside by any seasoned traveller. The dhow carried, like some receptacle filled to the brim, an ancient odour investing its timbers with the cargoes of decades, many of them of hides and of dried fish. Harder to endure were the assaults by innumerable mosquitoes, forcing us at night – despite the great heat – to cover ourselves completely by blankets. When the breeze fell away we lay motionless in the dark in a sea glittering with a great hoar-frost of phosphorescence, and for days on end the sun showed us a slow heave of oiled water clogged with the opened umbrellas of millions of jellyfish. The presence of familiar landmarks on the Yemen coastline, a rocky outcrop, a tower, reminded us that our position on the map had remained unchanged. Every day the ship's baker baked unleavened bread. This we washed down with kishr, a greenish, pungent-flavoured concoction boiled up from coffee husks, preferred in Southern Arabia to coffee itself. It was a combination which produced unappeasable indigestion.

A single incident stands out from the doldrums of this experience. The majority of our fellow passengers were from the interior of Arabia, and few had seen the sea until they reached Makalla or Aden to board the dhow. Fortunately however for us, when reduced to a diet of unleavened bread, we were carrying two sailors for Bahrain, originally pearl-fishers who now worked the coast, transferring from dhow to dhow and receiving in lieu of regular wages a very small percentage of the sale of the cargoes they handled. Despite a lack of proper tackle, these men set themselves to fish and caught a large and ferocious-looking barracuda destined to be cooked and divided up in the usual way. The big fish was left to leap and twist on the deck, and Ladislas, horrified at the violence done to it, pleaded for it to be thrown back into the sea. I remembered that he objected to the taking of animal life, living virtually on eggs, but he was the first man and probably the last I had ever known to be deeply distressed – on the verge of tears – at the plight of a fish on the hook.

In the end Hodeida was reached, a crystalline sparkle of dwellings on the dun Arabian shore, and soon a canoe paddled out to us bringing out a splendidly jewelled and be-daggered harbour master who announced that His Majesty the Imam Yahya had ordered a house to be prepared for us in the town, and that a committee of notables would shortly come out to take us ashore. They had been delayed by their civic duty to witness a public execution about to take place in a space reserved for this purpose on the sea front, clearly visible from the dhow. The delay had arisen, as we learned, over the necessity to obtain a confession of guilt before an execution could be carried out. This, it was explained to us, was always forthcoming as the accused man's penis was tied up and he was induced to drink water, while the waiting heads-man and the notables passed the time playing a simple game of chequers invented to combat the tedium of such occasions.

We were anchored rather more than a quarter of a mile off shore, from which distance little was to be seen other than the confused comings and goings of the crowd of onlookers that had gathered. Our captain who believed that attendance at such spectacles was a pious observance to be bracketed with a visit to the mosque, asked to be allowed to raise anchor and move the dhow in a couple of hundred yards closer to the shore. Most regretfully the harbour master told him that this was a request it was beyond his power to grant.

We watched, seeing nothing of the drama concealed by distance, and could judge only that it was at an end when, restless and sated, the sea-front crowd began to disband. Shortly a boat left the shore, making in our direction. It carried four motionless white-robed figures, and was moved by six negro slaves. In a moment the three dignitaries of the reception party, with their accompanying interpreter, were helped aboard, and settled themselves on the banked-up cushions ready on deck. They wore turbans curled like elaborate caracols, moved in a slow, almost dreamy fashion, and their skin was of that absolute pallor of people living in hot climates who never uncover themselves to the sun. The interpreter intoned a verse from the Koran, and this was followed by silence while the notables watched us a little sleepily, with thin, measured smiles, and an odour of camphor spread from them as they fanned their nostrils with delicate white hands to disperse the fetor of the dhow.

Kishr was brought; we sipped it and waited, while the notables summed us up slily and caressed the jewelled hilts of their daggers, then at a sign from their leader the interpreter posed a direct question. Where were the articles we had brought? His employers were ready to inspect them.

Articles? There seemed to be some mistake. We had

brought no articles but our personal baggage. A muttered conversation followed between the four men, and the interpreter tried again. The articles ordered by His Majesty, he insisted, for which a price had already been agreed, payment to be made as stipulated in golden sovereigns.

Now it was clear enough that we were the victims of a terrible confusion. The Yemeni had expected a cargo of arms, and the permission we had received to go to Hodeida had been intended for someone quite different. The harbour-master's face became clouded with coldness and suspicion. Further questioning by the interpreter had produced no motive to justify our presence there. We had no machine-guns for sale, we had shown no interest in hides or coffee. We desired to exploit no mines. What, then, did we want?

The notables and their interpreter rose to their feet, unfolding their bodies with the suppleness of cats. They pressed our hands and, drawing folds of lawn with gestures of exclusion across their faces, turned away. The slaves who had been swimming with a vigorous dog-paddle round the dhow struck out for their boat, clambered in and were ready with the oars.

We knew that we should never enter the Yemen.

Never, to sum up, was a journey richer in experience, and the fact that the avowed object of the expedition remained unfulfilled was of little importance, because such was the scope of power of Ladislas' imagination that he wrote a fairly convincing account of his adventures in the Yemen all the same (*The Riddle of Arabia*, London, 1939). For more than two months we had lived in the dazzling simplicities of the Middle Ages, and I had learned to do without all those things that distinguished modern times from the long past. In addition I was forced into an encounter with Arabic, filled immediately with a respect verging upon awe for the richness and subtlety of its vocabulary and the brilliant mathematics of its grammatical construction. The form spoken in Aden was rustic and deformed and sullied with many intrusions, yet it awoke the desire for a closer acquaintance. I came back with a great collection of words with no currency in any other Arab country. In an attempt to remedy this and introduce some order into confusion I began a course at the School of Oriental Studies, always realizing that there would never be time enough to explore more than a corner of this vast linguistic tapestry.

Chapter Twelve

IN MY ABSENCE Ernestina had been involved in some mysterious accident which had left the slightest possible change in her facial appearance, and a white scar across the septum of the nose just above the curve of the upper lip. Something in her spirit had changed, too. There was a slight scar there as well, which I could only hope would soon disappear. Florence, Franco's widow, still an occasional visitor to Gordon Street and an eager imparter of ill-tidings, was happy to suggest to me that she had been knocked down by a bus in a suicide attempt. It was significant that all reference to the small evidence of physical mishap was scrupulously avoided in the Corvaja household. I had long since been trained never to ask a potentially embarrassing question.

It was a time of some stress for the Corvajas as a whole. Eugene had gone off to the Spanish Civil War to drive an ambulance on the Republican side, which seemed doomed to defeat, and after the success of the Corvaja parents' return to Italy something had gone wrong with their plans for further visits which might have led in the end to a permanent move back to Sicily. One night, a month or two after the trip to Rome, the doorbell had rung and Ernesto's agent, Di Luca, who had come hot-foot from Palermo, was on the doorstep. Di Luca, with his stained eyes, his small, wistful face, and the arch-conspirator's high-crowned black hat, was always the carrier of weighty news. He spoke in the thickest Sicilian dialect, of which I was only ever to understand a single word *sangue* (blood), when at the time of our first meeting he kissed my hand and mumbled a conventional formula of allegiance. All Ernesto said on this occasion, after he had left, was, 'I have changed my plans.' The Corvajas, too, had watched Mussolini's badly-trained and ill-armed legions on the march again, and from conversations with such leading fascists as Count Giordano they were sure that war was coming and that Italy would be dragged in.

Ernestina's loss of satisfaction with life was symbolized by an increasing obsession with comedy in all its forms. Like so many in those days she had made a brief incursion into psycho-analysis, been assured by the analyst that she was without creative power, and been recommended to accept life as a spectacle. Now she was more isolated than ever, because a close friendship of many years' standing had come to an end. The friend, an Anglo-Indian girl, had moved into Gordon Street, being welcomed by the Corvajas as another daughter. Now Ernestina discovered that her friend had had a long-standing relationship, kept secret from her, with an elderly lover. It was a deception she was unable to tolerate, and although such were the rules of Sicilian hospitality that the ex-friend continued to live under her parents' roof, the pair no longer spoke to each other.

The spring of 1939 came, and with it I made my brief incursion into the world of serious motor-racing. Between us my friend Arthur Baron and I had bought a wreck of the Bugatti in which Mervyn White had been killed in the Ulster TT. This was a Type 51 and a celebrated car, for, driving it, Earl Howe had for a short time held the Brooklands lap record of 136 m.p.h. Arthur rebuilt the car with certain improvements and we entered it at the opening meeting at Brooklands on 17 March.

The car had performed excellently in minor events throughout the 1938 season, but on the day of my Brooklands debut the weather was bad, with mist and rain, and poor visibility, and I lacked the experience to handle an extremely powerful car in these conditions. On the second lap of the mountain circuit, I skidded, struck a sand bank, and nearly went over the top of the banking – an eventuality which, as far as I know, no one ever survived. Recovering, but going too fast, I was faced by the anarchy of several cars completely out of control at the fork ahead, and when I applied the brakes I spun the car several times before stalling the engine and coming to a standstill.

We consoled ourselves with assurances of the valuable experience gained. The truck, the car and the weather had each taught us lessons. Unfortunately they were lessons from which we were destined never to profit. This was the end of car-racing for us, when it had hardly begun. Very soon Brooklands was to put on its wartime camouflage, and when it emerged it was a race track no longer. I never sat at the wheel of a Bugatti again.

Now Ernestina was seized by a desire to go to Cuba, where a friend of her Spanish schooldays had taken refuge to escape the Civil War. They exchanged excited letters, and the friend begged her to come out. I waited for this mood to pass but in vain. Ernestina read everything she could lay her hands upon about the promised land, and her obsession became steadily more acute.

She was having treatment for nervous tension. 'Humour her,' the doctor said knowingly. 'If you can raise the wind, go. My uncle used to be a ship's doctor, and he was there once. It's a weird sort of disease-ridden hole. Probably change her mind when she sees it. Get it out of her system.'

It took some months to get together the necessary cash, then in July 1939 we were off by third-class passage to New York. All the New Yorkers were convinced that war was now inevitable; and many wore large badges of the electioneering kind, that said 'KEEP AMERICA OUT'. So universal was this lack of enthusiasm in the United States for embroilment in European affairs that the stewards on the Grace Line boat we took down to Havana admonished us, as English, on the dangerous likely outcome of British aggression. We entered Havana harbour, and suddenly all was forgotten. This was a different planet.

A norther, lifting the sea, had thrown a great curtain of spindrift over the city's façade, over the bay's curve of lean houses, granite-grey, pink, coral, pistachio as their owners had painted them in the colour of whichever political party they supported. Moon-faced negroes with dislocated joints were dancing down the Malecón, in and out and around the long cannon pointed out to sea. Music from drums banged at us from all sides as our carriage rattled through the streets. An altar with a black-faced madonna rocked on the seat at the driver's side. He took us to an apartment house of the cheaper sort, where we were asked to wash our feet before we entered. Then the lady of the house brought us sweet, tasteless fruit that stained our lips with indigo, and her son, standing by, played a flute while we ate it.

Much of the day we spent in the Central Park, watching. When we sat on a bench and kept quite still, doves no bigger than sparrows would alight on our arms, even our heads, in the search for crumbs. A bus rumbled by, every one of its passengers wearing an animal mask. An official hero of some old revolution, as a label he wore proclaimed, raised his cocked hat as he passed. A family dressed as if for a wedding escorted a manacled lunatic on a day-pass from the madhouse. Smoke spiralled everywhere from the finest of all cigars, and above us in the trees at least a thousand canaries, released to bring song to the city, twittered and chirped. Some time that afternoon I heard a sound recognizable only from American gangster films, the unmistakable heavy, slugging rattle of a Thompson sub-machine-gun. Following the crowd movement, we came upon three men in tattered clothing sprawled in their blood on a perfectly kept and weeded path. Their story was announced without excitement in the evening newspapers. There was an election on, they had agreed to sell their votes for a dollar apiece, then gone back on their bargain and demanded one twenty-five. For this, *pour encourager les autres*, a politician had killed them.

After this we stayed for a while with Ernestina's friends, the Castaños, in the new Vedado suburb. They were fascists living in Santander where Ernestina had been in school, and had managed to escape from this staunchly Republican town within days of the outbreak of the war. Now, following the Nationalist victory, they were making their plans for a return. In the meanwhile they enjoyed life in Havana, and had become hangers-on at 'The Palace', the name by which Batista's ornate villa was generally known. At this time Fulgencio Batista – for some years the real ruler of the country – was at the height of his popularity, the idol of the crowds. The worst severity he had so far committed was to have a magazine editor who opposed him thoroughly dosed with castor oil, and it was only in later life that he became addicted to murder and canasta. The Castaños were overjoyed to have been invited to a party at which Batista and his guests retired after dinner to listen to attacks on his character, which always greatly amused him, made by a communist radio station he never interfered with in the slightest way.

The dictator-to-be was a handsome, witty man, ready with a smile and a joke, and it did no harm to anyone to allow him to overhear a reference to his old nickname El Mulato Lindo, meaning 'the handsome mulatto'. There was no nonsense about him. In the old days when he was a sergeant, biding his time to smash the generals, he had taken up with a washerwoman. Years later she bore him a son and then became his wife, and now Doña Elisa was still to be seen most mornings doing her shopping in Havana's department store, Los Encantos.

On one occasion the Castaños arranged for me to be presented at 'The Palace', but something went wrong with the timing of the appointment. A chamberlain alerted the President-to-be to my presence, and after a while, taken by surprise, he popped his head round a door. His face was concealed by the bandages soaked in lemon juice he often wore when relaxing, in the vain hope of reducing the swarthiness of his skin. Through this covering protruded a substantial cigar. He gave a flip of the hand and slipped back out of sight, and I withdrew.

Thus life in Havana went on; a city always dressed for carnival in which the rich feasted in sedentary fashion and the poor danced and starved to music. On the first day by the purest of chance we had witnessed gross violence of the kind that was almost a national speciality. Thereafter, behind the mask of laughter, there were always small violences and tragic scenes in plenty, but soon we became inured to them – just as, by the coarsening of habit, a humane man may eventually come to tolerate the spectacle of a bullfight.

All the pessimistic predictions about the outcome of this expedition so far as Ernestina was concerned went wrong, for she did not tire of the pleasures of Havana, and showed not the slightest desire to go back to England. Suddenly, in this environment, she had developed a flair for a social life she found stimulating, and was the centre of attraction at parties given not only by Spanish expatriates, but by native patrician families, *gachupines* (wearers of spurs) who felt themselves a cut above Cuban colonists, most of whom had a dash of Negro blood. At such gatherings she sparkled, being a lively conversationalist, better read than anyone else in the room, and fresh with tidings from Europe, in the direction of which the eyes of all Cubans of the upper class were turned with yearning.

Suddenly we found ourselves a success, members of the Yacht and Jaimanitas Clubs, invited to country homes, and lent by somebody with a fleet of cars an enormous Cadillac in order to be able to accept such invitations.

Cuba, larger than one would suppose it to be, sprawls half across the Caribbean. Most of it remained off the beaten tourist track, and in these rural areas where the oldest inhabitants had childhood memories of the days of slavery, a strong servile whiff was still to be noticed. When we were shown the old slave-quarters of the great houses we visited, their dungeons, the fetters and the stocks, a kind of nostalgic pride was in evidence.

We stayed on a vast sugar plantation near Bayamó, and the owner, displaying his trophies, drew our attention to a case identical to those in which he kept his butterflies, containing at first what appeared to be scraps of shredded leather, pinned in position as the butterflies were. He was a man with a gentle deprecatory manner, who seemed to find life itself uncivilized, and he explained with a rueful smile that these were ears cut from the bodies of revolted slaves in the days of his great-grandfather. We went on to the veranda and looked out across the ocean of ripening cane to the great purple hump of the Sierra Maestra, lying between us and the sea. 'You can blame it on those mountains,' the plantation owner said. 'They had an unsettling effect on the field labour. They used to get away and hide in the woods, and the dogs had to be sent in to ferret them out. The best dogs came from England; the problem was to get to the quarry before they ate him. Perhaps I shouldn't have told you that. That's the way it was in a slave-owning society.'

'And were they all like your great-grandfather?'

'Of course they weren't. Some people wouldn't have dreamed even of thrashing a slave, let alone killing him. If you were soft-hearted and one of your slaves needed correction you sent him down to Bayamó where there were professional floggers to handle it. The main problem was with new arrivals, before they had settled in. Some of the estate owners had them flogged once a week. They claimed it helped them to adjust. Please don't think I feel anything but disgust for the kind of things that went on, but these are the facts.'

Now it was the quiet season, with the weeding done and the cane cutting still months ahead, and until work resumed no wages would be paid. Employers gave their workers occasional handouts. Our plantation owner, who made an issue of a kilo of bread a day per family, thought he was as generous as most. His negroes collected a certain amount of wild fruits, and were in his opinion accustomed to steal coffee beans from a neighbouring estate. They also, he said, chewed the butt-ends of cigars thrown away in the main square in Bayamó. For a moment I could not make up my mind whether this additional information was meant as a joke, but it was not.

We looked down on a yard surrounded by buildings in which the cane was crushed, and the juice treated. Here a few negroes in ragged cotton trousers were using up time, looking much as their ancestors must have looked before the emancipation in the seventies. 'This *is* Africa,' the plantation owner said. 'You might as well go and live there and have done with it.'

A drum was thudding somewhere out of sight. 'They've built themselves a cabildo – that's a voodoo temple – on the other side of the sheds,' the plantation owner said. 'You probably noticed the image of Santa Barbara in my study. They sacrifice white cocks, and a goat at Christmas to her. She's the same as Changó, their old god of war. You can buy all the stuff you need for her altar in Woolworth's in Havana. They have just as many White customers as Blacks.'

We asked the plantation owner why this should be, and he said, 'We made slaves of the Blacks and now it's their turn. They've done something to our minds. Half my friends are in one or other of the cults. This is a very strange place to live in. Do you know what a bocor is? They live in the trunks of cotton trees. They can raise men from the dead.'

'And do you really believe that?' I asked.

'You can't deny the evidence of your own eyes,' the plantation owner said.

When we left, the plantation owner said that there was some talk of bad weather on the way, suggesting that it might be wise to return to Havana by the Central Highway. Radio weather forecasts were extremely unreliable, he said, and to be on the safe side he sent a negro to consult the image of St John the Baptist in a local shrine, who as Ogun, African god of drunkards, was also a meteorological expert. The negro took an offering of the plantation owner's special reserve white rum in a cough mixture bottle, returning shortly afterwards with a message of thanks from the god – or saint – and warning us that a small hurricane was on its way and might be expected to reach the north-west coast later that day. I tried to telephone Havana in the hope of getting a second opinion on this, but the lines were unaccountably busy, so we set out for Nuevitas on the north shore.

Nuevitas was famous for the huge variety and numbers of seabirds breeding on a large cay just off shore, and as an occasional bird watcher I much wanted to visit this. In about three hours we reached the town, an eighteenth-century Caribbean survival full of colour, of rickety wooden houses and wayward streets, of boat-building and the smell of sawn mahogany planks, of saloons with swing doors and lean horses sagging at hitching posts.

Here, there was instant confirmation that St John's –

or Changó's – prediction had been accurate, for the population was engaged with saving their boats, which teams of mules were dragging over rollers up into the streets and as far as they could from the water. A dramatic change had come over the day, for although the sun shone brightly enough, there was something discoloured and yellowed about the light, as if this frantic activity around us, this manhandling of boats and nailing-up of shutters were being viewed through coloured screens.

We found an open space, a hillock from which we could look down through the coloured clapboard houses to the sea. It had fallen slack, but something seemed to be on the move under its polished surface as if a shoal of whales were about to surface. The sky curdled and darkened, throwing grey veils across the sun. There was not a flicker of breeze and the only sounds to be heard were the urgent tapping of hammers and shouts of the teamsters urging on their mules. Some miles out to sea a dark cloud, dense and fleshy as a negro's hand, pressed down on the water and was now rapidly expanding, and in a far corner of the field of vision the delicate wisp of a water spout joined sea and sky.

The small town of Nuevitas stretched into a promontory pointing at the great Cay of Sabinas and within minutes a wall of water charged into it. As it struck, the cay appeared to put up a crest of white water from one end to another, and we looked up to see thousands of sea-birds flying before the hurricane, like grey ash from a conflagration blown across the sky. As the shacks clustered on the headland caught the first lash of the wind, walls and thatches were snatched away. The next gust pelted us with airborne debris of all kinds, rocked the car on its springs and cracked a window. The moment had come for retreat.

The hurricane followed us for ten miles, then fell back, a clean-edged frontier of night behind the shining palms. Within the hour we were in Camagüey, where the news was that Germany had invaded Poland. By the next day, when we arrived back in Havana, England was at war.

Chapter Thirteen

NOTHING COULD HAVE been more remote than the sound of battle in Havana. Secretly, too, nothing could have caused more joy to the small percentage of Cubans who in reality owned the country than the news that war had finally been declared. The large British community besieged their Embassy, demanding to be enrolled in any capacity in the defence of their country, and the Embassy paid tribute to their patriotism in an announcement in the *Havana Post*, adding a recommendation, that they carry on, while maintaining watchful calm, with whatever they happened to be doing at that time in Cuba. The posture was to be one of heroic readiness.

The dismantling of Poland occupied here, as elsewhere, the headlines for a few days, before relegation to the back pages. Apart from lack of any real interest in such a remote country, there were more important subjects for public discussion. As a general rule, the only time when countries producing raw materials can expect a good or even fair price for their production is when a major war is being fought. Cuba depended entirely on sugar, produced largely under American control and sold almost exclusively to the United States. The Americans had devised a system for keeping the Cubans under financial control, and thereby reducing prices. This was done by introducing a quota system by which Cuba had a fixed share of US sugar purchases, the rest going to other producers, and in three years alone, 1930–1933, the

Cuban quota had been reduced from 50 per cent to 25 per cent.

The outbreak of war instantly and automatically put an end to this state of affairs, and even the visit to Havana of American film stars caused less excitement than the news, ten days after the German planes attacked Warsaw, that President Roosevelt had ordered the suspension of sugar quotas. Those who had pleaded to be allowed to sell even half the sugar they produced could now sit back calmly in the absolute certainty that there would be a scramble for surpluses held in warehouses. War bred shortages; armies in the field had to have sugar, and it was regarded as almost certain that Germany would enter the market. Acting as middlemen, the Americans were now prepared to take all the sugar they could get their hands on, and hardly had the bombs ceased to fall on Warsaw than the price shot up 1.5 cents a pound. Hope had returned to Cuba and the only slight remaining fear was that the Allies might come to an agreement with the Germans, causing the war to fizzle out.

Suddenly, with these rosy prospects, money had returned to circulation. The theatres were packed. Restaurant tables had to be booked days in advance, and rich men threw their half-smoked Coronas to the nearest beggar. Americans were flocking to Havana where it was forecast that the season would be the most brilliant on record. Temporary members enjoying a dip off the perfect beach at the Jaimanitas Club were served by waiters prepared to wade out into knee-depth water to bring them their drinks. The leading hotels connived with the system by which laundresses, straight from their work at such establishments as the Lavandería Tropicál, were on offer to guests, still in their working clothes and smelling of soap suds, as *trabajadoras auténticas* – 'genuine working girls'. ('Take a sniff of that, sir. None of your exotic perfumes there. That's nothing but pure soap.')

But the gaiety palled, and the excesses wearied. I was not of the opinion that the 'phoney war' – *la guerra fraudulente*, as the Cubans called it – would go on for ever. Patriotic fervour was hard to discover in 1939, and I was certainly not overendowed with it, but I had a feeling that I had placed myself in a position where great experiences might be missed. The psychological turning point for me came after reading a book on the life of Cervantes – never a one to miss an adventure.

While objecting to some aspects of life in Havana, Ernestina was on the whole happy there, while I was becoming bored. It was agreed that she should stay on with friends she had met there, but would almost certainly return to England in the spring. Such was the traffic in tourists between the United States and Cuba at that time that it was hard to get a passage out of the country. Finally on 10 November I boarded a vessel of the Grace Line for New York, transhipped there without delay to the SS *President Harding* bound for Tilbury, and arrived in England on 29 November.

Part Four

THE CAUSE OF WAR

Chapter Fourteen

AMAZINGLY, THE PROBLEM, after I had straightened out my affairs, was how to get into the Army. Mobilization at the beginning of this war, in which few seemed to believe, proceeded slowly. In the absence of any soldierly qualifications the advice was to await the call up of one's age-group. After a winter in the extraordinary doldrums of this conflict I was contacted by an old friend Oliver Myers, whom I had first met on a train in Italy on my way back from the Arabian débâcle. Oliver was an Egyptologist, director of the Sir Alfred Mond archaeological expedition to Armant from which he had been returning when I met him. He was a charming, enthusiastic man with an enormous range of interests, and spoke fluent though ungrammatical Arabic picked up from the Egyptian *fellahin* with whom he worked. Within minutes of our meeting on the train we had attempted to launch into a conversation in Arabic, from which we soon desisted as neither of us could understand a word of what the other said.

Oliver's news was that the War Office was eager to interview Arabic speakers, for whom it was expected there would shortly be a large demand. He himself had been interviewed, provisionally accepted for whatever the Army had in mind, and instructed to hold himself aloof from any warlike activity until sent for again. How was my Arabic these days? Oliver asked, and I told him that it was slightly better after the teacher at the School of Oriental Studies – unfortunately a Turk – had cleansed it of the worst of the Adenese barbarities. Once again we attempted to switch to Arabic but with total lack of success.

Next day I attended the War Office where an elderly lieutenant, clearly with an academic background, tested me on the basis of classical Arabic of the kind taught in theological colleges in Cairo, which bears little relation to the language as spoken by the man in the street. He was discouraged by the result but not without hope, noted down various particulars and recommended further tuition to which I agreed. Some months later, after the war had started in earnest, with France defeated and overrun, I was called for an interview in a Mayfair flat. This time, although I was bursting with new vocabulary and had conquered the ten forms of the common Arabic verbs, there was no linguistic test. Instead the captain examined my face with interest, commented with satisfaction on the aquiline nose and dark eyes, and asked if I'd ever done any amateur theatricals. 'We might want you to dress up a bit,' he said.

The upshot of this meeting was that I agreed to be enrolled in the Intelligence Corps, with deferred embodiment. It was a safeguard, he explained, as my age-group grew near to being called up. 'We'd like to keep you on ice,' he said. For how long might that be? I asked, and he replied, 'I wish I had the faintest idea.'

Slowly the months went by. The news from Ernestina contained no mention of a return. She now seemed to have joined forces with a Guatemalan family and moved to Guatemala, from which she wrote long letters full of the most fascinating details of life in that extraordinary country.

Last week we stayed on the Echevarriás' *finca*, which we thoroughly explored with them for the first time, and, found a previously unknown tribe of Indians living in some caves. Strange things can happen here. The current scandal is over the recent visit by General Nemisio Fuentes, the Mexican Chief of Staff. He was driving through Tapachula, the frontier town on the way home when a pretty *ladino* girl took his eye, and he decided to kidnap her. Five minutes later he was safe across the border. The President has heard all about it, and is said to be furious.

I stayed either with my mother or the Corvajas, who confronted the Blitz in London with their usual sang-froid. On 10 May 1941, in what was described as a thousand-bomber raid, a 1000-pound parachute bomb fell on the houses on the opposite side of the road from Number 4 Gordon Street, reducing half the street to a pile of rubble, and burying many of their occupants alive in their air-raid shelters. As the Corvajas' windows blew in, the period furniture in the front rooms was reduced to match-wood, the ceilings fell down, the partition walls collapsed, and Ernesto's decorated doors flew through the air like golden bats, he grabbed his wife and pulled her to safety under a table. The sound of the explosion was too great for the ears to encompass. 'The house shook, and there was a rumbling noise,' Ernesto said. 'It was like an earthquake.'

Fortunately Eugene was at home when this catastrophe took place, and he and his friends were able to make the house at least habitable, although the Corvajas camped out in it like gypsies until the end of the war. Eugene had registered as a conscientious objector, and I appeared to support him at the tribunal where – like the other half-dozen or so cases I heard – he was given a summary hearing and directed into the fire service. This proved to be far more arduous and – in the London Blitz – dangerous than military service, but he did what he had to do philosophically, in true Corvaja style.

Many bombs fell on Enfield, too – one fairly large quite close to my mother's house, although it did not explode. Spiritualists were under a cloud at this time because they had declared as a body, basing their confidence on information derived from the other world, that war would not break out. My mother was still in demand as a healer, though in this case too her following had fallen. Just as war lessened self-absorption and cut down the suicide rate, it also helped with bad backs, migraines and other disorders with a potentially psychosomatic content, which were highly prevalent in Enfield.

Some time after this I received call-up papers directing me to an infantry training unit in Northern Ireland, and I sent a letter in reply to this, explaining the circumstances in which deferred embodiment had been arranged. This produced a reply saying that deferred embodiment had been extended for a further three months. At the end of this period – it was now in the early winter of 1941 – a further and final notice ordered me, as before, to present myself to the depot of the Royal Irish Fusiliers at Omagh, to which I accordingly reported in January 1942.

I found myself one of a body of Intelligence Corps trainees. Whatever project that had called for a knowledge of Arabic and an ability to dress up had probably evaporated, or been forgotten, or I may have simply gone into the wrong file.

The first day at Omagh involved routine questioning. 'RC or C of E?' asked the orderly sergeant. 'You'd do better on the grub stakes if you're RC. They give you an egg every Sunday after mass.'

'Can I be a Buddhist?'

'No, but you can be a Jew.'

'What's the food situation?'

'Bad. No kosher cooking here, and you do the shit-house fatigues on Sunday.' After the first week at Omagh religion conversion became frequent.

At Omagh we received four months' basic infantry training, much of it absurd, some farcical. Endlessly we marched, saluted to the front and named the parts of the rifle, as the armies sent to the Peninsula and the Crimea must have done. It turned out that in this respect one was worse off in the Intelligence Corps than elsewhere for, leaving Omagh as a trained infantryman, it was only to be sent to the Intelligence Corps depot at Winchester, for three months of more or less the same thing. The outstanding novelty here was being taught, Army-style, to ride a motor cycle. Whether or not one already possessed this skill, it was a course that had to be gone through, and as most of the machines were grossly defective it produced many casualties. A ward in Winchester Hospital was reserved for the victims – of which I was one – and a Chinese-speaking White Russian in our intake, who was to be sent on a mission to Chiang Kai-shek, was killed in the first lesson riding a barely controllable machine on which he went under a lorry. Winchester, where the training was by the NCOs of the Grenadier Guards, was the shrine and museum of ceremonial marching, and the commanding officer in those days, 'Mad John' Rankin, prided himself on the fact that one form, invented by Frederick the Great, was practised nowhere else.

Three months at Winchester were followed by two weeks at Matlock in Derbyshire. Here for the first time the word intelligence came up, although the only instruction we received was in lecturing 'other ranks' on security. 'It's a good thing to get off on the right foot and put them at their ease,' the officer said. 'You'll find it helps to address them as "you fuckers".' He called me in at the end of the course. 'I've given you a commendation,' he said, 'but it won't make a scrap of difference. There's a dozen things wrong with you, including the colour of your eyes. You have to have blue eyes to get a commission. You'll go into the dustbin with the rest of them.' By the dustbin he meant the Field Security Personnel, and he was right, I did.

The letters arriving from Ernestina continued to hold the greatest interest for me, and I could not believe that any correspondent since Madame Calderón de la Barca, whose letters were published in 1843 under the title *Life in Mexico*, could equal them in their lively account of that part of the world.

I can't tell you how the Indians fascinate me. In the first place they are so mysterious. They remain an absolute enigma to the whites who have lived here for centuries. Take the symbols they weave into their cloth. Ninety-nine people out of a hundred will tell you they're no more than decoration. Actually they form a potted version of a tribe's history. I long to know more about them, but who to go to? Pedro Flores, the only man left in Guatemala who could interpret all the designs, died last month, and he could never be persuaded to write anything down. So slowly, everything is being lost. I've fallen in with a trick used by quite a few people here. When they go out into the mountains they carry an ordinary, good-quality blouse and a skirt with them. If they come across an Indian woman wearing a really marvellous *huipil* they try to persuade her to do a swap. Usually the Indians won't accept money, but sometimes an offer of sweets for the children does the trick.

Before I forget, Pablo Ruiz, the anthropologist I told you about in my last letter, speaks Maya Quiché fluently (I'm going to have a go at it myself), and he told me that the Indians believe Whites to be ghosts. His servants refer to him as 'the man ghost', and his wife Lupe is 'the woman ghost'. Imagine that!

The military treat them rather badly and we hear heart-rending stories of men being taken from their families, who are left to starve, and sent to forced-labour on the roads or the plantations.

There was no talk in this letter of any forthcoming return.

I had spent seven and a half months at Omagh, Winchester and Matlock, cutting the lawns with a table knife, marching ceremonially and falling off motor cycles, while the great battles in the East determined the outcome of the war. Now, ready at last, I was sent to join a section on active service at Ellesmere Port. It would be tedious to record absurdities of the kind shared by the soldiers of all armies, but duty at Ellesmere Port provoked frustrations of a special kind. For centuries the meaning of the word 'intelligence' had been changing, slowly assuming overtones of intellectuality it never originally possessed. Even the Army had fallen into the error of upgrading the mundane task of gathering information, suspected now of breeding a kind of sinister power. Plain NCOs who had gone through the mill as I had, with nothing more than a green flash to distinguish them on the sleeves of their uniform, were seen as knowing more than was good for them, of being too clever by half, potentially dangerous, and therefore to be kept under constant supervision. To ensure this, the preferred Field Security Officer in charge of a section had sporting qualifications, and the senior NCOs who wielded the real power were plain soldiers brought into the Corps, chosen for reliability (it was hoped) rather than imagination.

In line with this policy, the ten junior NCOs of 91 Section, of which I was one, found themselves under the orders of Sergeant-Major Fitch, who had looked after the boiler of a Liverpool cinema until September 1939 when, after the attack on Poland, and being convinced that Australia, where he had been born, was likely to be invaded next, he had instantly enlisted. 'They put me here to keep an eye on your spry buggers,' he admitted. Our duty in theory was to carry out a thorough search of every vessel entering Ellesmere Port, but even Sergeant-Major Fitch could see that this was a task to occupy a thousand men. 'Forget it, lads,' he said. 'There's nowt we can do.' He lived at home near the Nissen hut in which we were housed, and spent much of the time in bed, getting up in the evening to stagger through the blackout to the local for a half-dozen pints of porter. This man was strangely obsessed with coal, for which he had come to develop an affection while working in the cinema, and he always begged us when we went out to patrol the docks to take a haversack in which we could smuggle out a few 'cobs' from the various deposits in the dock area. He kept his treasure stacked in glistening black pyramids and ziggurats in his back garden. 'Take a look at this, you fuckers,' he used to say in a hushed voice. 'That's coal. That's a real fucking security. Better than having your money in the Bank of England.' So far as we knew, none of it was ever burned.

Having coped for some weeks as best we could with Sergeant-Major Fitch and his lust for coal, we were delivered over to Captain Merrylees, who had been appointed Field Security Officer of our section, now to be kitted out for service overseas. The captain seemed at first glance to be all that the Intelligence Corps expected of an officer, tall, ruddy, fair-haired, with a ready – if slightly aggressive – smile and eyes of the most intense blue. As a rowing blue at Cambridge, the selection board must have seen him as a prize indeed, but what seems to have been overlooked was that he had taken a degree in languages (Old Norse), and had actually translated a saga – an unimaginably rare combination of physical and intellectual achievement.

We were called in to Winchester, where he assembled us for a thoughtful chat about our shared future, which he expected to be adventurous. We were going on an invasion, although he had no idea where. He laughed and frowned alternately, in either case without evident excuse. Then he made what could have been a highly significant remark, and one to be frequently repeated. 'It's all rather unreal, isn't it? Play-acting. Each man in his life plays many parts, and now it seems we're soldiers. Ah well.'

Captain Merrylees was accompanied by a Sergeant-

Major Leopold with whom he seemed in some indefin-
able way ill at ease. The sergeant-major, although a
young man, was an old soldier who could be assumed
to know all the tricks, and there was something in
his handling of the captain that reminded me of a
snake-charmer at work. He was a tall man, with a long
nose and an exceptionally small head, and his manner
seemed to contain both ingratiation and menace. Later,
he too wanted to talk to us, receiving us in his quarters
where we found him in the act of shaving off his pubic
hair to rid himself of some infestation. This operation,
only suspended while Leopold addressed us, razor in
hand, may have possessed a symbolical intent. He
was probably showing us in his own quiet way that he
was very much down to earth. In the course of his
remarks he mentioned that he had been at Dunkirk, from
which – although he did not tell us why – he had been
brought back to England in chains. These were the two
men who would dominate our lives for many months to
come.

On 15 November 1942 we went aboard the *Maloca* in
Ellesmere Port to join the convoy assembled there for
the invasion of North Africa. This eventually steamed
westwards deep into the Atlantic before completing a
great arc to enter the Straits of Gibraltar. Rough seas
were with us throughout this voyage, and many men
were seasick for days on end. We travelled in the hold in
enormous compartments housing many hundreds of
men. As many as could be crowded in slept on the floor,
and above them had been constructed tiers of bunks. The
occupants of these were forced to vomit over those
beneath, and by the first night, as the ship ploughed into
a heavy sea, the floor had become a lake of vomit,

sluicing round islands of retching, groaning men and, whenever the ship gave a great slow roll to one side, pouring down to spill over the bedding of those placed at the edge of the hold.

When, many days later, we passed through the Straits, relief took on an almost religious fervour. All those on deck joined in singing 'Tomorrow Is Another Day', which was the nearest that the English could get to a thanksgiving hymn, after which a party of Welsh sang 'Rock of Ages'. On 5 December we reached Algiers, the terminal of the convoy for all but three ships. At Bougie our two companion ships left us, whereupon the corvette escorting us to Bône repeatedly attacked a U-boat that was dogging us, with apparent success, for after the corvette had released a number of depth charges the excitement was at an end.

We kept close in to shore, eyes fixed longingly on a rapturous pre-Raphaelite landscape, spring-like in winter, of fields sloping up to green hills through the deep, mossy shade of oaks. Among them glistened small white domes that marked the tombs of saints – a saint for every five or six square miles. Following the example of many others, I slept on deck that night, hoping to be able to swim ashore if we were struck by a torpedo. Next morning, shortly after dawn, we entered the harbour of Bône. My first impressions of Africa at war are conveyed perhaps more vividly by a diary kept at that time than by resorting to memory.

7TH DECEMBER 1941

Bône at last. Viewed from a mile or so, and at sea, a beautiful town with Islamic domes and minarets, although disfigured by several columns of black smoke, suggesting all is not well.

We soon learn that these are the result of a raid by German Stukas that has taken place at first light. We tie up and begin the immensely slow process of disembarkation of over two thousand men laden with their gear, down a steep and narrow gangplank to the dock, far below. Soldiers belonging to a docker company shout a warning to us to hurry as the bombers are expected back within the hour. There are great, smoking craters in the quay, and we see the bodies of several soldiers killed in the last bombing which have been tossed over the sea-wall. We stand in the great crowd of men pressing towards the top of the gangplank. Sergeant-Major Leopold seems in his element. He spent hours last evening preparing his equipment and now, his leather and brass starred with reflections, and blanco-ed to the eyes, he shows himself as the model soldier, equal to any situation.

After a wait of about two hours we are finally ashore, get our equipment together, place a guard over it and set out to see the sights. Although buildings here and there have been taken clean out of a street by a bomb, we find many shops open, the impression being that Bône cannot bring itself to believe it is at war. After three alcohol-free weeks we make for a wine shop, and are quite astounded when an unperturbed saleslady actually *gives* us all the bottles we can carry, thrusting away the few francs proffered. No more bombing but some rifle-fire, due – as explained later – to a member of the docker company going mad and sniping away at anyone within sight. Some of the men unloading the ship are in a state of abject terror, and understandably so, having just seen comrades blown to pieces. One rushes up as we are about to move off, and grabs me. 'Please, please, please,' he says. 'I have to get away from here.'

8TH DECEMBER

Night spent in a tobacco factory, like an enormous Kew Gardens greenhouse – all glass and likely to shatter into a million pieces if a bomb falls within a few hundred yards. In the morning collect motor bikes and set out for Philippeville where we are to take over the security of the port. Most section members drunk, and there are a number of spills – almost miraculously with no casualties.

On arrival at Philippeville go straight to Mairie where the FSO calls a meeting of all the authorities and addresses them in Latin. Ted Kingham, who is bilingual, is subsequently asked to translate, and produces a spirited version of his own which is loudly cheered by the assembled notables, who pretend not to notice that two section members have slid to the floor and gone to sleep. When the speeches are over we sing the two national anthems, and the French bring out more wine, which is gratefully accepted. After that we are escorted in triumph to the headquarters provided for us, a handsome seaside mansion, the Villa Portelli, on the route de la Corniche.

9TH DECEMBER

The FSO calls a meeting to allocate jobs. He is smiling and twinkling, and well turned-out as usual, but in some way remote, an actor in a play in which he does not fit the part. Leopold is at his right, boots clamped together, stick under his arm, regimental fashion, a churchy expression on his face. He does most of the talking.

Only two of us, Kingham and Brown, whose fathers are French, are bilingual. Their jobs will be to liaise with the French authorities. Three junior NCOs are sentenced to the boring sinecure of patrolling the port, two are assigned to visit the military units, one will run the office, one quickly jumps in to claim vehicle maintenance and ration collecting. This leaves one who will have to talk to the Arabs when necessary. Leopold's eye falls on me, and the FSO nods. 'Would that be just the Arabs in this town?' I enquire, and Leopold says no. He means the department. A wall map is unrolled which shows it to be a sizeable area, including the mountain range in Kabylie.

From seven in the morning when most of us are still dreadfully hung-over, French civilians are thronging at the door. It turns out that most of them are informers, and that they are drawn from all social classes, from Monsieur Gaudinot, *chef de cabinet* at the Mairie, down to a man who has a tobacco kiosk in the main square. Their message in the main, when someone can be found to listen to them, is that the town is a nest of spies. In the absence of our French speakers they hang about for most of the day in a morose fashion, seizing upon anyone in uniform who comes within range to pour denunciations into his ear. Monsieur Gaudinot speaks enough English to make it clear what it is all about. The population of Philippeville, with the exception of himself and a small band of devoted patriots, are all pro-Vichy, and therefore pro-German, and he is in a position to produce documentary evidence that about every person of substance, including his own brother – whom he particularly wishes to denounce – are in league with the enemy. He can also show evidence, often supported by photographs, that all these men are adulterers as well as notorious cuckolds.

One of our visitors, a smallish man with a red, polished face, sharp eyes and a severe expression, seems in some way invested with urgency and importance, and will have no truck with anyone but what he calls *le chef de l'équipe*. The FSO tries his Latin on him, and when this produces no results, orders an interpreter to be found. It transpires that the man is an executioner, who offers his services, complete with guillotine, to deal with any sentences of death passed on civilians who, he understands, cannot under military law be shot.

Later in the day there is a chance reference to him when Sergeant Brown confirms much of what Gaudinot has already told us about the persecution inflicted by the pro-Vichy majority upon the few heroic supporters of General de Gaulle, all of whom – barring our timely arrival upon the scene – would certainly have been wiped out.

Brown has spent some hours at the prison securing the release of Gaullists held there under an assortment of trumped-up charges. One of the martyrs to the Allied cause had had a close shave indeed, for through some fearful miscarriage of justice he had been sentenced to death, and the executioner from Algiers (as we knew) had already arrived. Brown tells us that this man, Michel Fortuna, asks to be allowed the honour of organizing a civic dinner to welcome us. It is becoming clear how little we know about French politics. Several of our team, including the sergeant-major, had never heard of Vichy or its government until we landed in Algeria, and whatever they say in praise of General de Gaulle, it is hard to forget that orders were passed to us at Ellesmere Port to arrest him if he ever attempted to leave the country.

The only other item of interest today was a visit to the FSO by the vice-prefect, accompanied by Captain Bouchard, head of the Gendarmerie, both of them speaking excellent English, at which security measures applicable to the civilian population were under discussion. Afterwards the sergeant-major tells us that it has been agreed that where arrests of French civilians or the search of their premises is deemed necessary, previous notice of such action should be lodged with the Sous-Préfecture. A face-saving formula, Leopold said, that does not apply in the case of Arabs, with whom we are to deal as we think fit.

Chapter Fifteen

As the days went by, we slowly began to grasp the realities of the situation. The friendly, expansive Algerian French appeared as wholly pleasure-loving opportunists, supporters at the bottom neither of Pétain nor de Gaulle, concerned neither with a collaborationist France nor an independent one. There was no intellectual life, nothing of the spirit to be discovered in Philippeville. No one picked up a book, listened to music, read poetry, or found entertainment in anything but the most mediocre Western films. The Algerians ate too much rich food, drank too much, slept too much, indulged in too much sex. Chronic complaints of the liver and stomach plagued them. They suffered from gout, hypertension, giddiness and worn-out hearts, and their life expectancy was in the neighbourhood of fifty-five years. It was the good life carried almost to its fatal conclusion. The preferred drink, for example, of Philippeville was *anisette* made instantly by dissolving a chemical supplied by any pharmacist in pure alcohol. Under the brief rule of the Vichy government this nefarious beverage had been outlawed, but with the restoration of democracy it was back, with dozens of glasses of it lined up on the counter of every bar. In the first weeks of our presence cases were reported of citizens going into a bar and drinking *anisette* until they died.

The full-blooded climate and the way of life took their toll of the character of all Frenchmen who had been born or settled in Algeria. They lost control of their passions, were prone to a kind of hysteria which drove them into mutually antagonistic feuding groups. Nowadays they were pro-Vichy, or pro-de Gaulle, taking furious sides in causes which were only old quarrels under a new name. The Algerians had become irrational. This was a country where ripe fruit hung for the picking on every tree and if a man wanted a woman there was always an unpaid Arab girl around about the house to be pulled into a quiet corner. The Algerian had grown to expect the instant satisfaction of his slightest desire. With all this, and perhaps inseparable from it – because in this interminable underground civil war every man was on the look-out for an ally – went a tremendous drive towards *camaraderie*. There was no more generous and firmer friend than the Algerian. He was willing to give, as well as take, on a scale no metropolitan Frenchman would have understood. There was something infectious in the atmosphere of this country, leading to a loss of Nordic restraint. Likes and dislikes tended to become coloured with love and hatred. I wondered how long it took to turn a man into an Algerian, always ready to hug someone or reach for a gun.

The common foe of all the Algerian factions was the Arabs. A tiny percentage of exceedingly tough-minded individuals formed the Arab bourgeois class. There was a doctor (one of two in the whole of Algeria), a few minor officials at the Préfecture, and a handful of sardine merchants who were prosperous by very low Arab standards. The rest of the native population lived in conditions inconceivable to Europeans. Most of the males observed on our arrival wore garments made from sacks, on which in many cases the stencilled mark of whatever produce they had contained was still visible. A woman forced for any reason to leave her village and go into town might only be able to make this journey after several neighbours had clubbed together to provide her with sufficient clothing.

We were assured by the French that the Arabs were pro-German, but what they really were was intensely and bitterly anti-French, after a century of intellectually planned subjugation. The French system was to rule through caïds, once democratically elected but now appointed by the government. They levied taxes, provided recruits for the Army, and labour for the colons' great farms. In return they were left in peace to pillage the villages as they saw fit. The weapon of the colons was unemployment, and therefore starvation, and a large surplus labour force was always there to see to it that the system worked. Suddenly – and quite by accident – with our arrival, the colons found themselves defenceless. As more and more Allied ships carrying warlike stores docked in the ports of North Africa, an ever larger supply of labour was required to unload them. Where the colons paid 7 'old' francs a day, the Allies offered 50 francs, plus two pounds of bread, several ounces of olive oil, and a little sugar and salt. Within the week there was not an unemployed Arab left in Algeria. Moreover, the Arabs were deserting the farms and flocking down to the coast. It was an inevitable outcome of the war situation that earned us the hatred of the colons, for, Algerians as they were, and subject to the passionate irrationality of this land, they saw in this nothing but an attack on themselves.

The Arabs shared with us this outburst of hatred, and although the colons realized there was little they could do to revenge themselves upon us, they made no secret to Brown, who was able to talk to several of them, that they planned drastic retaliation on their former labour force as soon as we had left the country.

Michel Fortuna's dinner for the section turns out to be extraordinary in every way. In the first place, the house of this supposedly rich and powerful man is rather like a barracks; vast, bare, and almost devoid of furniture. Secondly, it is next door to Philippeville's brothel, doing at the moment of our arrival lively business with the British soldiery, who have formed a long and orderly queue along the street. A woman standing at the door reminds me of a pantomime fairy godmother, and actually holds something remarkably like a wand with which she controls their entrance. The FSO pretends not to know what this is all about and seems amazed when the implications of this un-English sight are explained to him.

Fortuna, too, comes as a surprise. A small, thin man whose collar-bones stick out, dressed showily in a Palm Beach suit and bow tie, with a polka-dotted handkerchief protruding from his breast pocket. The jaunty attire contrasts with his expression, which is one of sorrowful resignation. Sergeant Brown translates for the benefit of our nine non-French speakers. 'He wants us to regard this as our house. All we have to do is to let him know when we want to move in.' Next Fortuna puts his arm round the FSO's neck and kisses him on both cheeks. After that he stands back, shakes his hand, and says, '*Tu es mon copain.*' Every member of the section, one after the other, gets the same treatment, and they show varying degrees of embarrassment. Next we are pre-

sented to Michel's wife, Madame Renée, an ugly woman
with an underslung jaw, tiny eyes, hair like copperwire,
and a perpetual suggestive smile.

We go in to eat and find a number of people already
seated at a narrow table stretching from one end to the
other of a vast, bare room, painted a depressing shade of
green. Despite the fact that Christmas is only two weeks
away, the weather is warm, and I am amazed to see bats
flying in and out of the open windows.

Among those seated at the table I recognize several
officials we have already met at the Mairie, including
Monsieur Gaudinot, *chef de cabinet*, all of them accompanied by dowdily respectable–looking women I assume
to be their wives. The impression I get is of an unusual
mixture of the social classes, which includes an extremely
distinguished elderly man with a square–cut grey beard
who is identified by Brown as a *chevalier* of the Legion of
Honour, and a member of the Académie Française on a
visit to the vice-prefect. Yet others are described by
Brown as small shopkeepers, and there is one villainous-
looking French *sergent-chef* with a hare-lip, and arms
covered by tattooing. Apart from the Academician these
people are like Breughel's feasting peasantry in modern
dress.

Inevitably a glass of *anisette* stands on the table before
each guest, and when emptied is instantly refilled by an
attendant Arab. My impression is that a number of those
present are a little drunk already and, downing an *anisette*
myself in an attempt to get in the mood, feel instantly
dizzy.

Such conversation as has any point is about the past
misdeeds and the evil intentions of the pro–Vichy faction
– claimed by this dedicated gathering of Gaullists to be

intensely engaged in treasonable activities – and the desirability of persuading the Allied authorities to permit the formation of a popular militia to deal with them. More and more though, under the influence of the raw alcohol, the gathering slides into a good-humoured, fatuous and rather noisy occasion. The meal is vast and interminable, the main course being wild boar saturated in garlic, and there are innumerable libations in local red wine of great body, but like most Algerian things devoid of finesse. The diners begin to sleep with their heads on the table, and fall on the floor where they are left undisturbed. Two of our comrades are out for the count, and the distinguished member of the Académie Française is carried off to bed. A moment later his lady companion who is somewhat younger than he is gets up and says in a ringing voice, '*Excusez-moi. Il faut que je pisse.*' At this moment Madame Gaudinot changes places to seat herself next to our youngest section member, offering in the coarsest of argot ('*veux-tu voir ma belle craquette?*') to show him her sexual parts. The FSO is well in control, and laughs with insistent politeness at bawdy jokes he does not understand. Sergeant-Major Leopold watches this scene with sardonic composure.

I find myself in the corner of the room, discussing with Michel the state of mind of a prisoner in the condemned cell. 'You know what's coming to you,' he says, 'because they've lined you up to watch it all happen before. They chop your head off in the courtyard. Last couple of times a fellow called Professor Dornier was there. He was doing some experiments about conscious-ness. He was got up in a rubber suit and rubber gloves, standing by the basket, and as soon as the head came off he would grab it up by the hair and shout into an ear,

"*Eh Jacques! Tu m'entends? Réponds!*" They say the eyes always opened once. Sometimes twice.'

'As I understand it, you were framed,' I said.

He laughed. 'Put it that way if you like. They knew I was for de Gaulle, so someone took a contract out on me. I decided to get him first, that's all.'

14TH DECEMBER

An urgent signal from GHQ Algiers to send an NCO to Bou Zafra in the Monts de Constantine, for an interview there with a Caïd Slalil. Several queries are raised. In the first place, surely this area is under the responsibility of 312 Section at Constantine? Leopold gets back to Algiers only to learn that the Intelligence major making this request has no idea of the existence of a Constantine section. After that it comes as no surprise to learn that there is no such place as Bou Zafra, and – according to the French – no such person as Caïd Slalil. The French point out that the name is not an Arabic one.

Much detective work is required before a Caïd Shallal is finally located in the village of Bou Zerqa, and GHQ confirms that this is their man. Captain Bouchard of the Gendarmerie, who has come to our help once again, calls the *caïd, entre nous*, a disreputable ruffian, to be approached with great caution, as he is believed to have been involved in several kidnapping and ransom incidents. He conducted a reign of terror, says the captain, in the Djebel Ouasch mountains to the north of Constantine, where previously he had to some extent been held in check by the presence of garrison troops in Constantine itself. Now, since these have been withdrawn, he is on the rampage again.

In discussing this business the captain appears shifty and troubled. He has made it evident, as best he can, that it would suit him if we left well alone where the Arabs are concerned. His distaste for them proclaims itself in an original way. When referring to an Arab he habitually garbles or mispronounces his name. Thus Gaudinot's immediate subordinate, Meksen – a man having some status in the town – becomes Meknes. Meksen is the name of an illustrious ancestor who made the pilgrimage twice, and gave most of his worldly goods to the poor. Meknes that of a dull little provincial town – an Algerian Bootle. Toukousch, another Arab notable, is always referred to as Touschkou, which most people find unbearably funny. To sum up this view on Arabs in general, Captain Bouchard concludes our meeting with the muttered verdict, '*C'est une race infecte.*'

15TH DECEMBER

Leave for Bou Zerqa at nine in the morning. So far as I understand, the Allied forces have kept to the main roads in their occupation of Algeria. Penetration has been shallow, hardly exceeding a hundred miles at any point, and I look forward with some excitement to a view of an undisturbed hinterland. Bou Zerqa could be reached more easily and directly through Constantine, along the main north–south highway, which is first-class, but for some reason Leopold fights shy of an intrusion into 312 Section's territory, as if they exercise exclusive rights over hundreds of square miles (little of which they will ever see). This means that I have the benefit of the main road only as far as El Arrouch, and am obliged thereafter to cross the Monts de Constantine by a second-class highway leading down through the gorge of the Oued-Zenati River to reach Shallal's headquarters, said to be in a feudal castle built over Bou Zerqa.

The day is one of perfection, like England in April at its best. The sluggish old Army Norton copes somehow with the gradients and carries me into an entranced landscape from the dawn of history, pristine and empty of humanity, massed with cork oaks, with deer and wild goats scrambling on the mountain sides and eagles swinging like pendulums in the sky.

Bou Zerqa, Shallal's capital, is a squalid place built by the Europeans, although long since abandoned by them, and his castle the shell of an old Esso filling station with great rubbish-filled caverns where the pumps have been uprooted. Several Arabs with inflamed eyes squat on the cracked cement with their backs to the sun. The *caïd* and three henchmen await me in what was once the office, now a void of stained walls smelling strongly of urine. Inbreeding has furnished them with identical triangular faces, and deeply cleft chins. Their sore, watchful eyes never leave my person, and after shaking hands the *caïd* scratches himself vigorously. The *meshwi* – the usual lamb roasted whole – awaits outside at the back, over the ashes of a fire, and we squat to pick at it with our fingers, and sip mint tea. A ceremonial silence is maintained for some minutes, then, after using his cloak to wipe his hands and his eyes, the *caïd*, who as a nominally French official is obliged to speak French, puts some questions from which it is immediately clear that he suffers from basic misapprehensions.

'You are German?'

'No, English.'

'Ah. So you are fighting with the Germans? On their side?'

'I'm on the other side. I'm fighting against them.'

'Then you are with the French? Their brothers? Their brothers in this war?'

'Yes.'

'Ah-h.' The *caïd* picks the sprig of mint out of his tea and chews it, eyes narrowed. The lean, brown, supple fingers are outstretched to stroke and tap on the blackened carcase of the lamb like a musical instrument before tearing away more shreds of flesh. The *caïd* rips out a blackened titbit and thrusts it into my hand. 'So you fight with them? The French? Ah-h.'

'They fight with us if that sounds better.'

'And tell me, oh my brother,' the *caïd* asks. 'Who will God give victory to in this war?'

'To us.'

'Ah-h. There are many of you?' he asks.

'Many thousands. We have many cannon, aeroplanes and ships. The enemy cannot resist.'

The *caïd* seems to be crossing himself in a gesture of astonishment, in the Christian fashion. To his three followers he says, 'They will win the war.'

He turns to me again, clicking his tongue as beggars do locally before imploring alms. 'You and the French, ah-h. You and the French. We all of us look for allies, for friends in a war. We could become your friends, too, my brother. We could come to your aid.'

The outcome is that, disappointed as the *caïd* and his followers are that we are on the wrong side, he is quite prepared to do a deal and send a hundred horsemen to strengthen our war effort, and naturally there would be some unspecified quid pro quo. I assure him that I will pass on this offer to the general.

At this point when I am ready to shake hands all round and take my departure, it suddenly becomes clear that the transaction is incomplete. '*Le cadeau*,' the *caïd* shouts, in his strangely thin, high-pitched voice, '*faites entrer le cadeau*,' and I realize that there is to be a ceremonial gift.

The door opens, a form wrapped in a blanket is shoved through it, and a moment later the blanket is pulled open to reveal the face of a girl of about thirteen. She is bright yellow from what I assume to be hepatitis, and covered in pock-marks.

'This present is for you,' the *caïd* says. 'To take with you.'

The best way out of this in a diplomatic fashion seems to be to point out that I lack the proper means of transportation, and this seems to be accepted with good grace. Perhaps it is only a polite and hospitable gesture, after all, and not intended to be taken seriously.

Chapter Sixteen

THE FIRST MAIL to arrive from England brought letters from my mother, the Corvaja parents and Ernestina. My mother had important news for me. She had been taken to a seance in London where the medium – she quoted her name as being a celebrated one – giving a demonstration of clairvoyance had asked, 'I'm being given the word mistletoe. Does it mean anything to anyone here?'

My mother had naturally claimed the association, whereupon the medium had continued, 'Your husband is on the other side. He is trying to reach you. He asks you to help him make contact by projecting your thoughts to him.' What followed sounded like a long-distance call on an extremely bad line, with the message given by the medium so broken up and intermittent that hardly any of it made sense. From what my mother could gather, and passed on to me, it seemed that my father had little enthusiasm for life after death, and had failed to shake off the boredom troubling him in his existence on earth. All he could say of it at best was, 'I am making progress,' adding that he missed his friends.

Spiritualism would seem from my mother's letter to have been on the upgrade again. First they had insisted that the war would never happen. After that, during the so-called 'phoney war', they had tried to explain it away as an 'astral confusion'. Then only at the start of the Blitz had they accepted the reality of the conflict, many of them, including my mother, taking the view that God had only really made up his mind and come down on the British side at the time the Americans had done so. The congregation at her church had doubled since then, my mother said, adding that she had been in the local newspaper after curing its editor of arthritis following two sessions of laying-on of hands. Finally she mentioned that a bomb had blown all the windows in and that in falling out of bed when this happened she had cracked a couple of ribs.

The Corvajas soldiered on unflinchingly in their shattered house. They drew water from a stand-pipe in the street, were able through the disruption of the wiring only to switch on the light in one room, and even this rarely, due to frequent power cuts. They kept out the cold by wearing several sets of underclothing, and wound crêpe bandages, of which they had a good stock, round their legs. Rats colonizing the ruins across the road had to be kept at bay, and Ernesto had acquired some skill with a catapult in order to do this. He mentioned having damaged a hand slightly while shovelling fire bombs from the roof in one of the earlier raids. They lived, like the rest of the population, on nine ounces of meat and three of butter per week, and one egg per fortnight, plus unlimited potatoes, and found their health much benefited from the simple diet. They had only suffered one major crisis since the great bombing: the dog Mazeppa's sudden and painful illness, reducing them as animal lovers to a state of panic. The vet diagnosed this as the result of a surfeit of condoms picked up in the gardens of Gordon Square, from which the railings originally excluding the general public had been removed to make weapons of war. This had become a death-trap for dogs without superb digestions. Fortunately, an operation had been carried out successfully, so all was well again.

Maria mentioned that they heard from Ernestina with increasing rarity, and put this down to the state of the mails.

Ernestina's letter spoke of a world that was as remote and unreal as Celtic Britain of Arthurian legend.

I was asked to a party at Ubico's new *finca* at Comalapa. Entertainment rather barbarous for my taste. The male guests were given horses but had to ride at a full gallop under a line from which chickens were hanging, tied by the legs. Winner was first past the post holding a bloody chicken's head in his hand. Prize: an Arab stallion. This is Central America, and it's the kind of thing you learn to accept.

The people I went with were the Iglesias. I believe I told you they invited me to stay with them as long as I felt I could. Nominally I'm paying my way by giving the children the odd lesson in English and acting as companion to Doña Elvira, who is perfectly sweet. Back to the General. The Iglesias' town house is only about a couple of hundred yards from the Palace and every morning he and his officers – all of them are obliged to ride Harley-Davidson motorcycles – come tearing past down Fourth Avenue. If you're one of the fourteen families, as the Iglesias are supposed to be, you can go out onto the balcony to watch them. If not you have to stay inside.

In spite of his fearsome reputation the Old Man, as

we call him, is really quite charming. His one outstanding weakness seems to be a hatred of criticism,
and it's suicidal to suggest he's a stooge of the Yan-
kees. Did you see the story in *Time* about the deal
with United Fruit? There was just the slightest sign of
hesitancy in Congress about signing up, and he went
in with a troop of dragoons. When a congressman
brought the thing up again last week the Old Man
walked up to him and broke his jaw.

We had another small earthquake yesterday. You
can count on a slight tremor every second to third
day. The latest fad here is earthquake parties. Most of
the houses are built on one floor of very light material,
so it's rare for one to suffer serious damage. You have
a rather glamorous-looking lightweight boiler suit to
put on if a quake starts in the night, and you take your
lamp and go next door, or maybe your friends come
round to you, and you have drinks, and pass the time,
and wait for it to stop.

With every letter Ernestina seemed to have gone farther
away, and she was changing.

So far our duties in Philippeville had been largely ceremonial. Three NCOs, as ordered, patrolled the port,
watched people fishing on the quay, occasionally boarded
a ship to gaze blankly at the crates holding the cargo,
then withdrew. In this way an hour might be used up
after which they would stroll under the bland winter sun
as far as the square for an illegal *anisette* at the Café du
Commerce, or the Café de la Marine. Here, sooner or
later, they might be joined by the pair who had paid

routine visits to military units and installations in the area, where there was never anything to report. Frequently Sergeant-Major Leopold would come on the scene. He spent hours every day scrubbing and polishing his equipment and was the most perfectly turned-out soldier in the area, but had taken to the most bizarre fashion of wearing two guns. Hangers-on would come up to our table to bow and shake hands, and occasionally whisper secret information which – unless a French-speaker happened to be there – would not be understood. At this time a French presence had begun to manifest itself by the arrival of a battalion of Senegalese, black automata so intoxicated with the military life, according to one of their officers, that field punishment took the form of depriving them of drills and fatigues, instead of imposing more of such exercises and penances upon defaulters in the way of our armies. Few sights could have been more pleasant than to watch from our seats outside the Commerce the sturdy approach of the Senegalese, led by their trumpeters, on parade. And no more delectable moment than the silence following the end of a musical phrase when, with a single corporate movement, a score of trumpets would be flung high into the air, turning smoothly as they fell, splashed by the sun with a row of brass stars, then deftly caught, pressed to the rich indigo lips in readiness for the next perfectly synchronized spurt of martial music.

Back at the section office the informers, with an occasional word of encouragement in Latin from the FSO, would be wasting their poison on the desert air. When one of the French speakers happened to look in he was instantly captured and compelled to listen to horrific stories of plotted treacheries and intrigue. There was really no point in listening to any of it, because it was always the powerful colons who were the villains, and they were beyond our reach.

Where to some small extent we could make our presence felt was in the case of the enormous base supplies depot established within the walls of one of the great farms owned by a colon called Redon. Here large-scale thefts were taking place, and I was called there after an Arab intruder had been shot dead by a guard. This man's grotesque dress – a time-rusted frock coat worn over football shorts – convinced me that he had been a beneficiary of a hand-out of old clothes shipped from England, for distribution among our contracted work force, and that therefore he had been shot by mistake. This turned out to be true, for a pass found in his pocket showed him to be employed at the base.

A number of Arab boys averaging about thirteen years of age had been picked up at the time. Nobody knew what they were doing there, and they could not make themselves understood. They were taken to a shed for questioning by one of Bouchard's gendarmes who as a preliminary measure – and he told me this was always done – had stamped on their toes with his heavy boots. I got rid of the gendarme, and took the boys – who had astonished onlookers by the stoicism with which they had supported the injuries inflicted upon them – to the commanding officer of the depot. He, horrified at this spectacle of crushed and bleeding toes, had them taken in a command car to Philippeville hospital. This incident opened a breach between myself and Captain Bouchard.

While at the base depot I took the opportunity of inspecting the stores that were being guarded so zealously. They included innumerable crates of non-freezing margarine, engine oil for use in sub-zero temperatures, and hundreds, possibly thousands – for they were crated up – of snow shovels without handles. The base unit's sergeant-major confided in me that these were supplies intended originally for the abortive Norwegian campaign and, after having been transhipped in turn to Malaya and the Gold Coast, had finally been deposited here.

No case was ever reported of the loss of Arctic stores but depredations upon petrol supplies were constant and severe. Much of the petrol was contained in five-gallon cans which were easy to remove, and on the black market such a can fetched about fifty times its regular price. Petrol had come to be regarded as a form of wealth at a time when the bottom had fallen out of every market, and we heard rumours of huge quantities stolen from this and other bases being hidden away in caves in the interior. The rich colons, we knew, were at the back of those losses, although the thieves could only be Arabs mingling with the labour-force the Army employed. The wild shooting that had taken place may have discouraged these but the ensuing panic among the legitimate workers virtually brought activity of all kind to a standstill at the base.

Intelligence Corps sections worked largely through informers of which Michel Fortuna was a valuable example. Nine-tenths of the information we garnered by one means or another was rubbish, passed on in most cases by persons seeking to use us to settle private grudges. But Fortuna revealed hard and often startling facts, and made himself indispensable to the section. Soon a few truths relating to his own personality and career began to be revealed, but by the time we began to understand the kind of man we were dealing with there was no question of cutting ourselves adrift from him. Moreover we were slowly becoming acclimatized to a situation where people took allies where they could find them, prepared if necessary to make a short-term pact with the devil. There was little British suburban respectability in Philippeville. A day or so after our dinner at the Fortuna mansion one of the town's upper-crust citizens happened to make reference to Madame Renée's firm belief in the value of church attendance, adding that she compelled all her staff to attend regular Mass. At this point we understood that she ran the brothel. It was not an occupation that caused the raising of local eyebrows.

Fortuna worked diligently for our cause, moved undoubtedly by self-interest, although possibly gratitude as well. Whatever information AFHQ called for, Fortuna could always unearth it for us, and in consequence the FSO was complimented for his efficiency. Captain Bouchard, who was turning sour, warned us, 'Always remember this man is a plain straightforward gangster.' That was his problem, Leopold told him.

Bouchard came to us to complain about his lack of transport. His old Citroën was out of action for hopeless, makeshift repairs one day in three, and the three men of his Philippeville half-section were riding bicycles. How was he to be expected to carry out his duties, including among them the protection of our supplies depot from thieves? The FSO asked him what he proposed, and Bouchard asked him to requisition Fortuna's car, to which our captain's reply was, 'We can't let our friends down.'

A small favour granted to Fortuna for his numerous services was a permit to drive his elderly but perfectly maintained car through the streets of Philippeville bearing a windscreen sticker that proclaimed its owner to be engaged in essential duties for the Allied forces. By this valuable concession he achieved the advantage of mobility. He had established himself as boss of an ill-defined area within a radius of possibly thirty or forty miles of Philippeville, of which he had lost control during his imprisonment. Now, with our aid, he was able to visit all the small towns and villages that had seceded and take over again. Anyone who opposed him – and this included several mayors – would be denounced as a pro-Vichy plotter, and placed on our blacklist, or that of any other section operating in the area. We only knew half of what was going on, but apart from that we did not greatly care. Let the Algerians settle their differences in their own way, was the general verdict, so long as they were kept out of our hair.

The theft of petrol continued to be the greatest of our problems and Fortuna promised to solve this, too. The worst culprit, he told us, was a colon of White Russian origin named Malakoff, the owner of a huge vineyard, producing an annual ocean of hard Algerian wine, much of which went to France for blending and bottling under a French label, while the rest was turned into industrial alcohol.

All the colons dealt in stolen petrol, and having notified the Sous-Préfecture, as agreed, of our intention to do so, we had already searched several farms. No petrol was ever found, but it was not unusual for the house to be filled with the stench of its disposal down lavatories. Clearly Malakoff was one of Fortuna's personal enemies, and this was his way of dealing with him.

Malakoff too had done his best to ingratiate himself with the Allies, and with some success. He had recently arranged a boar-hunting party for important British and American officers from AFHQ. They took part in this under the impression that Malakoff was the personal representative in Philippeville of General de Gaulle. He had shown our FSO a letter from the General, which Captain Bouchard assured us was forged.

By all accounts this hunt had been a singular affair, organized in such a way that however terrible a shot a guest might be, it was virtually impossible for him not to get his boar. There were no boars on the Malakoff estate, but Arabs had been sent into the interior to trap a large number of them which had been scientifically lamed in such a way that while able to walk without an obvious limp, they could not run. These were released from the top of a low hill after the guns had been stationed at intervals along a road that encircled it. Dogs then drove the boars down the slopes to their inevitable execution. A shortage of shotguns and cartridges at the time compelled some of the junior officers to use tommy-guns, or even pistols, but even these got a boar. At the end of the fusillade one of the guests was found dead with a bullet through the heart. With so many bullets flying about there was nothing extraordinary about this. The French were unaccustomed to take serious precautions to prevent sportsmen from shooting each other, and this they frequently did. Discussing the incident with Fortuna we learned, however, that the dead man was a French liaison officer at AFHQ who was known to have done Malakoff a bad turn in the past. 'He must have been weak in the head,' Fortuna said, 'to fall into a trap like that.'

However much General de Gaulle may or may not have sought to recommend Malakoff, he laboured beneath the disadvantage of being on our black-list, and therefore had been unable to obtain a sticker like Fortuna's to affix to the windscreen of the spectacular Delahaye mouldering away in one of his outhouses. He had lost ground too, according to the FSO, not so much because one of his guests had had to be taken back to Algiers in a coffin, but because he had directed the massacre of the boars in an absurd red jacket and peaked cap of the kind worn by French fox hunters. From other sources we learned that, some years before, Malakoff and Fortuna had been in a High Noon-style encounter, which Fortuna had lost. I tackled him about this and he readily admitted what had happened. Malakoff, having been warned by Fortuna to stay out of Philippeville, had strolled into the Café du Commerce one day, accompanied by two friends, and told the waiter to get a message to Fortuna that he was there and waiting. 'I got into the car and went down straight away', Fortuna said, 'making the mistake of taking with me a new Walther pistol I had never operated before. As I walked through the door Malakoff stood up. I pointed the gun at him and pressed the trigger. Unfortunately the safety catch was on. Next moment I felt a kick in the stomach. Somehow or other I dragged myself out, got into the car and drove home.' At this point he took out his most cherished possession – an X-ray photograph showing a bullet lodged against the wall of his heart. 'It's still there,' he said. 'They don't want to take it out. Funny about the pain in the stomach, though. It's all I felt.'

Fortuna directed the plan of attack against Malakoff. One of his contacts placed an order with him for petrol, to be collected on a certain day, and on that day we were to descend on the farm, this time without notice being given to the Sous-Préfecture. Malakoff's stock had fallen so low, we thought, that no one would particularly care what happened to him. To be on the safe side, Fortuna suggested, we might take a gendarme with us, although on no account revealing to him the identity of the target. To conserve the element of surprise he thought we should take the farm in the rear, and in this way avoid being held up by a man stationed at the gate, who might be able to give the alarm.

So often in the surgery of the Army is the wrong limb removed. The intelligence on which we acted was beyond question, our planning meticulous and our preparations thorough. Our weak spot was our maps. The large-scale maps issued to us were of the wrong area, and the small-scale ones we had been able to procure locally seemed vague, and possibly out-of-date. However we set out enthusiastically enough in the section truck, our sergeant-major wearing his two guns for this important occasion, and our accompanying gendarme with handcuffs in his haversack and an arrest warrant in his pocket on which a space had been left blank for the name to be filled in.

It was five days from Christmas, the weather eternally fine, with a thin, piercing sun and the pink laterite of the vineyards hatched with the innumerable lines of the vines out of leaf. Nothing is more anonymous than a vineyard, and the *domaine* houses, set well back from the road at intervals of two or three miles, seemed to have surrendered to this conformity, for they were alike in every detail of their architecture, and at this season devoid of all signs of life, except those that provided a temporary perch for storks migrating from southern Europe. We passed the Malakoff farm's guarded gate, on the main road, from which there was no building in view, and then watched for a side-turning, marked with dotted lines on the map as a track. When one came into sight a map-reading argument arose between those who believed that we were turning off too soon, and the old soldiers, led by the sergeant-major, whose word was law and who insisted that we were on the right road.

In a matter of yards a house came into view, porticoed, with a wide roof of shallow pitch, identical with all the other *domaine* houses, and – apart from a forecourt of crazy-paving – remarkably like a villa in a Roman mosaic. The sergeant-major posted two men to guard the rear of the house. The windows were shuttered and the atmosphere was one of abandonment. There was no one about but some excited Arabs who seemed to spring like startled genii out of the ground when we began to hammer and kick at the door. They received my Adenese-plus-School-of-Oriental-Studies Arabic with expressions of the most profound bewilderment, and many valuable minutes were lost before a French-speaker could be found to tell us that the Malakoff house was two miles away.

With this it was clear that the operation had collapsed. Nowhere do the jungle tom-toms of communication work more efficiently than in North Africa. We saw no remedy other than to return to the road and make our entry to the Malakoff *domaine* by the main gate, and by the time we arrived, Malakoff was ready for us waiting to open the door. He held out a soft, well-manicured hand: a young, bald man with an ivory, light-shunning face, a velvet smile and gold ornaments at the opening of his shirt and his cuffs. '*Messieurs,*' he said. '*Soyez les bienvenus.*' In the cool, vaulted background, a betrousered Vietnamese girl waited with a tray of champagne. Malakoff as an Arab-hater was known to recruit his female staff, as did many colons, in the Far East. The Algerian French called them *boyesses* and they were much appreciated for the extreme subservience of their deportment and the relative hairlessness of their bodies.

Malakoff did not long outlive this encounter. At about this time a number of severe air raids by German and Italian planes were carried out on the harbour of Philippeville and, in the course of one of these, a man seen wandering in the prohibited zone of the docks, said to have been signalling to the raiders with a torch, was shot dead by a sentry. This was Malakoff. Later, though, another version of his end was supplied by a contact. Malakoff, he said, had been kidnapped, drugged, carried by rowing boat into the port, and put ashore and abandoned, reeling and staggering about in the semi-darkness. After that someone had rung up the unit guarding the port and told them that a spy had just landed from a submarine. Whatever the truth of it, Malakoff died, and by local custom was buried within twenty-four hours, his funeral said to have been the most splendid since the outbreak of war.

The week of almost nightly attacks by dive bombers provided a classic, oversimplified vision of war, not devoid of its savage poetry. We had ring seats for these regular performances, for the Villa Portelli was close to the centre of the raiders' target. The planes came in, five or six in succession, flying at low altitudes, circling with premeditation, and clearly visible in the dusk. One after another, at intervals of a minute or two, they would carry out their bombing runs, going into their dive – as it seemed to us – when immediately above us. We would listen to the howl of the accelerating engines, interrupted by that of the high-pitched and penetrating scream of the approaching bomb. At this point the gunners operating the two anti-aircraft guns at the bottom of our garden would give up and jump for their slit trenches, although the pageant of fire and flame was kept going by many other guns placed round the harbour.

The glass fell away in an icicle shower from our windows and all that we saw through it had been balefully transfigured. Hundreds of guns were pumping thousands of shells into the sky, which opened up to spew fiery lava over ten ships sitting in a carmine lake. Our white arums in the garden had turned pink, and so had the naked, scaly branches of the plane trees. Tracers from the multi-barrelled 'Chicago Piano' came up out of a pink mist, only miraculously deflected in the last hair's breadth of time from our balcony. A near miss drove the gunners out of another emplacement, and they ran hunched like men caught in a driving hail-storm. We too were transformed, at one moment ruddy and grinning horribly in the light of a great vermilion explosion, and the next aghast in the white sheet-lightning of a magnesium flare. We heard the walls crack, and the villa shift and settle, breathed layered smoke and felt the concussion of the bombs in our eardrums and the soles of our feet. Our two worst cases of uncontrollable apprehension were clasped together under the table in the foetal position of twins in the womb, but even Sergeant-Major Leopold, our man of steel, seemed influenced by these happenings, revealing suddenly his Sephardic origins in an urgent outburst of *cante flamenco*. The FSO, after declaiming a passage from Ovid, bounded up to the roof, where he stood – as he admitted later, in a state of disbelief – while the shrapnel from anti-aircraft bursts tinkled around him.

The bombing was accurate and could be expected regularly to take place after the arrival of a convoy. Backed by the opinion of Signals radio technicians who detected the existence of clandestine transmitters, GHQ ascribed this to the presence of spies. We were ordered to drop everything and track these down, and to enable us to do so we were supplied with a van fitted out with the latest equipment, including a direction-finding aerial. It was quite a new toy for us, and at last after the wasted weeks we were to be put to effective use. Unfortunately, spy-hunting too soon turned into farce. Once again we were defeated by the system which surrendered all responsibility to our old soldiers. Only these were allowed to twiddle dials and perform the simple calculations necessary to locate the illicit transmitter. These, through educational limitations, were unable to cope with magnetic variations, and simple mathematics, so although we broke into a number of houses at the dead of night, and aroused their blameless occupants from their sleep – to confront them with wild accusations of espionage – no arrests were ever made, and the transmissions continued undisturbed.

Chapter Seventeen

TODAY I AM approached again by the Arab Sûreté agent Bou Alem, a man for whom I took one of my instant dislikes at our first meeting – these being so often discovered later to be without foundation. The aversion may have been based – regrettably enough – to some extent on the man's appearance, for he is rather ugly with some slight deformity of the arms and shoulders, giving him a somewhat cringing aspect. I was also repelled by the way he seemed ready to cultivate the good graces of French officials, in particular Captain Bouchard who evidently approves of his gendarmes' habit of crushing Arab children's feet.

Nobody particularly wanted to see him when he first called at our office, but in the end I was found and reminded that contacts with such as Bou Alem were part of my job. He asked me if I would go to prison with him, as he had something to show me. It was at least a way of using up too much spare time and I went along. He took me to a paved yard, raised a plate of metal like a manhole and shone down a torch. An iron ladder led into absolute darkness. At first I assumed this to be some sort of subterranean latrine, for there was a tremendous stench of faeces and urine. I then made out several half-naked Arabs stretched out on sacking spread over flagstones among piles of excrement. One began to crawl towards the light. Others stirred, as if in their sleep. We went down the ladder into the terrible effluvia and intense cold. 'This,' said Bou Alem, 'is a punishment cell. They call it "the grave". These men are dying.'

I told him I was horrified and disgusted, as I was. I added that we had received the most express orders not to meddle in French affairs, and that I personally could only be concerned with the security of our troops. 'There's nothing I can do about this,' I said.

'The first thing you did when you got into this town was to rescue the gangster Fortuna, who was sentenced to death for murder. These men haven't been charged with any crime. They're Arab village leaders, that's all. By this time next week they'll be dead of cold or starvation. You let Fortuna and his gangsters go. Why can't you free them?'

'We've reached agreements with the French. I haven't the power to.'

Shame has made me do my best to avoid Bou Alem all the more after this. Whenever I see him in the street I dodge down the nearest side turning, but once more he has turned up at the office and caught me before I could get away.

He says he has important and confidential news for me. It is not a good thing for him to be seen to frequent the Villa Portelli, he says, and he arranges that we should meet in a *gargoulette*, a cheap Arab eating-place in an alleyway which no European would ever dream of entering, and where he is among his own people.

Bou Alem's message is that the French are planning to massacre the Arabs, but that the killing is to be done by British troops, who will be used as their tools. In the first few weeks of our occupation the British had nothing but praise for the enthusiasm and diligence of their Arab labour force, and there is now talk that when the Allies withdraw from such base areas as Philippeville and advance into Tunisia, the best of their workers will go with them. It is a relationship the French are determined to break at all costs. The continuing British cause for complaint with the Arabs is the looting of their supply depots, the largest being at Philippeville, and the French plan is to induce the British to take bloody reprisals on the nearest village. In this way, Bou Alem says, the Arabs are to be taught a lesson they will never forget, and at the same time be detached from the Allies and therefore freely available once more on the labour market at 7 francs per day.

I listen to these revelations full of sympathy, but can only reply that whatever secret understanding has been reached – clearly at a high level – between the British and the French, it cannot be any concern of mine, and I can expect nothing better than a severe reprimand if I even put in a report based on his information.

12 JANUARY

The FSO called a section meeting today, appearing to be in a high state of excitement. He has just returned from a meeting at GHQ with the G2, and a commanding officer of the Royal Naval Marine Commando that has arrived in the area, and all he says confirms in substance Bou Alem's report. According to information provided by the French Sûreté, the Arabs responsible for the raids on the base depot are from the nearby village of Filfila, always a notorious den of thieves. The commandos have come straight from living rough in a Highland glen, chasing knife in hand after sheep before butchering and devouring them among the heather and snow. Now they are to be 'blooded', the FSO says, his blue eyes atwinkle – given a taste of the real thing. An invaluable experience, their CO agrees. Suddenly for Captain Merrylees, his lacklustre war of shadows has come to life, and there are fighting men among us, saga-warriors of the kind that skinned their captives alive after a Viking raid. He chuckles. 'To toughen themselves up,' he said, 'they mix piss with their beer.' Not a bad thing either, he seems to suggest. Something the Norsemen of old, too, were accustomed to do.

But there is a small intelligence involvement here too, for the G2, as willing as anybody else to unleash the dogs of war, has asked, before issuing the final order for blood to flow, for a routine account of the village, accompanied by a sketch map providing some physical identification to prevent any regrettable error, and a run-down of its population by age and sex. This I am ordered to do.

I go straight from this meeting to the lugubrious alleyway *gargoulette*, leaving a message to be passed on to Bou Alem to meet me there later in the day.

It is no more than he has expected, he tells me on his arrival. Now, he says, the time has come when something will have to be done to get it across to my superiors that the French are proposing to use them, that it is the colons and not the Arabs who are their enemies, and if the Arabs are to be punished it is only because of the energy with which they have supported the Allies' cause.

'We can forget it,' I say. 'Nobody will listen to me. I'd only be sticking my neck out for nothing. If we can stop the looting, they'll call off the attack.'

'Are you sure of that?'

'I'm sure.'

'The looting can be stopped,' Bou Alem says.

'How?'

'The saint will tell them to stop. All Algerians obey his word. Sidi Omar Abbas.'

'I've never heard of him,' I say. 'This is the first time I've ever heard you had a local saint.'

'He is a very great one. Most men become saints when they are old. Sidi Omar was recognized as a saint when he was able to read his parents' minds.'

'Ah.'

'Have you heard of the great influenza epidemic of 1918?'

'I have indeed.'

'Half of the Arabs of Philippeville died,' Bou Alem says. 'Sidi Omar was lying, about to die of weakness and starvation on a mountain top, when two crows fed him. They killed a newly born lamb and dragged it within reach of him.'

'Do you believe that?'

'Yes, I believe it. Certainly I believe it.'

'Is this miracle accepted by Mohammed Kobtan and Dr Kessous?' (Philippeville's two Arab intellectuals).

'I assure you it is. Not only that but we once suffered from a plague of poisonous reptiles, and Sidi Omar told all the people to go into their houses. He breathed upon the reptiles and they died. This was before my time. It is within his power to put a spell on the French and cause them all to fall asleep.'

'Why doesn't he, then?'

'Because God has a plan for us. He refuses to interfere.'

'Perhaps he'd refuse in this case.'

'We could ask him. There is nothing he cannot do if he agrees.'

Sidi Omar lives on a local mountain top, in a shrine

already built for him, in which his mortal remains will be buried, after – as Bou Alem explains – in the manner of Sìmeon, he has called upon God to draw his soul up to heaven. The upshot of this discussion is that Bou Alem will try to see him and implore his intervention, while I report on the possibility of a peaceful solution to the FSO.

13TH JANUARY

The meeting with Captain Merrylees comes as a surprise. Sergeant-Major Leopold has always preferred to arrange such interviews to take place under formal conditions, and to be present in person, having positioned himself in regimental fashion to the side and rear of the FSO's desk. This time he has been called away and, relieved of his faintly sardonic presence, the FSO is clearly another man. None of the usual flare-ups and barrack room explosions; on the contrary, he is positively mild, and seems quite to have lost his thirst for blood. Not only that, but apparently eager to find some way of holding the commandos at bay. 'Do what your Arab friend suggests,' he says. 'Why not? There's nothing to be lost.' It is the friendliest and most reasonable encounter that has taken place between us to date.

Pondering over this abrupt change of mood, I have hit upon a possible explanation for the two faces of Captain Merrylees. I have decided that he is obsessed with his own imaginary or real inadequacies as a soldier. The conditioning process we have all gone through appears to have done nothing to strengthen his self-confidence. He probably despises the foolishness with which, like us all, he is beset. So, over and over again he has to assure himself and us that it is nothing but play-acting, a kind of dream, something that will pass. Yet, as an ineffective and incomplete soldier, he feels threatened by the sergeant-major's martial presence, and above all by Leopold's total belief in himself. Leopold treats the FSO with an almost exaggerated deference, yet behind this a wordless domination seems to exist. It is a hypothesis providing a key to otherwise inexplicable behaviour, to Merrylees' increasing concern for his appearance which keeps his batman endlessly polishing his buttons and his buckles, and in particular the episode of the bombing when Leopold burst into song, while the FSO – perhaps determined to go one better – endangered his life by going up on to the roof.

In the evening I go to the *gargoulette* and see Bou Alem again. 'Sidi Omar agrees to see you and discuss your problem,' he says. 'He'll only see you if you're by yourself, and you have to remember he speaks nothing but Arabic. You speak a little, didn't you tell me?'

'But not the local variety,' I tell him.

'Say a few words,' Bou Alem says.

I trot out one of my sentences kept ready for such occasions, containing a few basic words common to all the dialects. '*Ana q'rait fil jerida al yom inna . . .*' ('I read in the paper today that . . .') He holds up his hand. 'I can understand you, but only just.'

'Couldn't something be worked out in advance which I could read to him? Perhaps you could help?'

'He wouldn't listen to a set speech. He wants to talk to you to test your sincerity.'

'This is a different language from the one I learned,' I say. 'Half the words are different, and even the ones I know carry a different accent which makes them unrecognizable. Everywhere else they say *bálad*, for country. You say *bled*.'

'And not only that,' he says. 'We have half a dozen different dialects in this department alone. If I go to Batna or Tebessa I have to take an interpreter. When you listen to some of these tribesmen they sound like sheep bleating.'

'What's to be done, then?'

'I brought this book along,' he says, 'It might give you some ideas.'

The book is Soualah's *L'Arabe Pratique et Commercial*, the only one to be found on Algerian Arabic, and it starts off with a casual mention of an extra letter in the alphabet, an extra tense and the fact that pronunciation has been much affected by the Berber language predominant in many areas. I have already studied it, lost heart and pushed it aside. On the other hand it is a school book produced in a stern direct fashion for the instruction of the children of another race, containing many cautionary sentences in French with their equivalent in Arabic which might have some application to these circumstances. There is even a chapter on '*Les Armes*', with an illustration showing fiercely moustached Zouaves firing an antique cannon.

'How much time have we got?' Bou Alem asks.

'Two days. Possibly three.'

'It's short. Read it through, and get what you can out of it. Sidi Omar knows the language problem as well as anyone else. Let him see you've done your best, and he'll make allowances.'

15TH JANUARY

Aïn Zouit is about five miles out of town, at the back of Stora, with the mountain looking rather like an enormous mine-tip rising among the oak woods, with the white unfinished shrine on its top. A number of Arabs live in the usual misery at the foot of the mountain, in the hope – Bou Alem mentioned – of imbibing the spiritual essences that roll down the slopes from the shrine. I see young marriageable girls, some of them pretty, who are too poor and demoralized to bother to veil themselves. They look away when I ride up.

I leave the Norton propped against a tree-trunk and start the steep climb up the track leading to the top of the mountain. After a few hundred yards I stop to rest, and a collection of villagers following me wait and watch. I go on again and after a while see a distant white-clad human form moving among the boulders below the shrine, and shortly it becomes clear that this is a man coming down the mountain-side at an amazing speed. He is leaping from rock to rock, scrambling across screes and dried-up gullies. At this point I decide to save my breath and wait, the semi-circle of villagers at my back, and a moment later an old man bursts through the scrub on the slope ahead, dislodging small landslides of loose stones, and comes towards me, hand outstretched. It is the saint in person, tall, lean, and immensely old, blue-eyed, with teeth set at all angles in his smile, a tattered but splendidly laundered *jellabia*, untidy turban, one of his sandals tied up with string, and a trickle of blood where he has grazed a toe.

He takes my hand in his grip, bursts into laughter, dismisses the following crowd, then gestures invitingly towards the summit, and we set off together. I scramble and haul myself upwards with bursting lungs, but for Sidi Omar this climb is hardly more than an act of levitation. He gets to the top a hundred yards ahead, and waits for me, laughing. Then we go into the shrine built a century before, as Bou Alem has told me, to house the relics of the most celebrated of all North African saints, Sidi Mohammed Ben Farhas, visited in his day by innumerable sterile women from all parts of the country, who infallibly conceived on their return home. Sidi Omar lives in the zuwiya, a partially ruined building that once housed the followers of the cult. He has set two plates on a table in a bare room with half the roof missing. A bowl of black honey encrusted with flies stands between us, and the saint opens up a hole among them with his thumb, gouges out a dollop of honey and drops it on my plate. Many flies that have avoided the temptation of the honey buzz round our heads, and occasionally one lands on the sagging inner surface of Sidi Omar's lower eyelids, although they do not bother with me. Chickens scuffle round our feet, and at one point a goat tethered in a far corner urinates.

The universally recognized greetings in Arabic pass between us and are repeated many times in the usual way. I shift my stool round to sit at Sidi Omar's side, pick up Soualah's book, in which numerous passages are underlined, and make a start with what I have to say, sticking to a dozen basic verbs covering this life's most important occasions, which appear in every page of the Koran. The saint listens attentively with the slightly wincing expression of one who hears great music being played badly. Sometimes he adds a correction, and rarely he even nods his approval. After a while he takes the book from me, closes it, and sets it aside. '*Parlons français,*' he says, and then in good French, 'I made a vow only to speak the language of my people, but God is very understanding, and will realize that exceptional circumstances can arise. Tell me about your trouble.'

I tell him, and he agrees to help. 'I'll go down to Filfila and talk to them,' he says.

'And I can tell my chief there'll be no more trouble?'

'Not from the Arabs. You'll have plenty from the French. We too, but soon they'll be gone.'

'They'll be gone, Sidi Omar?'

'Quite positively.'

'Why are you so sure of that?' The opinion voiced by an Arab of great prestige must be examined with respect. Based on the old adage that there's no smoke without fire, Field Security NCOs are instructed to be on the alert for rumours, and when there is little else to report, a kind of cottage industry springs up in many sections devoted to their manufacture. These in due course will be incorporated in the FSO's weekly report to GHQ, to be sifted through and analysed in due course by specialists in this nebulous area of intelligence. Sidi Omar's viewpoint can be taken as reflecting that of a high proportion of local Arabs.

'Because of the prophecy.'

This is a little disappointing. I hoped for some hint of an uprising, a *jihad* of guerrillas in the mountains, but I nod, hoping to make it evident that I am impressed. In these mountains a saint's prophecy is nearly as solid an affair as a battalion training in secret.

'God tested us with too many good harvests, and we were corrupted. People drank wine, they wore garments of silk and listened to profane music. Young men were permitted to see their wives' faces before marriage, and rich men selfishly refused to marry more than one wife.'

'I'm sorry, Sidi Omar, but what's wrong with a little pleasure? Why be so austere?'

'It pays,' Sidi Omar says. 'In the long run. We'll be here in a thousand years' time, and where will the French be? They were the lesson sent by the Almighty to cure us of our bad habits. My predecessor Sidi Mohammed Ben Farhas appealed to God to bring us to our senses. I imagine what he had in mind was a few bad harvests, but what we got was the French. But for a hundred years only, the Almighty made clear. And that's nearly up. A few more years, and we'll be free of them.'

20TH JANUARY

Visit to the base depot, where the news is that all continues to go well. I have seen a newly arrived Captain Rogers, second in command, and one of the few officers so far encountered to have a good word for the Arabs. He was astonished a few days ago by the arrival at the base of the saint in person, at which all the Arabs stopped work for a brief session of prayer, followed by a lengthy harangue pronounced by Sidi Omar. The saint was entertained by the officers to tea, served in Army style from a large brew-can, and asked with considerable dignity to be allowed to take the used-up leaves with him when he left. Rogers is inclined to judge people by the reception they get from dogs, whose powers of instinctive evaluation he believes to be more acutely developed than ours, and he was particularly impressed when one of their dog-handler's Alsatians made a beeline for him with obvious delight. At all events, not only has the thieving stopped, but work at the depot has speeded up since the visit. Rogers has had a pat on the back from AFHQ, and has put in a good word for us in consequence, news of which reached me in the form of lukewarm congratulations from the FSO – Leopold being present.

There was a singular footnote to this particular interview, for, before dismissing me, the FSO suddenly turned on one of his broad and crinkling smiles – a facial contortion from which the muscles take seconds to recover, accepted by us now as heralding momentous news. 'Ah yes, Sergeant. In future you will refer to me not as Captain Merrylees, but as Captain FitzClarence.'

'Is that order to cover all references made to you, sir, including those made to Allied personnel?'

'For the moment, no. But that in future will be my name so far as all non-Allied personnel are concerned.'

A strange business indeed.

12TH FEBRUARY

Relations with the Arabs continue to go downhill, as evidenced by the following incidents.

THURSDAY

British soldiers who had been drinking *anisette* in the Bar Jules came out and assaulted several passing Arab girls. Veils were torn from their faces and in one case a soldier put his hand up a girl's skirts. These assaults were encouraged and cheered by French passers-by.

FRIDAY

A party of drunken soldiers went into the mosque without removing their boots – as requested by a notice at the door. One of them pissed against a wall, and when the old Imam protested a mug of beer was emptied over his head. Later that day I visited the Bar Jules and saw the owner Vachon, who took me with evident pride into his kitchen where the *anisette* is made up in an operation taking no longer than five minutes. He laughingly said that it was lucky for him that the pharmacy happened to be next door.

SUNDAY

A jeep doing an estimated seventy miles per hour along the Charlesville Road ran over and killed an Arab child, and failed to stop. On the same day in the main street here an armoured vehicle smashed into the side of an Arab horse-drawn cart. The cart was wrecked and one horse suffered a broken leg and had to be destroyed. The sergeant driving the armoured vehicle threw about five pounds' worth of francs at the Arab involved, and drove off.

The fact is, we are beginning to copy the attitudes of the French who are out to persuade us that Arabs don't matter. The old recommendation that is said to have held good in Egypt – if you happen to run a gyppo down, be sure to back over him – has found its way here. The Arab has no rights. You can arrest one, go through his house, and no warrant is necessary, and if his womenfolk happen to be maltreated while this is going on, no one will raise an eyebrow.

Mohammed Kobtan's house was attacked, and all his windows smashed, one day last week. For two reasons. One, because he is an Arab, and the police are ordered in such cases to look in the other direction. Two, because he is the town's only successful Arab merchant. He buys and sells sardines, and this is the time – to some extent with our assistance – for his competitors, who employ gangsters to do their work for them, to settle old scores. Whether the FSO realizes it or not, our section supports the gangsters – posing with success as ardent Gaullists – and keeps them in business. Captain Bouchard is perfectly frank and fairly amiable about this. 'I am sorry, Messieurs. I am informed that these gentlemen are your friends. They take no notice of me. There is nothing I can do about it.'

In an attempt to close up the growing rift between us and the Arabs of Philippeville, I took up the idea put forward by Dr Kessous of giving our blessing to a species of friendship club to be started by a small number of influential Arabs. The object would be to provide an opportunity to make social contact with Arabs in their own homes. As it is, Arabs remain an unknown quantity to most Allied soldiers, and Kessous and many of his friends believe that there is no better way of re-establishing good relations and correcting damaging propaganda than by exposing us to traditional Arab hospitality.

When I mentioned this germ of a project to Leopold, he said, 'Steer clear of it. We're not interested,' and whatever Leopold says goes for the FSO these days. However, the section has no clear-cut policy in any direction, no fixed viewpoint, and very little direction. In fact we drift along, and mentioning to Leopold next day the possibility of dining at the house of a rich Arab, he was full of enthusiasm. This being so, I went back to Kessous, and told him that I thought his proposal was a very good thing.

Four founder-members are suggested for our friend-ship club, Dr Kessous, Mohammed Kobtan, Ahmed Meksen of the Mairie, and an engaging and enthusi-astic young taxi-driver called Hadef. Dr Kessous will represent the tiny handful of the professional élite, Mohammed Kobtan the almost equally limited business element, Meksen – so often addressed as Meknes – the Arab official world that little more than exists, and the exuberant Hadef the several thousand members of the proletariat.

Of these four men I have personal reservations only about one – Dr Kessous. I find him almost excessively ambitious, and therefore – so far as I am concerned – inevitably lacking in humour. Another thing that has not particularly recommended him to me is the display of a set of photographs taken while on the pilgrimage to Mecca, of the successive stages of the public amputation of a thief's right hand. These photographs, although technically satisfactory, are so gruesome that they have even been turned down by *Life*. I cannot bring myself to feel any deep affection for a man who could concen-trate on his photography at such a time, but for all that he is a natural leader, and much respected by his co-religionists.

Mohammed Kobtan and Ahmed Meksen are admir-able in every way, simple, dignified and generous, but of the men in our pilot scheme Hadef the taxi-driver is in some ways the most remarkable. He is exceptionally handsome – the double almost of the French film star Charles Boyer – and although he spends much of his spare time hanging about the bars round the port getting sozzled on *anisette*, he is a great reader – an intellectual by local standards – regarded by the French police as a potential subversive, not only because he owns a collection of *Reader's Digests* in the French version, but lends these to any seeker after knowledge who shows an interest in them.

A curious fact has emerged from recent discussions with these men when such matters as national prejudices are brought up. Something has convinced them that the main stumbling block to better East–West relations in their case is the seclusion of their womenfolk. They all assure me that the women themselves are responsible and are constantly chided by their menfolk for their backwardness in insisting on wearing the veil. Kessous, a Koranic scholar, says that there is nowhere in the Koran that the practice is upheld, and that the old Imam, who is greatly venerated through having elected to become a eunuch in furtherance of his religious life, has pronounced in favour of the veil's abandonment.

The current flirtation with Western freedoms is undoubtedly at the back of an extraordinary party attended by Kobtan, Meksen, Hadef and myself at Kessous' house. This was the equivalent of English five o'clock tea, at which in the normal course of events men only meet to talk politics, sip coffee and nibble almond and honey cakes. Something made me suspect that this was a special occasion, and sure enough, after a few moments of desultory conversation four black-shrouded and extremely animated forms burst into the room.

These were the wives, primed for a symbolical break with the past.

They were all young and spirited, two of them, Mesdames Kessous and Kobtan, although clearly not French, have non-Semitic faces, extremely pale skins, and light brown hair. I suspect them of being Berbers, and it also occurred to me that the possession of a wife of highly European appearance might have some status advantage for a prominent Muslim. Meksen's wife was undoubtedly an Arab, and Hadef's turned out to be a negress he had acquired while living in the deep south. All four girls seemed highly intelligent and had plenty to say for themselves. Madame Hadef had a great sense of humour. When she mentioned that it was the first time that any men apart from her husband had seen her face, and I asked her how she felt about it, her reply was, 'Well, at the moment I'm blushing, but my skin being the colour it is, I don't imagine you've noticed.'

The upshot of this meeting was that we should start the ball rolling with a typical Arab-style lunch, if this could be arranged, for members of the section, and take it from there.

23RD FEBRUARY

Called to AFHQ Algiers for a meeting with a Major Bright, who is somebody in an undisclosed branch of Intelligence. He is rather grand, and with the patrician manner – as is often the case – goes a certain informality. He tells me to 'grab a pew' and says, 'I've only just heard of you. I don't know why. They tell me you can cope with the lingo here.'

I tell him about my struggles with the Algerian brand

of Arabic, and he nods in sympathy. 'What do you people in FS actually get up to?' he asks. 'I imagine they keep you pretty busy.' When I tell him the true nature of our activities, he shakes his head in disbelief. 'Sometimes I ask myself,' he says, 'Can we win this war?'

Tea and biscuits are brought. 'To cut a long matter short,' he says, 'we need you here. We depend entirely on interpreters, and I needn't tell you how unsatisfactory that can be. I imagine you wouldn't be overwhelmed with grief at the prospect of being spirited away from Philippeville and given something useful to do with us?'

I show proper enthusiasm at the prospect, and he says, 'Very well then, that's a deal. I suppose you'd better go back to your section and keep them happy for a few days while I twist all the necessary wires together. I'll be getting in touch with your FSO.'

Leaving his office, I feel sure that no more will be heard of this.

28TH FEBRUARY

A mission to deliver supposedly highly secret documents to our Tunisian frontline section. They are extremely pessimistic about the outcome of the campaign, particularly after the rout of the Americans at Kasserine. We sit late into the night hitting the Tunisian wine and listening to the thud and thump of distant shelling. The section is no longer allowed to include any comment on the morale of the troops in its reports, and we agree that, whatever they may tell the people back home, we are facing an Army which is too good for us, which is better trained, better equipped, and above all better endowed with fighting spirit. There is no hope of an advance until we can build up a crushing superiority.

This FSO likes to dress up – or rather likes his section members to do so. A sergeant has just been induced to disguise himself as an Arab – without a word of the language – and try to reach Tunis and report back on the situation there. Nobody expects to hear of him again.

2ND MARCH

The get-together lunch with the Arabs has fallen through. After accepting, Captain Merrylees appears to have had afterthoughts, and made an excuse to pull out. Nevertheless, the FSO and half the section were entertained at a party for someone's *anniversaire* on the same day given by Fortuna at his house next to the brothel. Roast wild boar as usual, champagne by the bucketful, and quickest-on-the-draw contest between Fortuna and Leopold, which Leopold only narrowly lost.

A narrow escape for Hadef round about the time when all this was happening, when his taxi was sprayed by machine-gun fire at the moment of passing Fortuna's farm on the Charlesville Road. He heard nothing of the firing but suddenly saw a line of holes in his right-side door. A warning to him, he says, to keep his place.

3RD MARCH

Do any of the section members accept bribes or gifts from Fortuna? Something I'm never likely to know. Whatever's done in this direction would be with great discretion. Fortuna's not stupid enough to try to stuff thousand-franc notes in anybody's pocket.

I went to talk to him today at the farm from which Hadef may or may not have been fired upon. The subject for discussion was the *milice populaire*. He is the local commandant, and Bou Alem handing me a list of the membership mentioned that every single man had done a stretch in prison.

Reception affable in the extreme. He grasps me and it is impossible to evade his embrace. '*Tu es plus qu'un frère pour moi,*' he says. He is concerned about my appearance. I don't look well. '*Et la santé – ça va bien? Vraiment? Ah, je suis content.*'

We get down to business. It's about the *milice populaire*, I say.

'The *milice populaire*. Sure. Yes, go on.'

'Do you have any regular authorization to wear those armbands?'

'No. Should we?'

'I think you should.'

'Well, I'll see to it straight away. And thanks for bringing it up. To be on the safe side, I'll tell the boys to take their armbands off until the official say-so comes through.'

Unfortunately – hard as it is to admit it to oneself – he is likeable, this small man with his triangular, rueful face, his Chaplinesque shuffle and his *quatre-cents-coups* smile. The section as a whole are included in his blanket gratitude. '*Vous m'avez tous sauvé la vie,*' he says, whenever given the opportunity. We have all dragged him from under the guillotine, and this salvation has given him a kind of emotional claim on us.

He wants to show me round. The house is an ugly, tasteless villa with pretentious modern furniture in chromium, steel or glass. Several equally sad-looking, middle-aged henchmen mooch silently in the background.

'Something out here'll probably interest you,' he says, and he takes me to see an old oil-cellar in the garden. 'We cleared it out when the raids started, to turn it into a shelter.' We go down some steps and I find myself in a long narrow chamber with the most wonderful Roman mosaics lining the walls, the kind of thing I've only seen before in a museum. We stop in front of a panel showing a garden with peacocks and three Roman girls standing with their arms round each other's shoulders, listening to another playing a lyre.

'What do you think of it?' he says.

'I've never seen anything like it.'

'Would you like to have it?'

'I don't understand you.'

'Say the word, and it's yours. It doesn't interest me.'

I laugh, still uncertain whether or not he means it. 'I carry all my worldly goods in a kitbag,' I say. 'It's a nice gesture but you're talking about a ton of masonry.'

'That picture's on plaster only a centimetre thick. I could have it taken off for you in an hour or two.'

'I'd still need a truck,' I said.

'Well anyway,' he says, 'the offer stands. If ever you change your mind it'll be here for you.'

The matter of the *milice populaire* will go into my report, but I'm fairly certain that it will go no further than Captain Merrylees.

Chapter Eighteen

S PRING CAME TO Algeria in March, with a nightingale in full song among the empty shell cases in the dilapidated garden of our new villa in the outskirts of the town. A species of self-protective reticence had grown among our Arab friends, separating us from such as Dr Kessous, who had now come to the conclusion that they had little to hope from us, and that whatever the outcome of the war they were destined to remain as they always had been – second-class citizens of France. Since, in order to survive, the proletariat must at least cling to their optimism, our Arab workers remained unjustifiably in good heart, fully convinced that we should continue to reward their labour with our protection and take them with us when and wherever we went. This blind and unreasoning cheerfulness was their best weapon in the propaganda war waged by the French, and made them popular with our troops.

As far as we were concerned the war had ground to a halt, leaving us with absolutely nothing to do. Section members condemned to patrol the port did so, although there was really nothing there to watch over. Routine visits to units were quietly allowed to lapse. The FSO was rarely seen, remaining, according to report, most of the day in bed. Leopold now effectively ran the section, as I assumed he had always planned to run it; but having grasped at the substance he found he had caught the shadow. He held the power but there was nothing whatever to do with it. In despair he applied for a transfer to a divisional section, where whatever action the inert

THE CAUSE OF WAR

First Army had to offer was presumably to be found. When I asked what news there was of that job I was supposed to have been given at AFHQ, he grinned as if in secret triumph. 'You can forget about it,' he said. 'You've been lost in the files again.'

Fortuna and his friends circulated boldly as ever with our stickers on the windscreens of their cars, to be saluted by our MPs if inadvertently stopped at checkpoints. Most weekends he gave a party at which half the section would get uproariously drunk. If AFHQ wanted information about our area, it came through him, and any visiting nabob from Algiers would be respectfully escorted to one of his houses to be softened up with richly garlicked food and vintage champagne. Bou Alem of the Sûreté repeatedly warned me of the terrible reprisals arranged for the Arabs as soon as we were withdrawn, and repeatedly and with a feeling of cowardice and shame I was obliged to explain to him that while the Arab's fate might concern me personally, no one who had the slightest power or influence in our Army could possibly care less.

Left virtually to my own devices, there was nothing to prevent my going off on long trips of exploration of the Algerian hinterland, and this I did. Once again I was to discover how extremely underpopulated the country was, and I rode for hour after hour over empty roads without any sign of human presence.

In the beginning I was surprised to find how 'un-African' it was, but I soon decided that visually it was neither African nor European, but something unique. The outstanding feature of this landscape was its splendid oak forests, with glades stretched to infinity between the stands of majestic trees. This aspect of it reminded me of engravings in eighteenth- and nineteenth-century books devoted to the Italian scene.

The absence of human intrusion outside the coastal strip made for the presence of an abundant fauna. I rode as quietly as I could along the empty roads, coasting softly in neutral gear with the engine switched off down the long, winding slopes, and in this way frequently took the animals by surprise: a brace of elegant foxes and – I could hardly believe it – a single jackal, traipsing dutifully like a well-trained dog through the buttercups. Deer were everywhere, wild boars frequently spotted at the edge of woods, and once I saw a sow chased through an open glade by her litter of sportive piglets. The best of the birds were of the flashing sub-tropical variety, such as bee-eaters, rollers or orioles, displayed like bright toys or Christmas-tree ornaments against the rich but sedate foliage of the oaks. The surprise of the day, and of these trips taken as a whole, was a covey of great bustard, like colossal partridges, the largest of which might have weighed thirty pounds. Some were in the roadway and could barely hoist themselves into the air before I was upon them. The last of our native birds were hunted to extinction by East Anglian squires using greyhounds who could run them down before they became airborne. The Arabs told me that they were bold and aggressive birds that would attack any man who wandered near their nests.

Innumerable flowers grew in these untouched, lonely places. In early March blue dwarf irises invaded snow-fields of narcissi, but later in the month many orchids came into flower; the lilac or purple bee, fly and spider ophrys in the full sun, and butterfly orchids in the shade of the oaks which, as I coasted slowly down the road, looked as though thousands of white butterflies had settled among last year's fallen leaves.

On these expeditions I always took a packet of tea, and sometimes, about midday, spotting an Arab hut on a mountain-side, I would climb up to it, and if a male came out to meet me, show him my provisions and suggest we might share them. The offer was always accepted with enthusiasm. Quite often on these occasions an egg or two would be produced to complete the meal. And in this way – two simple men trying to make themselves heard, and understand each other above the vociferous singing of nightingales – a pleasant and indulgent hour would be passed.

Chapter Nineteen

IN THE MIDDLE of April I had a car accident, and when I awoke some time later in the 100th General Hospital it was to find Leopold's face, a vaguely sinister angel from an El Greco background afloat somewhere above me in the unfocused shapes of the tent.

'The story is this,' he said. 'You have a fractured skull and a few other things that don't count for much. We're going into Tunis right behind the assault troops in about two weeks' time. If you're on your feet by then, OK. If you're not, you're off the section. We've been picked out for the biggest FS operation to date. We're in business at last.' The long El Greco face sharpened with thoughts of military adventures, and acquisition. 'We can't afford to be a man short at a time like this,' he said.

'I'll be there whatever happens,' I assured him.

Some hours later I saw the MO and explained the situation to him. He was entirely sympathetic to the extent of agreeing to a minor falsification of the records. A skull officially fractured meant a minimum of a month in hospital, but if the nature of the injury in the register were altered to concussion I could go as soon as I could stand on my feet. The MO warned me that if this were done I should deprive myself of an infinitely small disability pension.

The section left for Tunis on 4 May, the first British troops entered the city on the morning of the 7th, and at about the same time I set off alone, riding a motor cycle. I suffered from no feelings of discomfort, but was handicapped by being obliged to drive the machine –

which fortunately possessed a foot gear-change – with one hand, due to fractured ribs on the left side. Apart from this I was inconvenienced by a loss of balance that only took effect when I got off the motor bike and prevented me from standing still.

On the whole I managed fairly well. The roads were perfect until Souk El Arba. I slept in a field there, got up at dawn, and within two or three hours reached Béja, sixty miles from Tunis. Here I had bad trouble with truckloads of Germans who had either been disarmed and directed to the rear, or were actually trying to escape. They were strangely exuberant and, seeing the lone motor cyclist in the road, one after another drove straight at me, and in one instance I landed in the ditch – this possibly being my nearest escape from death in the war. After Medjez el Bab the battlefield began, cratered everywhere, and littered with numerous shattered or burned-out tanks. The bodies – where they could be reached in the wreckage – had been removed, but in each case helmets had been left to provide a tally.

Casualty clearing stations had been established in the villages, each one with rows of bloodstained stretchers stood against the wall to dry in the sun, recurrent accents of bright colour in an otherwise drab and desolate landscape.

By mid-morning I was in Tunis, alert in a mind's eye anticipation of a Brussels after Waterloo, delivered over to the crashing of church bells, to flower-throwing, Te Deums and Caesarian triumphs. But what dominated the scene was a great sprawl through the streets and the squares of the city of thousands of unconscious British soldiers – I counted over fifty lying on the steps of a single church – a Goyaesque muddle of bodies and bottles and wine vomit. The crowds, surging without direction hither and thither, trod them underfoot, and the MPs dragged them from under the tracks of tanks and heaved them like sacks of potatoes over the tailboards of the lorries waiting to take them away. If this, I asked myself, was the British in victory, how would they have appeared in defeat?

The Army was on its way elsewhere, to Cap Bon where there was a final battle to be fought, and the crowds watching from the roadside seemed apathetic. In all probability to avoid the innumerable drunks, most of the young women had gone home, leaving a glum collection of the middle-aged and elderly of both sexes, who had had enough of the war. It was astonishing to discover that numerous German soldiers were included among these onlookers, still free to come and go as they pleased, and a greater surprise still, in the first bar where I tried to buy a beer, to be elbowed from the counter by the Germans that had taken over the place. A group of them were roaring a marching song. Thus it remained for the rest of this day and the next, the British celebrating victory, and the Germans making the best of defeat, each in their own way.

Movement Control directed me to our headquarters in an elegant suburb at the better end of the boulevard. This villa until a day or two before had housed Gestapo personnel, and they had created in it a little haven of pseudo-Bavarian *Gemütlichkeit*, with drinking-steins decorated with jocose faces, and rackfuls of carved pipes, beery wall-mottoes, and clocks from which small rustic German figures popped as the hour chimed to execute a few clog-dance steps before being jerked back out of sight.

This place was the reverse of sinister, and the hatchet-faced men – as we supposed them to be – who had lived here must have left it with real regret. They had gone off in a hurry, leaving a cupboard stuffed with a huge variety of jams, with innunerable condoms – some with fanciful additions – and an assortment of feathered hats. Personal correspondence had been overlooked too, in the haste of departure, including letters waiting to be posted. This showed the writers on the whole as sensitive men, caring sons and devoted fathers. 'Persuade Mutti to take regular meals . . . Magda's friends sound to me rather wild. Please take care.' Friends and relatives were reassured as to the correspondent's health and the future of the cause. 'The exercise is good for me. I've never felt so fit . . . of course the going's been hard, but I see a break in the clouds.' One *Kriminalsekretär* was distressed by the condition of the Arab population. 'I've never seen such poverty. To tell you the truth it thoroughly depresses me.'

It was Leopold's moment of triumph, his apotheosis, and he could hardly contain himself for delight. After so many barren months in Philippeville relieved only by weekly orgies *chez* Fortuna, this unimaginable prize had fallen to us. A great, mysterious and inviolate oriental city was ours for the taking. The first thing was to settle in and, overbrimming with good humour, Leopold allocated the sleeping quarters. Up to this we had lived to some small extent under the dead hand of the Crimean War, from which time we were assured a regulation had survived that prohibited Other Ranks billeted upon civilians from sleeping in beds. In each villa, therefore, which we had previously occupied, the beds were removed to allow us to sleep, as in the days of Florence

Nightingale, on the floors. But now it seemed even to Leopold unreasonable that we should be denied the modest degree of comfort that had been enjoyed by the Gestapo.

Amid this general euphoria a single note of warning was struck. Captain Merrylees – now FitzClarence – announced that to mark our entry into Tunis he would shortly be changing his name again, but had not decided to what. Next, smiling dangerously, he issued an edict imposing a curfew upon us. The front door would be locked at 11 p.m. He kept his pistol ready by his bed, he said, and might decide to fire through his bedroom window, overlooking the door, at anyone who tried to enter after that time.

No one was quite sure how to take this. Was it supposed to be some sort of stupid joke, or had this strange, confused man drifted so far from the shores of reality that he was capable of putting such a threat into action? As Leopold, shaking his head, remembered, even in the relative calm of the first days in Philippeville there had never been any question of working to a time-table, and that our duties there had occupied us as much by night as by day.

9TH MAY

Chaos in Tunis is in no way diminished, and as so far no duties have been assigned to us there is little to do but roam the streets. Yesterday the last of the drunks had been carted away before midnight, but today shows promise of producing as heavy a crop as ever, as fresh Eighth Army troops arrive, set up camps in the neighbourhood and soldiers flock into town. Sometimes there is more Hogarth than Goya in the aspects of intoxication. I saw soldiers streaming into a wine-shop, drinking from the necks of bottles as they came out, then almost within seconds falling senseless. One man, unable to remove a cork, smashed the neck off the bottle, and emptied it, the jagged glass to his lips.

The movement of our fighting troops along the avenue de Paris is settling to something more like a parade, with the top brass showing off. Every soldier must feel the need to do something to assert his individuality in the terrible anonymity of Army life, and this is an impulse that has led in the Eighth Army to unusual results. We get away with brown shoes, unorthodox headgear and odd badges. In the Eighth Army the officers go in for polka-dotted scarves and corduroys. Astonishing that even a general should suffer from the same ambition to stand out in the crowd, to the extent – as one does – of wearing in this sweltering heat a battle blouse with a fur collar.

There are as many Germans to be seen as ever – but not a drunken one so far. They form groups to sing their aggressive songs, some of them having removed their badges of rank, although inexplicably their uniforms remain neat and well-pressed. They treat us with amused disdain, rather as British officers at the time of the Indian Mutiny might have viewed momentarily victorious sepoys.

I go into a pub full of them, and attract a little cold curiosity by having to pace backwards and forwards to keep my balance. Hardly any of the British speak a word of German, but one in three of the Germans has a fair amount of English, and this can be even fluent and colloquial, as in the case of one of them who debars my access to the crowded bar and says, 'Fuck off.'

Served in the end, I make for a corner and there find a defeated adversary who has no objection to talking to me. He is small, and superior in manner with thick pebbled spectacles, and gives me the impression of never having smiled in his life. He appears to be short of cash, accepts a drink from me and a conversation in 50–50 German and English begins. Drinking my beer, he obviously tries to put a brake on his contempt, but starts off, 'As an army, you are nothing. This is an episode of no importance. An interlude.' He does not see the Afrika Korps as defeated. They have responded to the need for strategic adjustment. The outcome of the war, he says, will be decided in Russia, and at this point I agree with him.

His battle career has been a dramatic one, making him sound like the personification of some Teutonic myth. He volunteered for action on the Russian front, collected five wounds – 'I'm like a sieve with bullet holes,' he says – and frostbite that removed two toes. He was then sent to North Africa, where he found the war sluggish and unentertaining, and he had applied to be returned to Russia. Apart from the Germans, he says, the Russians are the only soldiers worth anything. 'When we advanced,' he says, 'we had orders to take no prisoners and kill all the wounded. If you left a wounded man alive he would come round eventually and start shooting again. I live only for war,' he adds. 'There is no other experience in life to equal it.'

Strangely, he is obsessed by the knowledge that

months will probably pass before his mother hears that he has survived after he disappears into a PoW camp, and he presses on me a piece of paper giving an address in Switzerland through which she may be reached with news of him. Suddenly the obsidian Teutonic heart softens. 'Do this for me,' he says, and he takes off his wristwatch and tries to make me take it in payment.

IOTH MAY

A chance encounter in the avenue de Paris with my friend Tennant of the Medjez el Bab section whose hunted expression seems much increased since our last meeting back in the winter. Dive-bombing induces in the end its own special melancholy, as I remember from our short experience of it in Philippeville, and Tennant has been under the bombers for six months. Faith and hope have drained from him, and gloomily he unburdens himself of depressing secrets.

'I suppose we outnumbered them ten or twelve times,' he said. 'In Medjez alone we had about 3,500 troops – British, American, French. In the end the Germans got tired of waiting for us and they sent a battalion of 300 men down the road from Tunis to get rid of us. We made an orderly withdrawal to previously prepared positions – in other words we pissed off as fast as we could. Three hundred against three thousand. Remember the stuff they fed you in the history books? Remember Clive of India? What's happened to us, for Christ's sake? Why aren't we heroes any more? – or perhaps it was all balls and we never were. Did you hear how the Americans lost half their tanks? I can tell you because I was there. They weren't knocked out. They heard the Jerries were coming, and they turned round and ran off the road and got stuck in the mud.'

'Never mind, John,' I said. 'We're here at last,' I said.

'Do you know why? Only because you can't go on fighting when you've run out of petrol and ammo. They had nothing left to fight with.'

11TH MAY

Action at last. A large operation is to be mounted for the search of the German security headquarters in the rue de la Marne where innumerable documents that have escaped a back-garden bonfire are to be collected and sorted out for study.

Amid huge excitement we prepare to take control. Captain Merrylees, stiffly animated after some hours spent by his batman polishing his leather and brass, leads our exultant convoy to the scene, where something strange in the atmosphere is instantly to be detected. No one has awaited our arrival, and no one seems to notice that we are there. Officers and NCOs, like flying ants in a disturbed nest, rush wildly about with armfuls of documents – some badly charred – dodging or sometimes colliding with us. We are mysteriously excluded from all this urgent activity, which in theory we should have directed. Captain Merrylees wanders away to look for a lavatory, and we suspect that is the last we have seen of him. A moment later a red-faced major comes up, twitching and frothing with anger, and yells, 'Who the hell are you?'

Leopold explains our business there, and the major runs his eye over us with something like disbelief. He stares down at our brown shoes, then at webbing and belts that have never known blanco, and the trousers that should have been tropical issue, but which in two cases have been made up by a civilian tailor in Philippeville, and now we realize that it is our un-regimental appearance that appals him. Some instinct of self-preservation has saved Leopold on this occasion from wearing his two guns.

It dawns on me that these interlopers must be members of a new section, or sections straight from England, for I recognize them, in their brisk bloodlessness, as men still stunned by their training. They all wear Intelligence Corps badges and caps set at exactly the right angle, where the North African sections have taken to berets, and their equipment is coated by the green blanco insisted on by the Winchester depot. The major stops one of these dazed automata to put some question to him, and the man comes to attention with a crash of heavy boots. He turns his attention on us again. 'You're an absolute shower,' he says, 'if ever I saw one.'

Coming closer to yank at a loosely hanging shirt button, his fury has sharpened by suspicion. The culprit in this case is Watson, one of our section drunkards, and the major sniffs incredulously. 'Have you been drinking?' he shouts at him. Half the section has been drunk up to half the time since our arrival in North Africa, and two members including Watson have been drunk every day from early morning until late at night. With huge concentration and practice they have learned in the end how to walk without staggering while in this state, but they are never free from the special odour of the so-called pure alcohol used in the manufacture of *anisette*. Watson, a journalist in civilian life and a persuasive talker, manages with practised dignity to flannel his way out of this situation. Fortunately the major's attention is distracted from our second drunk, Spriggs, who is notoriously incoherent, but who stands perfectly to attention with an expression of extreme alertness.

The major, in charge, it seems, of all the security personnel in the building, now assigns our duties for the day, which consist in opening and closing doors for these earnest, document-laden figures as they dash backwards and forwards from one room to another. The FSO and Leopold make themselves scarce, leaving us to it.

Next day, with excitement everywhere at fever pitch, beleaguered by clamorous citizens who cannot make themselves understood – for there are no French speakers in sight – we are on our door-keeping duties again. All we are allowed to do is to direct enquiries to a bewildered-looking young corporal who waves his arms hopelessly as if trying to disperse smoke while the petitions and denunciations pile up on his desk top, and supplicants try to trap his hands and bribe him by sticking banknotes between his fingers. We, too, are constantly assailed by plausible scoundrels who offer women, boys, gold, the kingdom of heaven if we will only find some way of smuggling them into the presence of the Allied Commander, who they are certain can be corrupted if only he can be reached. Some time in the morning a bomb is allegedly discovered, and everybody rushes out of the building, then back again when it is pronounced to be a harmless Gestapo souvenir. Every so often our enemy the major flings open a door and brays through it into the ruckus and confusion, 'This must be kept as a pool of silence.' Watson, immutably drunk, copes with all this imperturbably, but Spriggs manages at one point to go to sleep on his feet propped against a door, and falls over when it is opened suddenly.

Back at HQ for the midday meal Leopold makes a shattering announcement. 'We're being shunted into a siding,' he says, looking as though he has just listened to sentence of death being passed upon him. He goes on to explain that we are being pulled out of Tunis and moved to the port of La Goulette, six miles out of the city. 'It's a quiet place,' he says. 'Smashed up, with nothing working.' His theory is that GHQ Tunis may have had reports about Captain Merrylees, causing them to lose confidence in him, and they want to get him – and us – out of their hair.

Chapter Twenty

L ANK, SAD-EYED warehouses dominated the water-front at La Goulette. The sun had flayed the paint from all the façades, and bleached out all the words where the advertisements had once been, leaving nothing but naked silvered wood, lurching cranes and abandoned tackle; hawsers, pulleys, chains insisted that this was a working port, but the ships had gone elsewhere. Air-raid shelters stood like concrete wigwams among the bomb craters. A Renault car had been sliced almost in half and pushed to the water's edge, and the once bright red stains on its ripped upholstery had turned black. In the exact centre of this desolation the French had erected a won-derfully decorated iron *pissoir* and this was visited throughout the day by tattered but scrupulous Arabs carrying cans of water for their ritual ablutions. When not washing their private parts they sat fishing over the edge of the quay for small, obscene-looking fish that crawled rather than swam among the seaweed clogging the piers. Oil from a spill in La Marsa slithered over the sea-water, stifling the waves under its coat of many colours. The place smelt of baked bladderweed, oil and dust. The bombs had torn a gap in the harbour wall and through it Tunis showed its small ivory teeth along the horizon, and when the hot breeze puffed over us from the direction of Rades, which was only four kilometres away, it often brought with it the noise of trumpets and drums. Otherwise the war had passed us by.

The single distraction La Goulette offered was a water-front café-bar which, although seedy-looking enough, yielded a series of new experiences to those who frequented it. Tunisian Jews formed the backbone of the local middle class and owned most of the property, including this bar, where customers were waited upon with extreme solicitude by the owner's three daughters. They were beautiful, though extremely fat, with wonderful complexions of the palest gold and enormous soulful eyes. Their corpulence reflected old-style canons of taste in these matters still surviving in this remote corner of the once Turkish dominions, and, using their fingers with expertness and delicacy, the three sisters stuffed themselves with fattening foods to preserve their desirable fleshiness.

Spanish was their first language, and the family possessed genealogical charts written in old Castilian, tracing their origins back to Cadiz before their expulsion from Andalusia at the time of the Catholic kings. The parents were largely invisible presences but the girls were always within beck and call to cook oriental messes, and sing *cante flamenco* while we spooned our way through them gingerly. Leopold usually found himself inspired to join in the singing, wailing a few bars about the tribulations of a deserted orphan. This was the only *cante flamenco* song he knew, and although our Jewish friends received it with wild enthusiasm, we were heartily sick of it.

After the first few days of getting to know each other this relationship began to take an unforeseen direction. First we were informed by our young friends that as evidence of the Jewish community's huge gratitude in their salvation from the Germans – who were known to be preparing deportation lists – the Grand Rabbi had issued an authorization, considered unique in the history of the race, permitting Jewish girls to contract marriage with Allied personnel who were not of their religion. The next move was a formal invitation to several of the more presentable section members to a tête-à-tête held in one of the family's private rooms. These were intended as the first tentative moves in the exploration of matrimonial possibilities. One man was seen by each sister at a time and in one instance I was called in to interpret. The small room was densely furnished in oriental style with wall carpets, complex lamps, bazaar leatherwork, and brassware, and the inert air was heavily overlaid with the odour of incense. The girl had dressed herself up for the occasion like a Turkish cabaret dancer which displayed much of her substantial body, covered by her normal working clothes, through stridently coloured chiffon veils. The guest – guests in this case – were offered the usual sticky sweets, to be consumed while the girl put on display her dowry – consisting largely of several hundred gold sovereigns and *louis d'or*. While retaining her normal expression of the blandest innocence she then twisted and turned, rotated her stomach, set her haunches abounce, and produced a few sentences which sounded like ritual Spanish in praise of her amatory technique. There was no possibility of the visitor being spurred on to impropriety, because the mother was always present, only half-concealed behind a curtain, and making her presence all the more felt by an occasional squeal of admiration at the quality of the performance put on by her daughter.

Nobody married a Tunisian Jewess, although I am sure they would have made good, if over-indulgent wives. But they did much to lighten the terrific tedium of life at La Goulette.

★

We were housed in an opulent villa on the hill at Le Kram, looked after by an Italian couple who performed the daily miracle of transforming Army rations into superb Piedmontese food, but harrowed unrelentingly by the problem of how to kill time. Principally we played poker and waited for the phone to ring to report the presence of a spy. The first of such calls could be counted upon to happen within minutes of nightfall. Spy alarms were a barometer of morale. A unit on the move never saw spies, but as soon as they found themselves bogged down behind the wire in a camp with nothing to do but dig latrines, the spies began to move in. If one of our drunkards answered the phone, he would laugh into the mouthpiece and hang up, but sometimes a man who was bored out of his wits would get on his motor bike, ride a few miles to some desolate encampment and listen with what patience he could to a farcical story of lights flashing in the night. It would never be more, he knew, than an innocent householder lighting his way to a privy at the bottom of his garden. But it was something to break up the evening, a new face, sometimes a fresh and interesting form of mania to be soothed. After Captain Merrylees appeared to come suddenly to life again, and began demanding reports, such an abortive experience made something to put into them.

Captain Merrylees' personal resurrection followed several incidents which may have combined in their effect to shock him out of his lethargy. Life at the Villa Claudia, as our moral fibre collapsed, took on an almost western-frontier quality. Leopold claimed to have been warned at GHQ that for reasons undisclosed we could expect to remain where we were for the duration. It was a suggestion that gave rise to paranoia manifested in the emerg-

ence of a wild sense of humour laced with delusions.
Leopold was a man divided down the middle. Half of
him was schemer, the other half plain barrack-room
soldier, a man who had undoubtedly enjoyed the training
process in which he had been not quite reduced to an
automaton and who hated the shiftlessness and vagrancy
to which we had been condemned.

Now a craving seized him for the simplicities and
exactitudes of the old soldiering life, and he proposed to
us that – as a favour to him – we should allow ourselves
to be drilled. Inducements including local leave with
transportation included were offered. To us it was no
more than a joke but, under the threat of limitless leisure,
we agreed. He longed to put us through complicated
manoeuvres of the kind invented by Frederick the Great
and reverently preserved like museum pieces of
weaponry at the Intelligence Corps depot, but we were
too few. There were not enough army boots to go
round, so half of us had to march in our brown civilian
shoes, and we sloped and ordered arms with rifles
borrowed from the nearest military unit. From behind
their shutters our Tunisian neighbours must have
watched with amazement as Leopold, stick under arm
and two guns dangling on his thighs, put us through our
paces. After it was over, there was no mistaking his
relief, but it was short-lived and in a matter of hours the
pressures began to build up.

One of his delusions, or jokes – or perhaps a mixture
of both – was a belief that we were still under the risk of
surprise attack by the Germans – all of whom were by
this time safely locked away in PoW camps. He took to
propping a loaded sub-machine-gun against the leg of
the table when we sat down to dinner, and on one

occasion suddenly snatched it up and discharged a volley through the French windows into a clump of cactus among which imaginary Krauts were in ambush. Twenty rounds hissed down the table a few inches above the wine glasses, and riddled the soft flesh of the prickly pears. Leopold went to inspect the result. 'They've gone. They got away,' he said, with a disturbing chuckle.

It was something to be laughed off, but within days events took a more serious turn. He had invited the local MPs to the villa, and in the course of the meal Leopold said something to their sergeant-major and they both got up and went to the flat roof together. A moment later we heard a cry followed by a crash in the garden and rushed out to find that Leopold had thrown the MP sergeant-major from the roof.

This was the emergency that brought Merrylees in trousers worn with pyjama top on the scene. He tripped over one of our drunkards who was crawling about the floor wearing the crash helmet put on him to save him from knocking his brains out against the furniture, and rushed into the garden where Leopold, laughing uproariously, stood over the unconscious sergeant-major. An ambulance was called to take the MP to hospital, and a threatened court of inquiry was only evaded through the backlog of business occupying the department concerned.

With Leopold's sanity in doubt, there was no way out for Merrylees but a return to normality, and his recovery may have been assisted by the removal of whatever hold Leopold, as an assumedly sane man, had had upon him. Merrylees got up in the morning, shaved and dressed himself with extreme care, lined us up in his office at eight o'clock sharp and, as if staring into sunlight, deploying his always alarming smile, he issued his orders. Listening to them, we were plunged again into doubt. Merrylees wanted a full-scale report and Intelligence evaluation with suggestions as to how security measures could be improved in La Goulette, about which there was absolutely nothing to say, and Carthage – remaining roughly as it was after the Romans had dealt with it in 164 BC. The task allotted to me called for less imagination. I was to make a regular daily count of the vehicles using the La Goulette–Tunis road, under the headings, military and non-military, and if military, whether British, American, French, etc. This fatuous information was to be collated and condensed to form the body of a weekly report to GHQ. I wondered what the G2's feelings about it all would be after reading the first few paragraphs before it went into his waste-paper basket.

18TH JUNE

A letter from Dr Kessous in Philippeville carried by a member of 84 Section sent on detachment to Tunis. The Senegalese troops have run amok there and massacred the Arabs, with more trouble expected. Can I do anything?

Clearly nothing whatever. For all that, I feel an overwhelming urge to go to Philippeville to learn for myself exactly what has happened.

Leopold has suddenly turned reasonable again, calm and accommodating – even with his ferocious jokes pushed away out of sight. I told him I had to get away for a couple of days, and should I go to Merrylees about it? His answer was, on no account. If necessary he'd cover up for me. I get the impression the two may be taking up positions for their next private battle, and Leopold has made public his suspicions that Merrylees has blocked his application made back in April for transfer to another section.

I thought I had better tell him where I wanted to go, although not why. It was a good thing that I did because he immediately suggested that I should take my FS card to the airfield, show it to an American and try to hitch a lift on one of their planes. The FS identity card, which I had never used to date, is said to be the open sesame to all situations, and really adventurous FS personnel make free use of them to fly themselves back to England for the occasional weekend – a procedure which strikes me as dangerous. At the airfield I produce it with some diffidence hardly able to bring myself to study the American major's reaction as he reads the endorsement stamped at AFHQ, Algiers. This hints at the possession of huge, secret power. 'Authorized,' it says, 'to be in any place, at any time, and in any dress. All persons subject to Military Law are enjoined to give him every assistance in their power to facilitate the carrying out of his duties.' Little did the major realize just what these duties have been during the past few weeks.

He handed the card back to me, and I was seized by a kind of panic when he addressed me as 'Sir'. 'Sir, do you wanna leave just now?' It happened that there was a plane leaving for Algiers within the hour, and there would be no problem about an unscheduled landing at Philippeville to drop me off en route.

At Philippeville I went straight to Dr Kessous' house to hear the details of the atrocity. A company of Senegalese, normally the most disciplined of troops, had broken out of barracks, found the armoury mysteriously unlocked, and gone on the rampage killing every Arab they could find.

What had happened to all our mutual friends – to Kobtan, Meksen and the rest? – was my first question.

'Praise God,' he said, they were all safe. Someone had mentioned that Kessous had started his life as an unbeliever, but religiosity had fed upon success, and now the name of Allah was rarely out of his mouth.

It soon became clear that the massacre had claimed its victims entirely among proletarians – perhaps by design, or perhaps because they had no stone-built houses or walls behind which to take refuge. Kessous said the official figure for those killed was thirty-seven, but he put the dead at several hundred, most of them vagrant workers or distant villagers who could conveniently disappear without trace to be buried secretly in unmarked graves.

Listening to him, to the flux of angry rhetoric alternating with the persuasive smiles, I formed the opinion that he had suffered no more than a political setback, to be offset against propaganda gains, leading in the end to a bloodily satisfactory retaliation. What in the end, he seemed to suggest after the emptying of the vials of his wrath, did the death of a few nameless peasants matter, if by their sacrifice the cause of the Algerian people (behind their leaders) could be advanced? He was resigned to the fact that I could do nothing to impede the recurrence of such atrocities, but urged me to do all I could to publicize what had happened.

Madame Hadef, the vivacious taxi-driver's wife, had bad news. She spoke of her husband's last moments, as described by a European friend who had seen what had happened, displaying in the telling of this the simple dry-eyed fortitude possessed equally by an Arab woman of her calibre and the small boys whose toes were crushed by the French police at the base depot.

Every Arab in Philippeville knew that something terrible was about to happen, she said, and all those who could afford to do so left their offices or places of work, went home and locked themselves in. Since the withdrawal of most of the Allied troops, fares were few and far between, and most of the Arab taxi-drivers stayed put until a European drove up to warn them that the Senegalese were shooting every Arab in sight in the town's centre.

They decided to try to escape along the coast road to Jeanne d'Arc, but had only driven a few hundred yards before they found themselves cut off. They left their cabs and ran for it, but the Senegalese chased them to the top of a low cliff, bayoneted them, and threw them over the edge. The mass funeral, she said, had set off an extraordinary demonstration. All the French and Senegalese had been withdrawn from the town, and some irresistible impulse had sent the women out in their thousands into the streets. In defiance of custom among the Algerian Muslims, they followed the procession to the cemetery and held up their children-in-arms to see the coffins lowered into the graves, 'so that they would remember'.

Afterwards the bayonet-rent cast-off blazers and morning coats were carefully cleansed of blood, repaired, and passed on as heirlooms to close relatives, or in extremity sold in the market.

*

I took a taxi out to Fortuna's farm, passing several cars with MP stickers on them on the way. As soon as the taxi pulled up, Fortuna came out of the house, arms outstretched. The appalling fact was that he was unmistakably happy to see me – a man capable of lasting gratitude. He made a joke about pretending to assume that I had come to pick up 'the Roman thing', and said that I ought to have given him a few hours' notice to be able to have it ready for me.

'Were you mixed up in that Arab business?' I asked him.

'Not personally,' he said, 'but you know me – I can't stand the sight of them.'

I told him that a friend of mine had been killed.

'I'm sorry,' he told me. 'Maybe we could have fixed him up with a pass.'

For me this was a clear admission that the gangsters of the *milice populaire* had worked with the officers of the Senegalese.

This was the cloud, no bigger than a man's hand in the sky, that presaged the end of French rule in Algeria. Ten years of terrorism and counter-terrorism followed until, on 20 August 1955, Philippeville was the scene of the most atrocious massacre of the post-war period, carried out in reprisal for attacks on settlers elsewhere. French paras flew in and, aided by bands of vigilantes, began the task of destroying the Arab population. Here is a description of the action by Pierre Leulliette, a para officer who took part in it: 'We opened fire into the thick of them at random. Then . . . our company commanders finally gave us the order to shoot down every Arab we met. At midday, fresh orders, take prisoners. That complicated everything.' The prisoners were rounded up and kept in the stadium, but next day it was decided to kill them all after all. 'There were so many of them they had to be buried with bulldozers.' The total Arab death-roll was 12,000, a high proportion of them women and children. In the words of the Governor-General Jacques Soustelle, 'Between our two communities an abyss has been dug through which flows a river of blood.'

In this huge final tragedy our section in Philippeville, succouring through ignorance and gullibility such gangsters as Fortuna, played its tiny part.

22ND JUNE

Back in Tunis, where the shadows have lengthened, to find Leopold on firm regimental ground again, but – as was to be expected with his recovery – Merrylees once again fading fast. Merrylees sets his absurd tasks and Leopold, tongue in cheek, sees to it that they are carried out. The FSO has been taken with a sudden mania for numbers. Having counted all the cars, I am told to count the houses in Carthage, La Marsa, Le Kram and La Goulette. This I set about doing, handing in daily totals to Leopold, who nods gravely, and sets the information aside for incorporation in the weekly report. This, according to the section member who types the final result, is an extravagant absurdity. He is bound to secrecy, but goes so far as to admit that the last report was unintelligible to him, although several Latin tags included were familiar. In his effort to keep us, as he puts it, on our toes the FSO has decided that we should arrange to lecture the neighbouring units. We take this to be on topics such as security of access and the disposal of classified material, but this proves far from the case.

What Merrylees has in mind is morale-boosting get-togethers with veterans who have spent three years in the Western Desert, and are now reported as being, perhaps in consequence, somewhat cast down in spirit. He proposes we should remedy the state of affairs by readings of selected passages from the sagas, and by an account of the doings of Eric the Red, equally calculated in his opinion to have a tonic effect.

We all agree that one way out of this increasingly impossible situation would be for Leopold to ask to see the G2 at GHQ and tell him what is happening, but this he resolutely refuses to do, knowing only too well how the Army is accustomed to deal with bringers of bad news.

This sense of being confined in an open prison is heightened by the sudden dearth of letters from home from which we all suffer. Due to some breakdown in the Army postal service there has been no mail for weeks, but apart from this sudden stoppage, I am not the only one to notice that the bundles of letters collected for the section seem to be getting smaller. This is a situation calculated to turn men who hardly ever set pen to paper into excellent correspondents, and one section member – whether or not he has been able to post it – has written a letter to his wife every day he has been overseas. He is now tremendously depressed because it is two months since he has heard from her. It is five months since I have had news of Ernestina.

Today a letter arrived. I tore open the envelope and a half-dozen tatters of paper fell out, on which I recognized my own handwriting. Accompanying these fragments was the long awaited letter from Guatemala.

The enclosed gives you some idea of what's left when the censors have done their work. Once again, not a single comprehensible sentence. I know you're out there somewhere, that's all. The rest is silence.

It seems a long time since Cuba, doesn't it? I wonder how the years have treated you. They've had their effect on me, but it's happened so slowly that it's only when I look back I say to myself, my God, can I really have changed so much? Nobody should really stay too long in a place like this. People don't think here; first of all because they don't need to think, and then because they've forgotten how to. I read *Time* because there's nothing else to read, and that marks me down as an intellectual.

I'm afraid it has to be faced. I've given in. This is like a bullfight. I'm there for no other reason than that the others are, half-asleep, up in the *tendidos*. We go to the fiestas and throw confetti at each other, and the men get on their horses and pull cockerels' heads off. Remember when I told you about the first one I went to. You were disgusted, and so was I. Now I'm beginning to stop thinking, nothing has much effect. Last week they tied some Indian bandits up in chairs and shot them in the plaza, and the whole town turned out including every single member, male and female, of our legation – and guess who else? I've used up my protest, and that's what Guatemala does to anybody in the end, unless they're strong – which I'm not. Perhaps I see myself for the first time, and realize I'm a very ordinary sort of person. Just like a lizard, lying in the sun.

Chapter Twenty-One

FEW PEOPLE frequented the Chat Qui Rit, as the café-bar at the port of La Goulette was called, and those who did were from the depressed classes: fishermen who took their evil-looking fish there to be cooked, a man who watched over the plumbing of the local *pissoirs*, and a carpet-seller who admitted he was lucky to sell a carpet once a month.

One morning we had a customer of a different kind. He was intelligent-looking and a little sombre, and dressed in a dark, well-fitting suit that could have been made in Paris. Taking a seat, he sat bolt upright, thus – by comparison with the slouching regulars – giving an impression of alertness. When he beckoned in the direction of one of the Jewish girls, he expected and got service. In the matter of race he struck me as one of those borderline cases, either Arab or Jew – a man of the kind who had been in contact with power, which always seemed to me to have a deracializing effect, and provided its own international face. He ordered tea, and was served the usual stew-up of old leaves to which a sprinkling of new ones had been added. He took a sip, left it, paid, then stuck a tip under the saucer. I got the impression that the very special flies of La Goulette were bothering him. After a while he got up, came over and greeted me in Arabic, *salaam aleikum*. I acknowledged the greeting in the usual way, and he dropped into a chair at the next table so that we were seated side by side.

'So you speak Arabic?' he said in English.

'A few words,' I told him, and hoped it would be left

at that. One was always running into people wanting to talk to strangers, because they were lonely or curious, or had something to sell, or were just compulsive talkers, and without being rude I got rid of them as soon as I could. He paid me a routine insincere compliment on my pronunciation, and it was clear that this man would not be easily put off.

'La Goulette,' he said, 'is not very interesting.' I agreed with him, and this gave him the opportunity to ask what I was doing there, in reply to which I said the first thing that came into my head.

Next, as a matter of routine, it was the British royal family, always dragged in at such random encounters to keep up the conversation. 'You English are royalists, and we are royalists, too. All of us. You have a King and we have a Bey. This is the best system for us all.'

I said something non-committal.

He wagged a warning finger under my nose, and the sharp intelligent eyes mirrored mistrust. 'The French are no good,' he said.

'Why do you say that?'

'Because they are finished. Defeated.' He made a finicky gesture of distaste as if rejecting unsatisfactory food. Arabs frequently sought to curry favour with us by remarks of this kind, as if purporting to be aware of hidden tensions in the relationship between the two nations. I made no comment.

It was past midday and I was due back at our office in Le Kram. I made to get up, and he laid a hand on my sleeve. 'I will speak with you about a confidential matter. It is our wish for you to see the brother of our Bey.'

'Excuse me, but what on earth for?'

'It would be interesting for us. Also I think for you.'

'For me personally?'

'No, I think for your country it would be interesting.'

Mysterious approaches of this kind happened from time to time, and at Philippeville we had soon learned that they were rarely to be taken seriously. There was one chance in ten that there was something at the back of this to be investigated. I offered to pass the man on to Leopold and make an appointment for him, but he would have none of this. The meeting at the Bey's palace was to be with me, and questioning him as to why this should be, he became vague and evasive. I asked him who had directed him to me, and why, and he fenced me off with his secret smile. 'We know of you,' he said. 'That is why I have come to talk to you in this way.' He handed a splendidly engraved card. '*Jean-Claude Mélia, Conseiller à la Cour de Sa Majesté le Bey.*' I began to be impressed, and to argue with myself that there was nothing to be lost in such a meeting, which might at least prove to be a memorable adventure. It was agreed that we should meet later that day, when I would give him my answer.

Leopold wanted to know what exactly was a bey, and I explained that he was the ruler of the country under the French. In this case some confusion arose because there were two beys, one the royal figurehead and the second, Sidi Lamine Bey, the 'Bey du Camp', the power behind the throne and Commander of the Palace Guard. It was the Bey du Camp with whom the meeting would be arranged.

'And who's this man you've been talking to?'

'Mélia. Jean-Claude Mélia. He's some sort of adviser.'

'He's not in the book,' Leopold said. He was referring

to the book in which names of several hundred suspects were listed, and the fact that he could make such a positive announcement off the cuff suddenly made me suspicious. Could Leopold be in some way mixed up with this? I tested him with a pretence of lack of interest. 'Do you want to bother with this?' I asked.

'Go along with him,' Leopold said. 'I don't have to tell you what to do. You might get the section an invitation to the palace. Do us all a bit of good. Might even be a bit of harem going spare.' This enthusiasm only strengthened my suspicion.

I asked him if he wanted a report at this stage, and he said, 'No, why? There's nothing to report about.'

Next day Mélia drove me to the Bey's palace at Kassar Said, among the orange orchards five miles out of Tunis. He handed me over to a palace official who led the way into a garden and left me in a rose arbour, with an entrance guarded by an enormous negro in an old-style Turkish uniform, holding a drawn scimitar. Shortly the Bey came floating into sight in a cloud of billowing lawn. He was carrying a white cat with long silky fur which he handed over to an accompanying servant, before greeting me. He said *'Ahlan wa sahlan'* ('Welcome') three times, and asked with extreme politeness in a slightly disembodied voice after my health and that of the members of my family, before we settled facing each other at a little table covered with ceramic tiles, upon which another servant placed two glasses of mint tea.

The Bey du Camp, a man in early middle age, was saturated with patrician Arab restraint. All his movements were delicate and controlled, and through – as I imagined – a lifelong avoidance of displayed emotion, his face was strangely devoid of lines, and had about it something of a Madame Tussaud's model. Even the small, glittering eyes in their setting of white, unwrinkled skin, seemed never to move. 'Welcome,' he said once again, before we raised the glasses of tea to our lips.

Arabic, using a modest vocabulary, stripped of provincial barbarism, and the verbs confined to their simple form, is the easiest of languages, made all the more so by the emphatic pronunciation of its consonants. The Bey employed the language in the pellucid form of the Koran, minus its archaism. He spoke slowly as if to a young child and was miraculously understandable. Delivering his message, he came straight to the point. Tunisia, he said, was about to sever its links with France which, legally, had no longer any claim upon a protectorate which it had failed to protect. The choice that faced it was between a royalist or republican form of government, and the Bey clearly favoured the first alternative, mentioning that the republican Destour movement, if allowed to take power, would introduce socialism into a strategically placed Mediterranean country, which clearly nobody wanted.

A third servant, ebony-faced, in blue and gold livery stood like a graven image, holding a silver platter at our side. This held iced and perfumed squares of cambric, and between sips of mint tea, the Bey picked one up in his tapered, waxen fingers, pressed it to his lips and let it fall on the ground. I followed suit. The Bey sat with his back to the opening of the bower on a scape of lawns and flowering trees, and beyond the janissary in his braided gilet and tasselled cap, with his scimitar resting on his shoulder, a capering juggler, brought to entertain us, played on a pipe held in one hand and threw balls into the air and caught them with the other.

The Bey said, 'We are not prepared to surrender our country to socialism. Instead, we wish to become part of the British Empire.'

'What was it like?' Leopold asked.

'Like a film set.'

'How was the palace?'

'I didn't go inside. We stayed in the garden.'

'So what does the Bey want, then?'

'He wants us to take over Tunisia. We're going to win the war, he says, and he'd like his country to be in the Empire.'

Leopold let out a howl of delight. He danced all round the office, then opened the door and looked down the passage to satisfy himself that nobody was within earshot. 'Tell me about this man. Are you sure he's right in the head?'

'The Bey's nobody's fool, and he knows what's happening. For example he knows all about the Sicilian thing, including the date.'

'I don't even know that.'

'It's all set for the second week in July.'

'Christ,' Leopold said. 'We've really hit on something this time.'

'And not only that. He's in touch with the Sicilian separatists in this town. They don't want to stay with Italy, but they're ready to fight for the old Kingdom of the Two Sicilies. They'd turn the island over to us and ask to become a protectorate.'

Leopold shook his head. 'It's getting too big for us

now. We can't handle it. As soon as a word of this gets out they'll take it away from us. We'll have had it.'

I told him that I wasn't altogether sure of that. For reasons that still remained a mystery to me, the Bey had insisted that he was not prepared at this stage to discuss his plans with anyone but myself. I could only suppose he was under some terrific misapprehension about a powerful agent of Intelligence Service *britannique* sheltering behind the stripes of an FS sergeant.

He thought about this and agreed that it might be the case. In a burst of renewed optimism he decided that we all might come out of this with emergency commissions. 'So how's it been left?' he asked.

'There's to be another meeting this day next week. If we show interest he'll be ready with concrete proposals.'

'What are we going to do about Merrylees?' Leopold asked.

I asked him what he suggested, and he said it was essential to report the meeting that had taken place to cover us in case the whole thing blew up in our face. We had to find some way of playing it down, he thought – a sort of casual mention slipped into the body of the main report, that with luck might be overlooked. It was lucky that Merrylees had been out of circulation for a couple of days, giving out that he was ill. It might make him all the less likely to be able to concentrate.

Between us it was arranged that I should produce a voluminous and largely nonsensical report, stuffed with the meaningless statistics of which Merrylees was especially fond, and that among this a single vaguely worded sentence would refer to the visit to the Bey. At this point I asked for an outright assurance from Leopold that he had had no previous knowledge of this affair, and he used some sort of Sephardic oath to swear he hadn't.

I was left with an unsolved mystery. For an instant I was tempted to accept the presence in the Corps of some previously unsuspected rationality. Could it possibly be that the visits so long ago to the War Office, and the captain in the Mayfair flat, had led in the end through the long odyssey of stultification at Omagh, Winchester, Matlock and th coal-tips of Ellesmere Port to the palace of Kassar Said?

The credulous moment evaporated. I had every reason to know that in the Intelligence Corps there was no divinity that shaped our ends, no unseen but watchful eye, no enduring memory for its sons. Muddle ruled us. We were lost in the files, sent to the wrong country, inevitably innocent of what we would encounter when we got there. I came to the conclusion that the most likely solution to this riddle was that I had been chosen to play a part in a crafty game permitting the Army to reap what benefit it could from a potentially embarrassing overture, while not appearing to be involved. For a general to have talked to the Bey might have been a dangerous matter, a motive for recrimination between allies, even scandal. A sergeant counted for nothing. He could be instantly repudiated, explained away as having interfered without authorization in what did not concern him. The more I thought about this the less I could believe that it was likely to end well.

Collapsing confidence sent me back to Leopold for reassurances. 'I don't want to put myself in a position where I could be thrown to the lions for free-lancing,' I explained. Leopold told me to leave it to him. He'd make absolutely sure that I was covered in the report. Some way had to be found of playing it down, he said, or Merrylees would be sure to wreck everything. 'Just suppose he doesn't pick it up,' I said. 'What are we going to tell the Bey? That the British are interested? How can we do that?'

'I don't know,' he said, 'but we'll think of something by next week.'

This was a Tuesday, and the weekly report to which we were all supposed to contribute something went in to Merrylees next morning. On the rare occasions when an item took his eye, he might send for the author of the information and ask a few desultory questions. The report was put together by Leopold and what usually worried Merrylees was its lack of style, but apart from a little chiselling away at the grammar and punctuation, it normally went through untouched, to be typed out in final form by the section clerk for presentation to the G2. No more, and no less, Leopold found out, had happened in this case.

Some time on Wednesday afternoon Merrylees sent for the couple who looked after us, and after a few words to them in Latin – which he assured Leopold that as Italians they understood perfectly – he set them to work with brooms, mops and pails to clean his office up. This, with the furniture polishing that followed, occupied the rest of their afternoon and part of the evening, in consequence of which they were unable to cook the evening meal. As soon as Merrylees had dismissed the Italians, his driver-batman was called on to press his uniform and polish his equipment. This signified to us that the FSO proposed to visit GHQ for once, and hand the report in in person. It was something that happened on average once a month. Otherwise Leopold deputized for him.

Next morning, Thursday, before leaving for GHQ with the report, Merrylees paraded the section for a morning meeting. With most sections this was a daily routine, but with us it had only happened four or five times since the section had been formed. We filed into the office and lined up, and Merrylees watched us intently with a tiny glint of canine teeth in the fixed grin we had come to regard as a warning of strain. The office was usually in a mess, and anyone who called in to see the FSO could expect to find him rummaging through the papers strewn over his desk, and piled on the floor. Now, wherever we looked, there were empty, polished surfaces. The files were no longer in sight, the notices had been removed from the notice board, and the in-and-out trays had gone. In their place on the desk-top stood two toy-soldiers in uniforms of the last century, and the framed portrait of an elderly woman.

Captain Merrylees got up, came round the desk and walked towards us. He walked slowly down our line, stopping in front of each man for a prolonged scrutiny of his face. The muscles round his mouth seemed to have twisted it into a kind of cramp over which he had no control. There was anger in his expression but also a kind of bewilderment, and when his lips moved as we stood facing each other and he seemed about to speak, I half-expected him to ask the question, 'Who are you? Do I know you?' Leopold at attention, and stick under his arm, watched from beside the desk, and as Merrylees moved on we exchanged a quick, puzzled glance. A moment later this eerie episode was at an end, without a word having been spoken. Leopold asked for permission to dismiss, and we filed out.

The rest of Thursday and Friday passed without incident. Our bilingual senior sergeant, who was the only member of the section Merrylees showed any liking for, saw him on several occasions and reported him as not only calm but unusually cheerful. The Italian servant was delighted to receive a substantial tip for the extra work he and his wife had done, and showed his appreciation by presenting Merrylees with a splendid bouquet which was now in a vase on Merrylees' desk, along with the two toy soldiers and the portrait.

On Saturday evening I found Mélia in the Chat Qui Rit, attended by one of the Jewish sisters called Rebka, who was seated at his table strumming a bandurria. As I came in she got up, whispering as she passed me, '*Es un señor muy grande – muy importante.*'

I sat down with Mélia, who wanted to know if there was any news, and when I said there was not he asked if I was hopeful as to the way things were progressing.

To this I replied that I was as much in the dark as he was, and that we should have to be patient until Tuesday, when there should be something to report. This seemed the moment to tackle him on the subject of my doubts, and I told him I felt disinclined to involve myself any further unless it could be explained why I should have been singled out for the approach.

'On Tuesday,' he said, 'you will be seeing His Highness again. If you ask him, I'm sure he will tell you. Why should he not?'

The Jewish girl came with her bandurria and sang *cante flamenco* to us, and we sat drinking and listening to the music for an hour or so, and then I saw Leopold beckoning to me in the doorway of the café. I went out, overpowered suddenly by a tremendous premonition.

'Nice night,' Leopold said. 'Let's go for a walk.'

We strolled down to the water's edge. Suddenly Tunis had come to life again with a fresh movement of ships, and a few that had not been squeezed into the main harbour had been sent to La Goulette. By daylight they seemed little better than hulks with the paintwork everywhere bubbling over eruptions of rust. Night in Tunis was kind to them, and at a distance they could have been ocean-going liners with all the passengers asleep in their cabins. 'Have to take a look over them in the morning,' Leopold said, but something in his voice warned me that this was no more than a private thought spoken aloud, from which I should have been excluded.

Everything in Leopold's manner was slightly abnormal. Above all, whether or not he really had anything to say, he was a man who fought shy of silence. We walked on a few more yards under the shapes of the ships, and suddenly – speaking as if something has just occurred to him – he said, 'Things all right with you, then?' Why the solicitude? I wondered, beginning to understand that something had gone wrong.

'Things are all right with me, but what's happened?' I asked.

'You've been posted,' Leopold said.

'Couldn't you have told me before?' I said. By this time I already knew what was coming.

'I only just heard myself. It was written on a slip of paper Merrylees handed to me. That was all. Not a word out of him.'

'What's it all mean?' I asked. 'Is this the high jump – or just another muddle?'

'There's no way of knowing. I'm in the dark as much as you are.'

'Can I see him?'

'What's to stop you? But it won't do you any good. Anyway, what have you got to worry about? It's a wonderful let-out for you. We're going to be stuck here for the rest of the war. You'll be where the action is. It'll be like starting all over again. I only wish I were in your shoes.'

'What section is it?'

'A new one. One-o-one. Coming up from Algiers.'

'And going to Sicily?'

'Where else? It looks like your friend the Bey was right.'

'What's the objection to my waiting for them here?'

'Because it's not the way the Army works. You have to go all the way to Algiers and come all the way back again.'

'Are you going to do anything about the Bey?'

'No,' he said. 'I'm not in a position to.'

'If he knows about the invasion, just about everybody else does. Even if we don't want him in the Empire, surely that's something to worry about.'

'Fuck the Bey, and fuck the Empire,' Leopold said. 'The report went in, and that's the end of it, so far as I am concerned. What more do you expect me to do?'

I watched him go, taken by surprise suddenly by the realization that it would come as a wrench to leave this place. Suddenly I admitted to myself, with shame – as if to a weakness – that La Goulette in its sly and diffident fashion had won me over. And more than that, for now, late in the day, I accepted that if there were a place in which to take refuge, in which to go to earth while the spirit renewed itself, and the eye corrected its vision, this was it.

Calmly and surreptitiously La Goulette turned its back on the world. The drums thudded across the pink waters of the lake but it might have been for a dance. When the planes took off at El Ariano the flamingos stood up in our shallow lagoon, flapped their wings and skipped defiantly into the air, and that was about as much as we heard or saw of the war. People here, whatever their race, were linked together by a kind of low key, unself-conscious amity. The Jews played their bandurrias at Arab weddings, and the Arabs sat down to eat at the tables of the Jews. Living in La Goulette was like breathing in the smoke of opium that slowed the movements, pacified the thoughts and replaced the noxious habit of action with a taste of introspection. All the Algerians had found reason for hating someone, but in reality Algeria was Europe. Here in La Goulette the East began. The Tunisians were the calmest of the Arabs, ready on the slightest pretext to embrace a stranger in an unemotional way. For me it had been the best of both the Eastern and Western worlds, remote yet not cut off, and the lines of communication between La Goulette and home remained intact. In the end the letters would have arrived with an explanation of why they had been so long delayed. Utter silence awaited in Sicily. Silence, and a long banishment.

Leopold's footsteps had died away. The time had come to take leave of my friends in the Chat Qui Rit, and then I saw the man coming with his ladder to light up the mosque ready for the call to prayer, one of the many small routine entertainments that La Goulette offered.

No one here, except for the Jewesses in making their music, did anything well, and this man's inefficiency never failed to enchant me. He carried a ladder with several rungs missing, stood it against the mosque's wall, climbed up and began to twist wires together. The fishermen, still at the quayside, who seldom caught a fish by day, let alone by night, turned to watch the performance. A dozen or so lights came on, then, in a shower of sparks and a wisp of smoke, went out again, while on the ladder the electrician had done something to the wiring of the public address system over which the call to prayer would be made. We all waited and in a moment the call began. Through faults in the system I had never known the affirmation of the Muslim faith to be given in its entirety, but at least hitherto it had got as far as 'There is no God, but God'. This time it spluttered into silence after the atheistic declaration, 'There is no God—.' Beliefs were held lightly in La Goulette and fanaticism unknown. Everyone, including the electrician, laughed. 'Tomorrow,' he said, 'they will deliver the new transformer at last. Come back tomorrow, sir, and you will see the whole mosque lit up as never before, and for once not a single word of the call to prayer will be lost.'

'Tomorrow,' I told him, 'Destiny had decided that I shall not be here, but be sure I'll be with you in the spirit.'

Chapter Twenty-Two

I LEFT LA GOULETTE at the end of June, joined the new section in Algiers, and arrived with it back in Tunisia in the middle of July. The rest of that month was spent in a field hospital at Sousse with malaria. In this way I missed the Sicilian invasion, being, as things turned out, reserved for the later one of the Italian mainland. In August, shortly before this took place, shuttling back once again to Algiers, I found an opportunity to call on my old friends at La Goulette. They were without an FSO following a dramatic episode in the previous week, when Merrylees had called another of his surprise morning parades which proved to be the last. Marching into the office my former comrades had found Merrylees waiting for them. Apart from his well-polished Sam Browne and his boots he was stark naked, and he held his pistol in his hand. He proposed, he said, to shoot one of them and then himself. Leopold, who had caught a glimpse of him preparing for the meeting and suspected that something of the kind was about to happen, had slipped away to telephone, and within minutes a medical officer arrived, accompanied by an infantryman with a rifle, and Merrylees was persuaded to dress and go with them. Thus ended his military career.

On 9 September 1943 I landed with the Italian invasion force at Paestum, south of Salerno, there finding myself involved largely as a spectator in a long-drawn-out, confused and untidy battle, ending for me in the first week in October with the occupation of Naples.

No other experience of the war made as deep an

impression upon me as the first days spent in this devastated city in which so many people dragged out an existence amid the remnants of modern urban surroundings, comparable perhaps to that of the pre-Middle Ages. There was a curious deadly matter-of-factness in the air. Grief had worn itself out, to be replaced by a kind of sullen resignation, and the pressures of utter necessity had enforced the suspension of many restraints. Thus in the municipal offices of Torre del Greco, where queues had once formed at counters under notices about the municipal taxes, rows of blank-faced housewives waited in the hope, there and then, in the most public of places, to prostitute themselves for army rations of corned beef and Spam. Down at the water's edge they were experimenting with weird machinery in an attempt to distil drinking water from the sea, and gnawing at raw limpets scraped from the rocks, while other citizens grubbed for edible roots in the parks, and bombed-out families harnessed to carts piled with their possessions poked among the ruins in search of shelter. These people were bowed and bent like troglodytes, silent and expressionless, as though they had just emerged from holes into which they would soon creep back again.

The tragedy of Naples has been overshadowed by the fire and brimstone holocausts of the cities of Germany, of Dresden and Hamburg and Cologne, and the slow strangulation of Leningrad. Naples' sufferings were less in the world's eye, but they persisted for months after its liberation. Thousands were buried under the rubble of largely working-class districts destroyed, on 4 August and 6 September, in the carpet-bombing raids preceding our occupation. These brought ordinary civilized life in the city to an immediate standstill with the cutting off of electricity and water supplies, and the loss of food stocks to a point when outright starvation began.

Twelve of us NCOs plus an officer arrived to deal with the security problems of Naples, while the delayed-action bombs left by the Germans were still exploding all over the city. We had little idea of what was expected of us and neither had our superiors. Never before in the short history of the Corps had one of its sections been confronted with an emergency of this order. Our training had been based on the static simplicities of the First World War. This was chaos, Babel, anarchy; the streaming of a million distraught human ants in their shattered nest.

We were instantly besieged in our headquarters by innumerable Italians bringing news of the desperate crises that surrounded us. Our allies the Moors were on the rampage, killing, looting and raping in outlying towns. Soldiers wearing our uniforms were breaking into Italian houses. The relations of imprisoned anti-fascists came clamouring to us for their release, and those of vendetta victims wrongfully incarcerated on trumped-up charges of co-operating with the Germans as soon as we entered Naples, now demanded they be set free. Informers of every stamp flocked to us with their denunciations. A sinister priest with a letter from the Vatican applied for permission to carry a gun; a nobleman, head of one of Naples' most illustrious families, arrived with his aristo-cratic-looking sister, explaining that she wished to enter an army brothel.

AMGOT – the Allied Military Government of Occu-pied Territories – largely officered by Americans of Italian origin, stood between us and justice and truth. They had made a start by replacing all fascist-appointed mayors with the nominees of the Mafia, freshly released from gaol. Vito Genovese, ex-head of the American Mafia, now their principal adviser, was ready with his list of names, and soon these sinister ruffians became the real rulers of Southern Italy. The Mafia which Mussolini had come within a hair's breadth of crushing back in 1923 flourished as it had never done since the days of Garibaldi.

In theory we were a counter-intelligence force, charged with the frustration of saboteurs and spies, but in reality half the battle was with AMGOT's black market, into which was diverted one-third of the military supplies unloaded at the port of Naples. Medicines in short supply were sold under the counter of any Neapolitan pharmacist with a connection with Vito Genovese. I went to discuss the theft of penicillin with one of his underlings, who set forth the hopelessness of my position in a conciliatory fashion. 'Sergeant, I have nothing against you in person, but frankly this will do you no good. Who *are* you? You are no one. I was dining with a certain colonel last night [this would have been Poletti, head of AMGOT]. If you are tired of life in Naples I can have you sent away.'

Thus it went on, the weeks and months crammed with bizarre and tragic adventure. In 312 Section every member was obliged to keep a daily 'log', for incorporation with the FSO's reports. Nobody ever asked me for the return of my old notebooks, and they were still lying undisturbed at the bottom of a drawer twenty-four years later when one day I turned them out and began to leaf through them. I was amazed that the episodes recalled by these notes, which had seemed so unexceptional at the time, should now appear so extraordinary. When so many years ago I made some diffident reference to my friends about my aspirations as a writer, there was a general outcry of 'At least spare us your war memoirs. That's something nobody wants to hear any more about.' I took them at their word and wrote fourteen books before the day when I got out the old Naples notebooks and diaries once again. But now it seemed to me that here was a small, obscure corner of history upon which perhaps the time had come to throw a little light, and I put aside whatever I was doing and settled to write *Naples '44*.

On 24 October 1944 an order came through that I was to leave immediately for Taranto, to embark on the *Reina del Pacífico* where I was to pick up 3000 Russian soldiers who had been fighting with the Germans and gone over to the Italian partisans. These were to be repatriated with evident discretion to the Soviet Union, via the Red Sea, the Persian Gulf, and Khorramshahr in Iran. Instructions, as usual, were vague to the point of cryptic and there was nothing but Celtic intuition to warn of what awaited me at the port under the heel of Italy.

At Taranto a major saw me at Movement Control. He wore no Intelligence green flash, but the faint aroma of lunacy and the fierce but vague eyes identified him almost certainly as a member of the Intelligence Corps. 'They're all shits,' he said. 'Absolute bastards. My orders are these: if any man so much as attempts to escape, you personally will shoot him.' I remonstrated gently with him, pointing out that this was an illegal order, and he quickly simmered down. 'Well, anyway,' he said. 'They may try to commit suicide [several of the Russians had already done so in the camp]. If they do, just let them, and a bloody good riddance.'

The *Reina del Pacífico* provided stark accommodation for troops and 'third-class families' and, going below to inspect the prisoners, I found a dispirited rabble in rumpled German uniforms. Up to this point they had been treated as prisoners of war, being among other things fed on the reduced scale of rations supplied to the captured enemy. Most of the documents that should have accompanied them, including the nominal roll, had been lost, but sufficient proof remained to show that these men had fought against the Germans before their surrender to the partisans. I discussed this matter with the OC Troops commanding the infantry company acting as escort, following which he telephoned AFHQ and it was agreed that the Russians' status should be changed, and that British uniforms should be issued to them as soon as we reached Port Said.

This was done and I next persuaded the OC Troops to allow the Russian senior lieutenant commanding the battalion, and his two junior officers, to put up badges of rank. In this way they were able to restore discipline, and within a few days parties of ex-prisoners were allowed up on deck where they were drilled by their NCOs and subjected to morale-building speeches by their officers. Hope was restored, and attempted suicides ceased.

My Russian at this time was fair only, although it rapidly improved in the course of the voyage. I was assisted by three British Army interpreters, all of them Jews of Russian origin, and interrogation where necessary was assisted by the fact that many of the Russians spoke some German. With three or four exceptions,

including the battalion commander, Ivan Golik, a Mus-
covite of strikingly English appearance, all these men
were Asians. They had been members of the 162nd
Turkoman Infantry Division, composed of Uzbeks,
Khirgiz, Kazakhs and other Muslim racial groups which
had fought in Northern Italy under the command of Lt-
General von Heygendorff. The Turkoman Division had
fought well under German officers but, committed to
battle in July 1944 against American armour, it began to
disintegrate, and after a bad mauling near Mass Maritima
many of the Asians changed sides. They were terrified,
they said, of falling into the hands of the Americans who,
as they had been told, believed them to be Japanese
auxiliaries under German command, and – as the rumour
went – ran over such prisoners with their tanks. For this
reason they took care to surrender only to the partisans,
and it was to the partisans that most of the 3000 in my
charge had given themselves up on 13 September after
shooting their way out of encirclement by German
troops who already had reason to suspect their loyalty.

Starvation, the most atrocious treatment in German
PoW camps, and the knowledge that the alternative
facing them was certain death, had induced these men to
serve in the German Army. I spent many hours listening
to these ultimate survivors' experiences and came to
know that for every Russian who had come through the
fiery furnace of the PoW camps, a hundred had found a
miserable death.

The Germans had captured whole armies intact in a
series of pincer movements as they streamed eastwards
into Russia and were faced with vast human surpluses –
amounting to many millions of men – to be cleared as
speedily and economically as possible. A Tadjik herds-

man taken at the age of nineteen within days of joining the Army had been among those rounded up by soldiers in unfamiliar uniforms he had not at first even realized were Germans, and taken to an enormous barbed-wire enclosure. Here he and his comrades remained for three days without food or water, before a body of Germans arrived, accompanied by one who addressed them in Russian through a loud-hailer. The Tadjik remembered him as short, bespectacled and mild in his manner. 'There are far more of you than we expected,' he explained. 'We have food for 1000 and there are 10,000 here, so you must draw your own conclusions.'

The Russians were then lined up, and the order was given for officers, communists and Jews to step out of line, but no one moved. All the prisoners had by now torn off their badges of rank. The bespectacled German then invited any prisoner who wished to do so to denounce any of his comrades belonging to these categories. He promised that those who co-operated in this way would receive favoured treatment, including all the food they could eat, and after some urging and more promises and threats on the German's part a number of men stepped forward and the betrayal began. Those selected in this way were marched off to a separate enclosure, and at this point the bespectacled German said that a further problem had arisen through a shortage of ammunition. The men who had betrayed their comrades were given cudgels, and ordered on pain of instant death to use these to carry out the executions.

The Germans on the whole contrived to have Russians kill Russians. There were not enough SS 'special squads' to go round, and it was found that regular army soldiers were reluctant to engage in mass murder.

In the disorder of those early days of the German push to the East, I learned from my informants that the method of selecting Jews for elimination was both rapid and unscientific. Prisoners, as soon as taken, were ordered to drop their trousers, and those found to be circumcised were shot on the spot. As all the Muslims composing the Asian units were also circumcised, these too were butchered *en masse*.

Between four and five million Russian soldiers died in these camps, most of them of starvation, but for those men of iron resistance who were determined to survive come what might, the first hurdle to be cleared was an aversion to cannibalism, and I learnt that all the men on the ship had eaten human flesh. The majority admitted to this without hesitation, often, surprisingly – as if the confession provided psychological release – with a kind of eagerness. Squatting in the fetid twilight below deck they would describe, as if relating some grim old Asian fable, the screaming, clawing scrambles that sometimes happened when a man died and the prisoners fought like ravenous dogs to gorge themselves on the corpse before the Germans could drag it away. It was commonplace for a man too weak from starvation to defend himself to be smuggled away to a quiet corner, knocked on the head and then eaten. One of the Asian Russians I interviewed displayed the cavity in the back of his leg where half his calf had been gnawed away while in a coma.

Cruellest of the camps, from which my informants had sought *any* way of escape, was at Salsk in the Kalmuk steppes, on the railway between Stalingrad and Krasnodar. Here prisoners were prepared for what was to come by seven days of total starvation. When bread finally arrived they were forced to crawl on their hands and knees to reach it under the fire of German soldiers who were being trained as marksmen. Jews were buried alive by their non-Jewish comrades, force-fed with excrement, and very commonly drowned in the latrines. There were spectacles here from the dementia of the Roman empire in its death throes, when naked prisoners were compelled to fight each other to the death with their bare hands, while their captors stood by, urging them on and taking photographs.

At Port Said the Russians were kitted out as promised as British soldiers, were transferred to the *Devonshire*, with some accommodation for 'second-class families', and their spirits continued to rise. Many of these Asian tribesmen were poets. They wrote verse in their native language in a vein of tender surrealism, which Golik working with one or two literate NCOs translated into Russian, and I did my best to render into English. Alas, all this work came to be lost. Most of the soldiers were excellent musicians too. They had been able to dismantle simple musical instruments, and carried these in their rectums. There was a British Army issue of things like zinc water bottles, mess cans, toothbrushes, nailbrushes and combs, and these they dismantled, pierced, spliced, and amalgamated in such a way that in the first concert they gave when we were a day past Suez they had a full-scale orchestra of thirty or forty varieties of miniature musical instruments; of strange little antique-looking fiddles, lutes, pipes and rebecks; and the bowels of the ship quivered with the wild skirl of oriental music. Somehow costumes were improvised from such unlikely basic materials as camouflage netting and gas capes, and supreme theatrical art transformed a man who had tasted human flesh into a tender princess, stripping the petals from a lily while a suitor quavered a love song, oblivious of the drumming of hoofs (as the men pounded on the deck with their heels) of a Mongol horde on their way to sack the town.

Ten days later we tied up in Khorramshahr. I looked down over a glum prospect of marshalling yards under the soft rain. All was greyness, befitting the occasion. In the middle distance the strangest of trains came into sight, an endless succession of pygmy trucks, like those used in the West to transport cattle, but a quarter their size. It was drawn by three engines, the leader of which gave a sad derisive whistle as it drew level with us. It stopped, and this was the signal for a grey cohort of Soviet infantry to come on stage and go through a routine of changing formation on the march, before deploying to form a line between us and the train.

The escort party and the returning Russians now disembarked, and there was more ceremonial shuffling of men, slapping of rifle stocks and stamping of boots. The OC Troops and the Soviet commander then strutted towards each other, saluted, shook hands, exchanged documents formalizing the completion of the handover, and the thing was at an end.

One of the interpreters came back. 'No problems?' I asked.

'None at all.'

'Any idea what's to be done with them?'

'Probably be shot,' the interpreter said, 'most of them anyway. I had a chat with the major. Turned out to be quite a character. Full of jokes. Took a great fancy to Golik's coat.' (As part of the morale-boosting programme I had given Ivan Golik permission to have a

superb greatcoat made from two Australian blankets,
Red Army-style.)

'"Whatever happens," the major said, "I must see to it
that they don't spoil that." It may have been just his
sense of humour, but I don't think it was.'

The mission to Khorramshahr was seen at Intelligence
Corps headquarters at Castellammare di Stabia as a heavy
responsibility to be undertaken by an NCO. A mention
was made of the likelihood that I should be com-
missioned on my return before a posting for liaison
duties with the Russians on the Eastern front. Back in
Naples in December, this move was announced to be
imminent, and I was told to prepare myself for a winter
to be spent in a cold climate.

Weeks and months followed in tedium and inactivity,
with no more news of the expected posting, and at the
beginning of April I was sent to headquarters to join a
highly secret course for British and American personnel
for the study of an elaborate security plan worked out
for the occupation of Germany. Put simply, it was
proposed to encircle the whole country with radar-
equipped strong-points joined by a fence. Behind this the
population, both military and civilian, would be contained in something like a vast concentration camp, while
Alpine redoubts and any other such pockets of resistance
were demolished and a huge Anglo-American security
task force, in which I was to be included, worked at their
leisure to sort out the German sheep from the goats.

Armed with this impressive information I joined
forces with a Sergeant Hopper, also roped in for the
operation, took over a lorry, and set out for the north of

Italy to await the German collapse. Hopper's military career had been a remarkable one, for he had been sent to Canada by mistake, and there lost, and after various interim adventures had finally ended up in Trinidad where he spent three years boarding and carrying out a nominal search of the same small ship used to transport tropical fruits between one port and another. He was a PhD and had been a lecturer in Hellenic Studies at Aberystwyth University, and with the outbreak of the communist revolt in Greece and the consequent rush to find Greek speakers, his name had been unearthed in the files. Hopper spoke only the classical version of the language, and knew little of the happenings in the country after its eclipse by Rome in the first century AD. Needless to say, by the time he reached Europe on his way to Athens, the emergency had been at an end for some two months. 'What the hell are we going to do with you? Whatever induced you to come here?' the selection officer at Castellammare wanted to know. A week or so later he was to find himself on his way to Austria.

The operation we were supposed to join proved one of the most spectacular farces of the war. All the thousands of pages of secret material did not produce even the proverbial mouse, and the electrical fences, and the strong-points scanning the countryside with their radar beams, existed only in the imaginations of their planners. In due course the German resistance caved in and Hopper and I drove our lorry (laden with trenching tools, camouflage nets, anti-gas equipment, and so forth) over the Brenner Pass into Austria, forced sometimes to reduce speed to a walking pace by the hordes of Austrians and Germans streaming towards us over the pass into Italy.

We established ourselves at Köflach near Klagenfurt, where we were joined by a charming but confused officer who refused to be persuaded that the long war was really at an end and insisted on taking precautionary measures against surprise attack. We were supposed to be there to look for war criminals and for high-ranking German officers, who were automatically arrestable, and this we did in a desultory fashion, but found not a single one. The men with dark secrets on their consciences had long since gone to earth, or were on their way to South America, and those we rounded up for investigation proved nothing but small fry. By the purest chance I ran into a man with a knowledge of atomic secrets, and whatever he might or might not have done as a member of the Gestapo, he was happy to co-operate, and too useful to prosecute. Perhaps it had always been intended that this was the way it should be.

Of the experiences of the early days of the occupation, one alone may have been of importance for the light it throws on a controversy that never seems to have been satisfactorily settled. I was in Cologne on the day when the Allied authorities put up posters for the first time reproducing photographs taken at Belsen at the time of our entry into the camp. My instructions were to mingle with the crowds of German civilians gathering wherever the posters were on display and to listen to their comments – basically to be able to decide whether this form of propaganda was effective. The Germans' reaction was one of total incredulity. The onlookers were wholly in agreement that the pictures had been faked, and that this was no more than a cynical attempt further to undermine their morale. In 1974 Walter Kempowski published a book entitled *Haben Sie Davon Gewusst? (Did You Know About It?)* which argued, on the basis of an opinion poll taken of 300 persons living in the days of the Third Reich, that the generality of the Germans of those days knew of the existence and function of the extermination camps. From my experience in Cologne, and from some hundreds of previous interrogations in Austria of average, unimportant civilians and soldiers of low rank, I formed the opinion that this was not the case.

In 1946, as soon as I was free from the Army, I made a quick trip to Guatemala to see Ernestina. I was not surprised to be told that she had had a long-standing relationship with a Guatemalan, a member of one of the fourteen families, and a relation of the President of the day. I received the news with philosophy. Few marriages, I imagined, remained intact after a separation of six years. Living together, people could to some extent evolve together, influencing each other in their development as human beings, sharing and interchanging tastes, antipathies, prejudices, attitudes and ideas. As the years of severance stretched out, the points of contact were inevitably lost to sight and new directions followed. A deadly consideration had entered into our relationship. Ernestina and I had become strangers.

Following this meeting she went to Mexico to obtain a divorce – which were readily and cheaply available there – and she and Rafael Aparicio were married. Shortly after this he was appointed Ambassador to Haiti, and Ernestina naturally accompanied him there. Haiti may not have been considered as in the first rank of diplomatic appointments, but the local colour and interest of this extraordinary island must have compensated to some extent for any drawbacks of the posting.

Guatemala was, and has remained for me, the most beautiful country in the world, and I saw all that I could of it while I was there. There is hardly a part of it that is not embellished by the view of a volcano, and there are charming and pacific Indians everywhere; half the population of five millions being composed of Mayas of a number of tribes. In these days they conducted their religious ceremonies, and retained the ancient speech and many versions of pre-Columbian dress, but recent governments have embarked on a policy of doing all they can to destroy such evidence of 'Indianness'. In 1954 I wrote my first modestly successful novel, *The Volcanoes Above Us*, based on the overthrow of democracy in Guatemala by US intervention. This, greatly to my surprise, was not only well received in this country but sold six million 'magazine edition' copies in the Soviet Union. Although no royalties were paid I was rewarded by a free and lavish trip through Russia and some of Central Asia.

The tragedy of Guatemala lies in its geographical location in the US 'backyard', and the consequential subjugation of its rulers to American political interests. There have only been two democratically elected civilian presidents in the country's history, the second of whom, Jacobo Arbenz, being swiftly removed to be replaced by a military puppet after he had most ill-advisedly broached the question of land reforms which might have damaged US investments in fruit. Since then a series of iron-fisted military dictators have governed without recourse to popular opinion.

With the arrival on the scene of one of these – Ydígoras Fuentes – Ernestina and Rafael were in trouble, and one of the last letters to be received from Ernestina described the affair with sparkling relish. Rafael had made the mistake of falling in love with Ydígoras Fuentes' niece and shortly found himself called to the palace for a discussion with the President over the matter of his intentions. He was put in a chair so low that he was almost sitting on the floor, this being a regular device employed to place visitors at a psychological disadvantage. Seated above him at a vast desk flanked by a pair of dog-faced bodyguards, the President, a sinister old buffoon, questioned him in cat-and-mouse fashion about the pregnancy laid at his door. 'My boy,' he said, foaming, smiling and twitching, 'tell me, what do you propose to do about this child?'

'Give it my name, sir,' Rafael replied, and Fuentes – said Ernestina – went possibly quite unconsciously through the motions of a man sharpening a knife. 'That is not enough,' the President said. 'You will marry my niece forthwith.'

'I already have a wife,' Rafael told him, beginning at this stage, as he admitted to Ernestina, to break out into a cold sweat.

'So they tell me,' Fuentes said, 'but that is the least of our problems. You will leave on tomorrow's plane for Mexico City, where you will divorce your present wife, after which you will return and marry my niece. The marriage will take place within two weeks, otherwise you will be found dead in a ditch.'

The expression '*muerto en un arroyo*' was, and is, familiar to all Guatemalans. Their city had been built, following the destruction by earthquake of the two previous capitals, on a tongue of rock surrounded by deep ravines, in the fallacious belief that these would cushion it from seismic shock. Now the ravines were used as a temporary place of concealment for those who died by violence, and since there have always been so many of them, no day dawns in Guatemala without an inspection of the ravines by a special fire-fighting team equipped to remove the victims of the night in that supremely violent land.

Rafael therefore complied without demur. Ten days later his wedding to the President's niece was celebrated, and although the wedding could not be held in the Cathedral, Ydígoras Fuentes graced the reception by his presence. Perhaps the enforced marriage with the niece, who was difficult to live with, rankled, but for one reason or another a few months later Rafael was involved in one of the plots against the presidency that are a feature of Guatemalan life, and he, his new wife, and Ernestina were banished from the country. The three of them went to Madrid. After that correspondence between us dwindled, then ceased.

Returning to England I confronted not only the normal problems of psychological resettlement, but more unusual ones of a psychosomatic or even physical order. After the doldrums of Tunis I had entered a phase of incessant, almost frenetic activity, of an improvised life full of emergencies. Now even the nerves and the muscles were in revolt against the torpor of peace. Medical advice was that I should make no attempt to come to terms with a regulated and sedentary existence, but go into action again in any way I could.

I stayed for a while with the Corvajas, with whom I remained on excellent terms, and with my mother, still cheerfully occupied with her healing mission. Then, deciding to go rock-climbing, I moved to Tenby in West Wales, and took over the tenancy of St Catherine's Fort. This was a military folly built in 1868 with the encouragement of the Prince Consort by the whimsical Colonel Jervois, Inspector General of Fortifications, whose obsession it was that, despite a peaceful relationship with France at that time, the French were secretly preparing an invasion of Britain and that such an attack was likely to be launched in the Tenby area.

For a rental of £6 per week I enjoyed the amenities of four main bedrooms, sixteen rooms in the four turrets, a banqueting hall – including in its furnishings a lifesize marble statue of Queen Victoria, and the skin of a twelve-foot grizzly bear. The fort had been built on an island in the bay and was cut off by the tide for six hours at a time. For this reason and because of its reputation for being haunted by the ghost of a previous tenant, who had hanged himself from a hook still in position in the ceiling of the banqueting hall, domestic help was ruled out, neither even would tradesmen deliver supplies. For all that the fort was perfectly situated as a centre for rock-climbing, bird-watching and for marathon walks along the splendid – and at that time quite unspoiled – cliffs of Pembrokeshire, and in such activity I spent many rewarding months.

In 1947 I carried out a reconnaissance of the coast of Spain in search of a remote village providing no temptation to entice me away from an energetic life, and eventually lit on Farol, a small fishing community tucked among the cliffs at the end of a bad road on its north-east coast. I contrived to be accepted by the fishermen, moved into a local house, took out a fishing licence, and spent three seasons there fishing. It never occurred to me that I would write about this place, and although I filled many notebooks with my observations, they were largely to do with catching fish.

Some time after I left Farol I wrote a novel, *The Day of the Fox*, drawing for its plot on incidents of the village's life, but over twenty years passed before I got out my old notebooks again and read what I had written in those days before the tourist influx brought so drastic a change to southern Europe. I found that in setting down data about the weather and the winds, the movements of the sea, and the arrangements of nets and lines I had, rather by accident, been led to describe the remnants of an archaic Mediterranean society of Chaucerian scenes and pilgrimages, village enchanters, fishermen who spoke in blank verse, pre-Christian credences and taboos, and none of us would ever see its like again. *Voices of the Old Sea*, published in 1984, was my attempt to record the vanished experiences of those days.

In 1950 the take-over by the communists in China convinced me that the world had embraced a phase of rapid and irreversible change. It had always been my ambition to travel in the Far East, and now that the frontiers of China were closed I decided to make no delay in visiting such countries as were still accessible, and embarked on a journey of some three months through Laos, Cambodia and South Vietnam. Nationalist rebellions were in full swing against French colonial rule in all three countries, and this made travelling conditions sometimes arduous. For all that I was just in time to see what remained, as travellers in the last century and before would have seen of it: its mandarins, its warlords and their private armies, above all the hill tribes retaining so much of their ancient custom and ceremony, on the brink of disappearance when the limited anti-colonial struggle was transformed into a modern war, with its free-fire zones, carpet-bombing, napalm and defoliants. I had gone to Indo-China with the intention of writing a book, and *A Dragon Apparent* appeared in 1951. Most unfortunately, it was at this time when I was out of touch with home news for three months that both my mother and Ernesto Corvaja died quite suddenly, and it was a matter of great sorrow to me that I was unable to be with them at their end.

A journey to Burma followed in the same year. This too was a difficult country to get around in, and so it has remained ever since, being the only Far Eastern land that has wholly and successfully resisted change. I spent about two months travelling in the interior, finding myself so exhausted by the time I returned to Rangoon that I went to bed in the Strand Hotel and stayed there for nearly a week. *Golden Earth*, describing the confrontation I experienced with this withdrawn and contemplative corner of the Buddhist East, was published in 1952.

This was almost the last of my eastern peregrinations – I visited Thailand and North Vietnam the following year where I witnessed the prelude to Dien Bien Phu and US involvement in the affairs of South-East Asia – but although I switched for some years to the writing of novels, I found that I had picked up the habit of travel, and that it had become an almost indispensable stimulant. I catered for this form of self-indulgence by undertaking occasional journalism. This has taken me, writing for one or other of the Sunday newspapers, to many parts of the world, but especially the countries of Latin America. In 1968 I went to Brazil for the *Sunday Times* and helped to publicize that country's massacre of its forest Indians.

This always seems to me to have been the most effective episode of my life. News had leaked out of the massacres perpetrated against the Indians of that vast country, and what appeared as almost incredible was that these atrocities had been committed, not only despite the efforts of the Government's Indian Protection Service, but with its connivance and frequently its actual co-operation.

It was discovered that in many cases where there had been thousands of Indians, there were now hundreds or even tens. To quote an example, where 19,000 Munducuras had been included in a census conducted in the thirties, only 1,200 were counted in 1968. The Indians were close to extermination because they were seen as being in the way of loggers, gold and oil prospectors and land-grabbers of assorted kinds. Those who were charged with their protection had been bribed to look the other way, while the tribes had been wiped out by mass inoculations with the virus of smallpox, the distribution of poisoned food supplies, bombing from the air, and mass murder by professional gunmen organized in full-scale expeditions. A Government White Paper blamed in part the post-war flood of American fundamentalist missionaries into the country, who by destroying the Indians' cultural identity had deprived them of the power to defend themselves.

It was an investigation in which difficulties that were to be expected arose owing to the involvement of powerful interests. The results published in the *Sunday Times* provoked a world reaction, a change in the Brazilian law relating to the treatment of Indians, and the formation of organizations such as Survival International dedicated to the protection of aboriginal people.

A strong stomach is called for in the pursuit of investigations of this kind, for although one is rarely at the scene of the crime at the time of its commission, its aftermath presents only too often a sickening spectacle. This was certainly the case in Brazil, yet none of the incidents I described at that time affected me in the way of a single experience in a mission camp in Paraguay. I had gone as a result of a report that the Aché Indians in the east of that country were being hunted by armed American missionaries. This proved to be the case. Not only had members of a fanatical sect captured many naked and wholly peaceful Indians at the point of the gun, but they had profited from their victims' misery. Able-bodied males were supplied as forced labour to local farmers, for which the missionaries were paid, and young girls were packed off to the capital, Asunción, for what purpose we can only guess.

Some, however, were quite simply shot down, and Donald McCullin, who was with me, was able to photograph a woman who had been wounded in the side while attempting to escape. What made this episode in a way more haunting and macabre than the violences of battle he had photographed in Vietnam, was that oppression and cruelty here wore a pseudo-religious mask, that crimes were committed in the intervals of prayer, and that voices raised in praise of God drowned the screams of terrified children. This sombre and unforgettable episode was the genesis of a book, published in 1988, entitled *The Missionaries*.

Part Five

ISOLA FARNESE

Chapter Twenty-Three

I HAD REMARRIED, and with three small children now to consider, the future assumed new dimensions and warned of new problems. We had settled in rural Essex, in a house with a large garden, in pleasant village surroundings. Then, suddenly, the great environmental change took place. East Anglia, with an economy based on cereal crops, discovered the use of herbicides and of defoliants developed in the Vietnam war. For some years thereafter, road verges and hedgerows everywhere were scorched brown throughout the summer months, the flowers began to disappear, then the birds, the rabbits, the hares, even the frogs. There were periods when not a day passed when we were not obliged to put a poisoned pigeon out of its misery, and hardly a week without burying a dead owl. School children called upon to recite Shelley's 'Ode to a Skylark' from that time on had never heard one sing.

There was the problem of education. A determined effort had been made with what the State provided, but the time came when we had to admit defeat. Neither of us cared for boarding schools and the irrevocable commitment to the class attitudes they appeared to dictate.

With this I was overtaken by an urge to go and live in Italy. The children would be brought up in an environment in which class played a lesser part. In due course they would become bilingual and modestly cosmopolitan, and I would fill in the years writing books in surroundings which had become comfortable and familiar during the eighteen war months spent in this most engaging and civilized of all countries.

Being always at the mercy of sudden impulse, little planning preceded action. Someone told me about an international school near Rome. I rang them up a week before the beginning of the school year, and was offered two places. Two days later I presented myself at St George's, La Storta, just off the Via Cassia, nine miles north of the capital, which, as hoped for, was large, cheerful and up to date, and staffed by teachers from England who had acquired Mediterranean gestures and boxy Italian cars. The only remaining problem was to find somewhere to live. From my experience the city itself had become an inferno of battling traffic and noise, but at La Storta, within easy reach of the school, the green fields came into sight. My eye was drawn to Lake Bracciano, shown on the map as about five miles to the north. This, by reason of its considerable size, and the many lakeside villages marked, offered possibilities, and with a mental picture of the choice offered by an array of picturesque and romantic settings I hired a car and drove over to inspect the lake.

It was in the first week of October and I had not fully understood until this moment how completely and finally summer is effaced in southern Europe by this time, and what a sensation of abandonment replaces it in all those areas where pleasure has reigned during the long season of clear skies and jubilant sun. Never was this sad transition more in evidence than in Bracciano. The map had shown twenty miles of villages where the visitors in their uniforms of pleasure had thronged throughout the five months when the long sun-saturated days subsided so softly, almost imperceptibly into scented and lucent nights. Where there had been laughter, music, bronzed bodies endlessly in action, now there was silence and a disheartened peace. A beauty of an austere resurrected kind might be said to have returned, but the life of recent times was extinct. The lipstick had faded from the mouths of the village girls stranded by the passing of summer now halfway to slatterns on listless waterfronts. Here in the late afternoon the day was already worn out. Down in Trevignato Romano, backed by the Sabatini mountains, fifty boats were moored under tarpaulin with long-legged lake birds picking round them in the mud and a poster for water-skiing ripped by the wind from a wall. There was a bar open here and I joined the last of the boatmen to sip a cloying marsala which was all they had to offer. He was of no help in the search for accommodation to let.

'Nothing here,' he said. 'They lock these places up and forget about them. Try Anguillara.'

'I have,' I said. 'I looked over the Villa Claudia. It was a sad place. Bad atmosphere.'

'Understandably,' he said. 'The man drowned his wife last year. They'd pay you to take it over.'

'Am I likely to find anything at Bracciano?'

'You won't find what you're looking for. Maybe a couple of rooms over a shop. Only two buses a day to La Storta. The morning one is 6 a.m. They're on their winter schedule now.' He tossed the remains of his cheroot into the sallow water and a seabird scuttled across to snap it up.

I drove back to La Storta and explained my quandary to a master who knew the area well and suggested I

343

should go and talk to Conte di Robilant in the nearby village of Isola Farnese. 'When he's hard up he sometimes lets a wing of his castle,' he said.

'Somewhat more than I could run to,' I told him.

'I don't know,' he said. 'No harm in seeing him. He might let you have it for nothing if he takes a liking to you. Go and put your case to him. You've nothing to lose.'

I spent the night in a motel full of whimsy of the kind I had previously believed to be exclusive to the United Kingdom, with joky notices and plaster elves that even invaded the bedroom, and in the morning called on the Count. What was remarkable about Isola Farnese was that it was built on a ridge overlooking the ruins of the great Etruscan city, Veii, destroyed by the Romans in 359 BC, and every house on the north side of its single street had a stupendous view through its back windows of what the Romans had left. The village was confusingly called an island because it was nearly encircled by two rivers, from which soared a massive escarpment with the Count's Hohenstaufen castle built on its top. The Count was at home when I called, a genial man who would have passed anywhere in manner and dress and speech for an Englishman, but for a Venetian cragginess of feature, including a great, aquiline nose possibly inherited from a Doge ancestor.

We discussed the matter of my possible tenancy, in an environment of dishevelled magnificence. The first impression was that this vast vaulted chamber was the storeroom of an eccentric antiques dealer into which every item that could not be put on display had been remorselessly shoved. Vast ancestral portraits, many of them punctured in various ways, or with strips of canvas flapping from them like scrofulous skin hung on the walls, or had been piled up in odd corners. Mildew or attack by moths had left the motifs of ancient tapestries hardly decipherable. There were marble cupids and Venuses that had lost fingers or toes. An eagle stuffed, with wings spread, viewed us with a single saffron eye in the melancholic illumination of stained glass.

'You could have this if it's the kind of place you're looking for,' the Count said. 'Plus a few bedrooms to go with it. The view is rather pleasant.' Together we admired the prospect through the narrow thirteenth-century windows. Below us vast weeds clung to the ledges of the rock face, brandishing garish yellow flowers over the valley. Wide Etruscan fields curved away into the distance, through which, now out of sight, the Cassia plunged in the direction of Rome. Glittering white spots sparkled everywhere in the grass and were in constant movement as if caught up by the wind. These, I was later to discover, were discarded plastic bags.

The Count seemed almost apologetic for a reference to the question of rent although the amount suggested for what was on offer was low. A small difficulty arose. I had in mind a trial period of six months but family trustees came into this, he said, who stipulated a mini-mum rental of one year. As an alternative he offered a building once used as a small convent, and now a castle annexe which I could have for six months. This, he pointed out, possessed a spacious garden – something the castle itself lacked. We crossed the road for a quick inspection and I took the ex-convent on the spot. In its concentrated way, this, too, had once been grand, although now a little time-worn. There were a dozen or so rooms and many passages, all with marble floors, a

large subterranean kitchen with Latin verse scrawled over
the walls, a scorpion either dead or moribund in each of
the four baths, and a stunning fourteenth-century fresco
across one wall of the main sitting room showing a
scene, on the verge of erasure by time, of foot-soldiers in
armour going to the assault of an airborne fragment of
fortification which might have belonged to our castle
itself. This room was dominated by a statue of a Japanese
samurai grimacing fiercely at its occupants. Otherwise
the furniture repeated the decayed splendours of the
castle: the great chairs deeply imprinted with the poster-
iors of the past, the tattered sheepskin bindings of books
on religious themes, a case with a stuffed bittern family,
the male and female birds surveying their nest with their
young realistically set up in the act of emerging from the
eggs.

The garden was undoubtedly the feature of this dwell-
ing for it occupied all of a hillside sloping, in places
dangerously, to the river. Paths wound steeply down
through thickets and coppices of ancient trees, past a
shattered summer house, and at one point over a reeling
bridge across a tributary of the Cremera, and thence on
to the river itself, where, beyond the further bank, the
few stones that were all that was left of the great Etruscan
city glinted among the green sward and through the
branches of the forest at its back. It was the opinion of
Doctor Pecorella, to whom the Count introduced me,
and who spent more time on archaeology than on
medicine, that the convent occupied the site of an Etruscan nobleman's villa. I noted that the cavern now used to
accommodate the central heating equipment and oil-tank
had, in the memory of the oldest villagers, contained a
number of sarcophagi.

Three days later the family arrived, to greet the arrangements made for them with huge delight. By the purest of chances their arrival coincided with the celebration of a local festa, for which the Count had procured masked Venetian dancers on stilts, who plunged up and down the single street blowing their horns, and shouting obscenities in an incomprehensible dialect. It was a fortunate coincidence indeed, for the villagers of Isola Farnese were not on the whole given to displays of this kind, and suffered from a tendency to matter-of-factness and taciturnity.

There followed an interlude for exploration in which the children, transported from Essex mundanities, wandered entranced through the excitements and mysteries of the ancient south with its castles, its tombs and its fields dominated by magnificent white cattle with mild eyes and hugely spreading horns. 'I keep them', said the Count, speaking of his own small herd, 'not for profit but for effect. There is no money in such animals, but just to look at them is enough. We pretend to ourselves that they are descended from the race shown in neolithic cave paintings. You may know better than I do about these things, but please don't destroy my illusions.'

From the great isolated crag of Isola Farnese we looked down across a spread of fields, some of them prairies in miniature with pockets of woodland with chestnuts crammed together in the corners and hollows of the landscape as tightly as the trees of the Mato Grosso of Amazonia. From these leafy refuges flocks of crows were continually discharged into the skies. They were the only birds to be seen, all the rest having been shot by Roman

sportsmen. There were burial chambers to be investigated everywhere, not only in our garden but in the deep
banks forming the barriers of the fields. We made our
way from tomb to tomb, and the big white cows,
shaking their horns to dislodge the flies, followed us,
consumed with curiosity, wherever we went.

Great excitement was generated when poking about
with her stick in a cavernous interior my twelve-year-
old daughter, Kiki, accidentally unearthed a large fragment of decorated pottery. Back in Isola Farnese this was
identified as Etruscan, and led to a great deal of digging
activity in which several more coloured fragments were
brought to light.

These were submitted for inspection to Dr Pecorella
who held surgery in the village once a week. He was
busy with a patient, but he immediately got rid of him
before raking through the collection we had brought. I
apologized for disturbing him, and he said, 'The man
was wasting my time. Every week I have to put up with
him. He wants to be injected – they all do – and I ask
him what for? "It's just something that comes over me",
he says, and I tell him to put himself on a diet of chicken
soup with weekly enemas. As for the stuff you've
brought me, it's interesting but the colours won't last
more than a few days. What's the matter with your lips?'

'The local wine,' I told him.

'It's the chemical preservatives they use,' he said. 'Dab
them with vinegar after you've had a drink. The fellow
in the bar keeps a bottle on the counter.'

'I noticed it.'

'How are things going with the Count? Nice fellow
isn't he? From Venice. Just as much of a foreigner here
as you are. Descended from the Longobards. All of them

have enormous noses – penises, too, so they tell me. Note the difference in a typical Roman face like mine. They have a bust of Caligula in the National Museum I'm supposed to be the image of. I mean when I was young, before my hair fell out.'

Up to this time I had hardly more than heard of Veii, but Pecorella, as an expert on its history, now took me in hand. Dennis's *Cities and Cemeteries of Etruria*, published in 1880, was still the classic work on the subject, he told me, and I managed to borrow a copy from one of the teachers at St George's. From this I learned that what we considered as no more than our extensive garden was part of one of the great necropolises of history. 'The rock', said the book, 'is hollowed in every direction by sepulchral caves and niches.' At a time when Rome was no more than a cluster of villages, Veii, Dennis tells us, was the exact size of Athens, being seven and a half miles in circumference. Subsequently as Rome grew in size and power, fourteen wars were fought against the Etruscans of Veii. In the end, after a siege lasting ten years, the forces of the dictator Camillus entered through a mine excavated under the city's ramparts, and the silence of total defeat settled down. Local patriotism insisted that Isola Farnese had been the citadel of Veii, and Pecorella, in other directions a human monument to disbelief, supported this point of view, and subsequently took us to a local hill where from studying the accounts of Plutarch and Livy he had identified the situation of Camillus's camp. Both this and the reputed entrance to the tunnel appeared to us as no more than meaningless irregularities in the rocky terrain.

The villagers of Isola Farnese came as a surprise to us all. After the eighteen war months in the exuberant south

I was quite prepared to accept the Neapolitans as far from temperamentally characteristic of the Italian race, but was quite unprepared for the discovery that these Romans were a match for the natives of Essex in matters of stolidity and reserve. First contacts with our neighbours, apart from the Count and his wife Alice, were with the couple who ran the small bar across the road, and the owner of the village shop in the square. In the first case I bought very bad local white wine, and in the second all the essential groceries, finding it extraordinary that in Italy of all places these transactions could be accomplished with the complete absence of the usual pleasantries exchanged elsewhere on such occasions.

Kiki and Gawaine, two years her junior, were delivered to St George's which contributed to their favourable impression of Rome. A three-course lunch prepared by a first-rate Italian chef was yet another Roman adventure and many pupils at this school agreed that they ate as never before, and might well never do again. They were unaware at the time that a few of the senior pupils who behaved in so pleasantly eccentric a fashion, and could expect no more than a gentle chiding from a teacher, were on drugs. This became more apparent later when their antics sometimes assumed dangerous and spectacular forms. There were times when the otherwise easy-going and gratifying existences of children drawn largely from the moneyed classes appeared as far from sheltered. Shortly after the children joined the school Paul Getty III, a pupil in an upper form, was abducted. His grandfather at that time was reputed to be the world's richest man. The grandson was much in the public eye for his somewhat stereotyped rebellion against a materialistic society, which nevertheless provided for him a life of

pleasure and luxury. His family connections, his partici-
pation in the drug scene and public extravagances could
not fail to land him in trouble. He was kidnapped from a
Rome nightclub, probably by the Mafia, and held for
five months while an attempt was made to extract a
ransom of seven million pounds. When this failed one of
the boy's ears was cut off after he had been stunned by a
blow on the head. The ear, accompanied by a note
threatening to amputate further bodily parts, was sent to
the office of a Rome newspaper. After some haggling a
ransom of one and a half million pounds was paid, and
the boy released. A few of the richer parents decided at
this point that it might be prudent to send their children
to school elsewhere.

Chapter Twenty-Four

O N THE TWENTIETH of the month we were all awakened shortly after dawn by the most tremendous racket. It was the rattle of small arms, a battlefield sound of the kind to be heard when a fighting patrol has run into difficulties, its members have become separated, and are letting fly in a sporadic and unconcerted fashion, usually with little result, at anything that moves.

I got up and threw open the shutter of a rear window, with partial views of the fields to the left and the right and most of Veii below showing through the oaks and chestnuts across the river. In the distance I noticed, spread across this panorama, several small groups of two or three men carrying guns. At the bottom of the garden itself two men crouched in a kind of trench which had not been there the day before, while a third, hidden behind a shrub a few yards away, cranked a handle attached to a piece of apparatus like an adjustable lamp standard which flashed the sun's rays in all directions through mirrors fixed at its top. Guns were popping all over the landscape, some far off and some from concealed positions quite near me in the garden. The targets, I realized, were certainly birds, although minutes passed before I spotted one under concentrated fire, and this was very small. There was no doubt about it that a large number of guns were involved, of which not a few had not hesitated to violate our privacy.

I went up through the house and crossed the road to the bar. The lantern-jawed and introspective owner,

352

Primo, was filling tiny glasses with brandy to be served to customers kitted out in the most extraordinary sporting gear, one of them, with a markedly Italian cast of features, in a kilt. The owner gave me a dank look and said, 'Eh?' I held up a finger and he passed over a glass. A daughter had been called in to help, and I managed to catch her eye. 'What's going on out there?' I asked. 'The season', she said, 'starts today.'

The Count was off on his morning walk down the Via Baronale with his grizzled asthmatic Alsatian called Hannibal which he had imported from England and allowed no one to address except in English. 'It's purgatory,' he said. 'Lasts at least two weeks so you may as well get used to it. Better buy ear-plugs if you enjoy a morning lie-in.' He felt it necessary to warn me. 'These people are a law unto themselves. Of course they've taken over your garden. Your problem is to keep them from taking pot-shots through the windows of the house. The vineyards have to employ guards to keep them out. They not only shoot all the birds but eat the grapes. Better not complain. In this village they grin and bear it.'

For half the day the guns popped and crackled, shot pattered on the roof and occasionally tapped at a window. Someone brought my binoculars, and I saw a fat man throw down what looked like a modern assault weapon to chase after a tiny fluttering bird with some life still in it, and then lose part of his trousers on a wire fence. It is normal for participants on such Roman occasions to shoot each other, and one of the guns went down as though poleaxed, although I was later to learn that he had only lost the top of a thumb.

Suddenly a silence that had hardly been disturbed in

2,500 years settled about us. It was midday when by immemorial custom shooting stopped until two hours before sundown, when birds would be prospecting among the surrounding trees for somewhere to roost. The second part of the day's entertainment awaited in the form of ritual spaghetti already cooking in cauldrons over fires stoked with wood confiscated by foraging parties in local gardens. The scarifying wine accompanying this was by tradition an early pressing of the year's vintage, its fermentation arrested by chemicals, and charged with raw grappa. The exaltation close to fury produced by a mug of this lasted for about half an hour, and was followed by sedation and often sleep. In the lucid interval the hunters dashed about reliving their recent experiences, boasting of triumphs, recalling the extraordinary rarity of birds who had narrowly survived their fusillades, and describing how others, equally rare, had fallen from the sky when outside what was accepted as effective range.

Besides binoculars I was carrying a camera and was implored by the hunters to photograph them holding up the little bundles of blood-splashed feathers, averaging, they said, 150 grammes in weight, which the morning's sport had yielded. The migrants which had chosen this precarious route to the safe havens of Africa were almost all small, speckled, unremarkable birds of the bunting family, although mixed in with them an occasional goldfinch or a warbler dangled from its tiny claws. Separate were the water wagtails shot from cunningly prepared ambush along the river bank, and the perquisite of a sporting syndicate having some affiliation with a charitable group known as 'The Drop of Milk'.

I was called away at about this time to deal with the

first garbage collection from the house. This was remarkable for the livery worn by the two men employed on the job, and the grandeur of their vehicle. I took it at first to be a fire engine, except that it had an electrically raised and lowered top. Resplendent in scarlet paintwork, it was lettered in bold black initials SPQR, standing for the Senators and People of Rome, and was clearly some miles off course at this point. Annunziata, the maid we shared with the Count, who had arranged the collection, explained that the villagers themselves simply threw their rubbish and unwanted objects into the nearest field, and that this service was only available to the upper crust of La Storta and the castle of Isola Farnese. 'That's the way it is here, sir. The rich and the poor. If you're rich you do nothing. If you're poor you work for nothing. Take the case of the Count. With respect, what does he do? He grows parsley and when it's ready the priest's horse jumps over the wall and gobbles it up.'

At round about six in the evening the shooting started again, and although Annunziata warned me that most of the guns would still be drunk I wandered down the garden to see what was going on. There were fewer birds than in the early morning, but they were larger and more important by local standards, many of them being starlings whose small, mangled corpses would attract admiration and command a high price when they hung among the dishevelled bunches of sparrows on the stalls of the local markets in the days to come. The starlings foolishly congregated in the hope of roosting in the trees of the wooded ravine to the north-east of the house, and here the hunters blazed away at them as soon as they settled, but with little success. While studying this action through the binoculars I was suddenly aware of the presence of the Roman garbage lorry stationary in the road running along the ravine. It would shortly be dusk and the blatant scarlet of the municipal lorry was dignified and enriched in the waning light. Now only rarely was the sound of a stray shot to be heard, and it was evident that the day's sport was at an end; cars' horns bleating impatiently summoned the last of the laggards from the slopes. With that, faintly, I heard the lorry's engine start up, watched it manocuvre into position with its back to the ravine, saw a door lift and the following cataract of black sacks and broken furniture go over the edge.

Back in the Via Baronale I was lucky enough to witness an extraordinary ritual. A kingfisher had fallen to one of the guns, an event of extreme rarity likely to happen once in a season, and at the moment of my arrival a crumpled handful of feathers, still glistening in the half light, was being passed from hand to hand amid cries of astonishment, congratulation and delight. The custom in such cases was for the successful sportsman to swallow the eyes, and this he did, washed down in a glass of brandy, to the sounding of car horns and shouts of applause.

The shooting party departed, watched in silence and with on the whole expressionless faces by the men of the village, whose only voiced criticism was that 300 lire could be spent on a single cartridge required to kill a sparrow offered for sale in the market for one sixth of the price.

Annunziata was on her way back to her house carrying the Countess's personal garments to be laundered at home where she could keep an eye on her children. Her wash-house was fitted with the laborious Victorian equipment her employer insisted be used in this case. She had been a beautiful girl, but was now greying, with a distraught expression, and over-muscular arms, and carried with her an inescapable odour of soap.

Staring after the departing cars, she said, 'Good riddance to the sods.'

'Don't you like them?'

'Well, who would? Did you hear them down by the river? They ran out of birds, so they shot all the frogs. Can you wonder we vote Communist?'

I brought up the matter of garbage being tipped into the ravine. She seemed surprised. 'Naturally,' she said. 'It's the easy way.'

'They'll fill up the ravine in the end,' I said.

'Not in our time.'

Chapter Twenty-Five

I T CAME AS a relief that bombardments did not follow
on a strictly daily basis. The report was that bad
weather sometimes held up the migrants in their passage
round the Western Alps, so there were peaceful mornings
when scouts posted by the syndicates along the migrant
routes telephoned in with the depressing news that no
flights had been sighted making for Rome. When the
weather lifted and the passage cleared it was natural that
a more than average number of birds was to be expected,
and the shooting continued almost without pause
throughout the day. Following these intervals of glut Di
Stefano's, the smart restaurant at the end of the village,
put out a placard announcing that *ucellini* were on the
menu. Four of these per portion were served grilled on
skewers and patrons were provided with pretty porcelain
receptacles painted with pasque-flowers into which
osseous remnants could be surreptitiously spat. It was an
expensive course; nevertheless, the rumour spread
through the village that the *ucellini* were not buntings,
skylarks or pipits that had fallen to the guns but in reality
were no more than sparrows netted in the Pontine
marshes.

The house was separated from the castle by a small
but dense shrubbery. In this, inexplicably, scorpions
congregated among the leaves in quantities I have never
seen before or since. It was an attraction in consequence
for weary and famished birds, in particular warblers,
who seemed by some extraordinary instinct to detect the
presence while in flight of the succulent morsels awaiting

them below. Inevitably the birds caught the eye of the marksmen and a few days on in the season a close-quartered early morning fusillade awoke me once again. From the window overlooking the street I saw that two men had placed themselves behind the garden wall from which they fired into the bushes. Soon after, they moved off and another arrived in a car from which he alighted carrying a most elaborate and costly looking gun which he set up on a tripod. He adjusted the sights, took aim and fired just at the moment when the Count, followed by Hannibal, came through the castle gate. With that he dismantled the gun, climbed back into the car and drove off. The Count had stopped to watch these proceedings before joining me, while Hannibal limped away for his morning visit to a stone projecting from the base of the wall bearing an obliterated Etruscan inscription. 'Anything wrong?' he asked.

'I wish these people wouldn't shoot into the garden,' I said. 'I have children to think about.'

'All the same, it's better to grin and bear it,' he said. 'If you complain you're likely to make enemies, which is something to avoid. I'm off to my garden to collect some rather special parsley. Why don't you lock your family away in a safe place for an hour or two and come along?'

Chapter Twenty-Six

L IFE FOR THE pupils of St George's was pleasant. Relations with the teaching staff were informal and relaxed. The older children dressed as they or their parents pleased and in the top form first names for all concerned was the order of the day. The midday meal was something to look forward to – spaghetti in one of its innumerable forms, followed by meat or fish, then a sweet of an exciting and inventive kind, usually based upon some regional models. Students in the top form could ask for a glass of local wine if they wished, despite its tendency to produce a scaliness of the lips. In the afternoon juniors like Kiki and Gawaine dozed gently through readings of the poetry of Petrarca and Leopardi by which it was hoped to introduce them to the Italian language. At weekends they were offered sailing instruction on Lake Bracciano, and there was a promise of skiing in the Gran Sasso D'Italia when the first snows fell.

The village satisfactions to which the children were returned by the school bus at the end of the scholastic day were of a solid but different kind. This was a community devoid of onward and upward pressures. The villagers saw themselves as guided by destiny into the paths they trod, and this they accepted with a sort of spirited calm. Take no thought for the morrow, the Bible adjured, and had they been able to read it they would have agreed. Apart from a short repertory of obscure oaths the expression most frequently in their mouth was 'pazienza' usually accompanied by a weary smile. An absence of ambition in childhood had its advantages. The young of Isola Farnese could live for the day, because there were no future summits to be climbed. Within reasonable limits they were left to their own devices, and the village school released them in the afternoon to something close to absolute freedom.

Boys and girls formed separate groups with little contact with each other. In the evenings the girls took over the doorsteps of the village, escaping to fairyland in little rustic soap operas of the imagination. The boys fought down their huge reserves of energy with endless activity in mock wars. Unlike the girls, who were companionable and democratic, the boys chose a leader who exercised stern discipline over the rank and file, and demolished the silences of Isola Farnese with their outcry that persisted long into the night. It was a scene the Count very much enjoyed, and to foster it he had installed powerful lighting throughout the village which was not switched off until midnight – or even later on demand. 'Let them play,' he said. 'Why shouldn't they? I like to see it, and how much I wish I could join in.' To complaints from village adults who were being kept awake, he would say, 'I have ear-plugs for you. Wear them as I do, and you will sleep well.'

Our arrival in Isola Farnese gave rise to a curious breach of custom among the children. After a few weeks a scattering of Italian words they had picked up provided the open sesame to the tribal life of the young. At this point Kiki would normally have taken her place among the little coteries of girls on the village doorsteps, but after a discussion among the leading boys it was decided that she was to become an honorary male. This may have been no more than the highest compliment that could have been paid, or it might have resulted from some local fallacy on the subject of Anglo-Saxon competence. Following a brief speech by the leader, nothing of which was understood, the boys pressed forward to congratulate her and shake her hand. '*Adesso sei uomo come noi altri* (now you're a man like the rest of us),' she was told, and invited to take part in their energetic and sometimes dangerous games. Apart from simulated warfare from which Kiki was excused, the most popular game was nascondino – hide and seek, for which there was endless scope in a landscape full of Etruscan tombs.

This freedom of the streets granted to the children might have caused doubt in a similar environment in northern Europe but the Count assured us that the crime of mugging, so far, was unknown in these parts and that child molestation was exceedingly rare. We had heard through Annunziata a garbled account of an assault on a child said to have taken place in or near the town of Viterbo, some thirty miles to the north, and followed by a lynching of the culprit. 'I heard some mention of it,' the Count said, 'although it may be no more than a rumour. I'm afraid we suffer from a tendency to take the law into our own hands. In this case there was talk of the man being hung by a hook through his throat, but whether there's any truth in it I can't say. Such punishments can be barbarous.'

The juvenile military campaigns of Isola Farnese provided Kiki with a splendid opportunity for exploration of the countryside and the innumerable secret places in the fields and woods. At first it struck her friends as strange that their honorary boy would want to poke into dark and uninviting places that they had previously overlooked, but in the end she managed to enthuse them in the search for pottery collection, and while the craze lasted we were showered with coloured fragments, most of which lost all trace of decoration within days of disinterment. A special interest in my case when I was allowed to accompany some of these trips was the autumnal flora of the area which was remarkable. The country people stripped this landscape of everything that was edible, from the tiniest snail lodged in a crack in a wall down to the most insignificant nut. On fine days families streamed out from Rome and went over the fields yard by yard cutting out dandelion plants by the thousand for incorporation into salads. Flowers – apart from a few known to have edible bulbs – they seemed to regard almost with distrust. At most they bought chrysanthemums in the market, but the wild variety they left alone. It was through this indifference that all these fields in autumn were enamelled with countless cyclamens, colchicums and crocuses, some species being of great rarity elsewhere.

Our most exciting find in the matter of archaeology was quite accidental, arising from a quest, for once, not for fragments of Etruscan pottery but for rare flowers. The Count had suggested a location some three miles away and Kiki and I went there in the car. It was a field under a steep slope with flowers sprouting everywhere from among the rocks. Followed by a white cow full of amiable curiosity, prepared to wait while we botanized and then move on with us to the next outcrop of flowers, we began to explore the area, soon discovering a cave. Pushing through the ferns at its entrance we saw to our amazed delight a marble sarcophagus, in perfect condition and missing only its lid. It was empty apart from a deposit of the finest chalky dust.

On returning to the car and trying to drive away we promptly stuck in the mud and seeing that there was nothing to be done we left it and set out to walk back to Isola Farnese. The grocer's shop seemed the best place to enquire where to look for help. We went in and the grocer, Antonio, vacant-faced as ever looked up from a customer he was serving, 'Eh?'

I explained the predicament, asking if Antonio knew of a garage in La Storta where they would be prepared to come and pull the car out of the mud. 'There's a festa on, they're shut,' he said. I thanked him, turned round to go, and he called after me, 'Wait.'

He finished serving the woman, and then came to the door with us. A notice hung on the glass door panel facing the street. This said 'Open', and he turned it round so that despite the early hour he was now shut. 'Let's go,' he said.

He gestured to us to get into his Land-Rover parked outside, and we set off. I started protestations about putting him to trouble, and he said in a flat voice, 'This happens all the time. Where is it?'

We drove off in silence, leaving the road for the cart track I'd originally followed, and thence after crashing through numerous potholes, into the field.

'What sort of car is it?' he asked.

'Fiat 127,' I told him.

'For going to the beach in,' he said. 'For this road a car needs to have entrails. You're lucky. The garage at La Storta doesn't come out to a place like this.'

We ploughed into the field where, guarded by our

white cow, the Fiat leaned over in the churned-up mud. 'Sticky,' the grocer said.

He hitched the tow-rope he had ready over the front bumper and pulled us clear with a single jerk and I followed him back to Isola Farnese where a small collection of customers waited at the door of his shop. A little ironic cheering was silenced with a glance as he unlocked the door and turned the notice round. I stood at the back of the customers at the counter trying to mouth my gratitude and he held up his hand in acknowledgement without raising his eyes from the rice he was weighing. A grumbler was put in her place by *pazienza* – a wry acceptance of the frustration of life in another village mouth, but in this case a stern command.

We were turning away to leave the shop when he called after us 'Buon giorno'. The incident brought us closer together. From this time on we became almost friends and for the important Feast of Befana, immediately following Christmas, he presented us with a bottle of Asti Spumante, a salami and a jar of excellent olives from his own trees and pickled by himself.

Chapter Twenty-Seven

O NE OF THE attractions of Isola Farnese was that apart from our own intrusion and the conspicuous idleness of the Count and his family, this was a working village devoid of parasitism. The doctor came from La Storta, there was no policeman, a single shopkeeper, a taciturn couple who ran the bar, and a baker who turned out enough fresh bread every day to go round. The local wine came from a tiny triangle of vineyard on a hillside. It was doused with sprays from time to time, and when harvested the grapes still carried a bluish veneer from the spraying and were tossed into a vat without any attempt to remove this or sundry foliage snatched up by the machine that did the picking, before the wine-making took place.

The thin and acidulous white wine of Isola Farnese was sold in the local bar, but bottled with an impressive label, featured also in the wine list of the Di Stefano restaurant, the sole enclave in the village of the outside world. Di Stefano remained a bit of a mystery to the locals, because only the village women who were called in to clean the place up after business was at an end on Sunday had ever been allowed to put their noses inside its inner rooms. Di Stefano's opened on Saturdays and Sundays only, and Sunday lunch was the great event of the week for middle-class Italy, here as elsewhere. Every table for this meal was always booked, and occupied in the main by men in dark suits who arrived in black Alfa Romeos. These customers who travelled here from Rome and consumed enormous amounts of food in the hours between midday and four were supposed to be members of the Sicilian Mafia known to have established itself in the capital. They were highly popular with the staff for their courteous and considerate behaviour and the generosity of their tips.

The restaurant was splendidly sited on the far end of the enormous rock supporting the castle and offered an unequalled prospect of the slightly unearthly landscape I had viewed in part through the narrow windows of the castle itself. Bronzed and burnished autumn fields had been flung over the low hills in a way that identified this as Etruscan country. Sharp-edged black patches marked hollows in which chestnut groves grew. Most remarkable was some atmospheric trick by which for an hour or so around high noon a deep blue boundary divided the horizon from the sky where the salt wind blew in from the sea.

It was a setting that enchanted the Count, who had invited me to join him here for lunch on his saint's day. Much of his early life, he said, had been spent in an attempt to escape the flatness of Venice. 'This,' he said, 'is a landscape that takes wings.'

The waiters, silent, swift and starched into their outdated uniforms, transported us into the vanished kingdom of Victor Emmanuel III and its servilities that had survived in this environment. 'If I am not disturbing the gentlemen,' the head waiter said, 'may I present our menu of the day?' What was on offer, in its elaborations and absurdities, also recalled an exaggerated past. Cardollini prati di Lazio (goldfinches from the fields of Latium), four on a skewer, baby octopus no bigger than a large spider – of which a sample was produced – pig's snout Viterbo style, braised with assorted fungus; testicles of milk lamb in saffron rice. The Count swept the suggestions away with patrician contempt. 'A decadent imposture,' he said, in reference to the Di Stefano cuisine. 'I am a simple eater.' To the waiter he said, 'Give me a woodpigeon, if you can assure me that it is not from the deep-freeze.' The waiter returned a slight bow. 'It can be feathered in Sir's presence if Sir desires,' he said. 'At least the flesh is wholesome,' the Count assured me. 'At this time of the year the birds feed on nuts.' I agreed to follow his example.

Cautiously I watched the men in dark suits, who hardly raised their eyes, absorbed with food. They were stamped with a strange uniformity in clothing, facial expression and gesture. A few were accompanied by glamorous women from whom they seemed strangely aloof and who were on show here rather as part of the accepted setting of mafiosi lives. Surreptitiously I studied the nearest couple as the man chewed thoughtfully on the tiny black carcase removed from a skewer before raising the little flower-painted bowl to his lips to dispose of the inedible aftermath. His friend displayed in profile the sweet emptiness of a Meissen shepherdess as she raked on a lobster shell with a silver claw. A musician in medieval trappings moved quietly into position behind them and began to scrape on his violin, and the man instantly dropped a 5,000-lire note on the table and dismissed him with a flick of the forefinger.

'He is eating a sparrow in the belief that it is a goldfinch,' said the Count, sotto voce, and almost without moving his lips. 'On the same principle he pays dearly for the kisses of a courtesan to convince himself they are those of love. You have heard of men of respect?' I told him I had. 'This is the Rome style. Even those who manipulate the rulers of our country can be deluded. Even they can be made fools of.'

Below us a boy and girl moved into sight on a short length of road visible beneath us skirting the rock as it unwound uphill. The girl was the Count's seventeen-year-old adopted daughter, Zo-Zo, and the boy her fourteen-year-old village admirer whose father followed the profession of wheelwright, still much in demand in an area where metalled surfaced roads were few, and farm carts still in use on the rough country tracks. The pair were inseparable, a situation which appeared to cause not the slightest surprise among our phlegmatic village neighbours. It was an imperturbability that appeared to be shared by the Count and his wife. 'There they go again,' he said on this occasion. 'I cannot understand where the attraction lies in long walks under the midday sun, especially with Zo-Zo's fair skin.'

'What's the news of her?' I asked. 'Will she be going to university?'

'We've given up the idea. She wants to stay here.'

'How do you feel about that?'

'Both Alice and I have decided she must do as she pleases. She's on drugs. We have to keep an eye on her. It's better she stays where she is.'

I was staggered. I shook my head. 'You amaze me. Zo-Zo – she seems such a quiet girl. I'd never have believed it. What a problem for you.'

'The top form at the school was full of junkies. I imagine it still is. A dolce vita while it lasted, but what comes next? Dr Pecorella broke the news to me, but we'd suspected something of the kind.'

'Wouldn't one of the small provincial universities be something to consider?'

'They wouldn't have her, and in any case she wouldn't stay. She'd take the first train back. I know her only too well.'

'So you put up with the attachment. It can't have been an easy decision for you and Alice to take.'

'It wasn't really difficult. The boy's good for her. He keeps her quiet. I should explain both Alice and I are followers of Epicurus and he always comes to the rescue in situations like this.'

'Didn't he favour a luxurious style of life?'

'Far from it,' the Count said. 'His doctrine was one of moderation. He recommends the pursuit of sensible satisfactions and a calm approach to emergency. Whenever it is possible, he says, take the easy way out, which is what we are doing in this case. Zo–Zo is home. She is here to stay, and we cannot rid ourselves of our responsibility, even if that were possible, by burying her in a university. This being the case, let her be as happy as she can.' He pointed to a verse in archaic and barely readable lettering fixed to the restaurant's wall. It was by Lorenzo Il Magnifico, regarded by some as the great man's inevitable descent into triteness when he took time off from statesmanship to venture on the more difficult path of poetic composition.

> Quanto e bella giovanezza
> – Che se fugge tattavia,
> Chi vuol' essere lieto sia,
> De doman' non v'e certezza.*

* How beautiful is youth,
  As it escapes us,
  Take what joy you can of it.
  Of the morrow there's no knowing.

At this moment the waiter appeared with a trolley with a covered dish over a low burner containing the pigeons. A junior followed at his heels with another, charged with a great variety of *contorni*, momentarily inspected by the Count who showed a trace of irritation before waving them away. 'Just the pigeons,' he said to the waiter. He turned to me. 'How extraordinary', he said, 'that the Master's reputation in Italy should be as it is despite his complete indifference to food.'

Chapter Twenty-Eight

THE SEASON OF the shooting of birds came to an end and the sportsmen from Rome, having disposed of the only remaining targets in the way of stray dogs and cats, went their way. Such sport as the area now offered was on a depressed level, attracting a few enthusiasts to the shores of Lake Bracciano where they fished for a unique and primitive fish sheltering in its muddy depths, described as of repellent flavour, but beneficial in the treatment of genito-urinary complaints. We were now in the season when the pigs were killed and turned into fearsome-looking sausages gorged with chilies, fat and blood.

It was to the pig-killing that the superstitious attributed the coming of the rains which were as violent here in their uninterrupted downpourings as anywhere else on earth. When the rains stopped with a sudden finality – as if by the turning off of a cosmic tap – the weak sunshine of the pre-Christmas lull illuminated the land, and in this period of decline of the year small dramas that might have been overlooked in the grand drama of high summer drew attention and excited comment. At Monte S. Vito one of those gentle, white bulls that despite their outward placidity were said to bear grudges, turned suddenly on the farmer who owned it and skewered him with a long, elegant horn. An epidemic of stomach trouble with several near fatalities was traced to a wine producer who added various chemical intoxicants as well as quantities of banana skins to his grapes. In Tarquinia a man, having been arrested on a charge of grave-robbing and selling Etruscan antiques to a friend of the Count, was able to prove that he had manufactured these himself. Fregene was the scene of a freak storm, quite unexpected at this time of the year, which picked up a small yacht and dumped it in a field, and then, with a switch round of the wind, floated a car out to sea. Pilgrims hastening to a hill village behind Tivoli where the Virgin was reported in a newspaper as having appeared to the locals on several occasions, found that these miracles were no more than part of a plot to sell land in the vicinity.

Isola Farnese was subjected to its own minor sensation. Bruno, Zo-Zo's young suitor, had been sent off to Rieti on a short course designed to prepare him for entry into his father's profession. This left Zo-Zo, otherwise without friends in the locality, very much at a loose end. One evening a loud outcry from the children playing outside sent us rushing into the street to be confronted with the sight of Zo-Zo promenading on top of the thirty-foot-high outer castle wall, flapping her arms in imitation of a bird in flight. This was shortly after an addiction to LSD had spread to Italy, and some of those who had experimented with its use, becoming victims of the delusion that they were able to fly, had jumped or fallen from high places to their death. It was a spectacle that brought the whole of the village's inhabitants into the open. Implored not to move she cavorted, pranced and flapped and laughed shrilly. The fire brigade in La Storta could not be reached on the phone in the bar, so a man was dispatched on a Lambretta to raise the alarm, but by the time the fire engine arrived it was all over, and with a final flap and a titter Zo-Zo had disappeared from sight.

Suddenly an ebullient and vociferous Christmas was upon us, blending under Roman influence the celebratory styles of all the Christian world. In the Piazza Navona the shepherds brought down from the Abruzzi wheezed their prehistoric bagpipe music against a tableau of Santa Claus drawn by reindeer on his sleigh and nativity cribs peopled by pseudo-Palestinians of the first century. The crib had been introduced from Byzantium. The masked dancers on stilts, most applauded of all the strolling players, had arrived via Venice, from their place of Saracenic origin. The *Corriere* reported that a hundred stalls selling sweets, toys and seasonal souvenirs had been counted in the Piazza. Visitors consumed ritual nuts, sugared almonds and torrone by the hundredweight. Most popular with the children was licorice, hung in thin strips like long black bootlaces from many stalls, and those who overindulged were hurried away to a little vomitorium concealed in a corner of the square.

The Count and his wife spent much of the holiday in Rome in their penthouse flat, possessing from its windows over the Spanish Steps one of the most superb prospects of the urban world. Throwing open the shutters for us to look down upon the endless multitudes ascending and descending the steps the Count, as he frequently did, quoted Dante: *I had not thought death had undone so many*. At his back incunabula in antique bindings spilled from the bookshelves among the feet of statues deprived of noses, ears or toes. Alice looked forward to an orgy of shopping. The feast of the nativity and the great winter solstice was also that of consumerism, with the shop windows baited with seasonal extravagances of every kind. It was alleged by Annunziata that she hired a car with a driver for the period to be driven slowly backwards and forwards up and down the main shopping thoroughfares, exultantly studying through binoculars what was on offer behind the glass sprayed with plastic snow.

For their Christmas dinner itself, to which we were invited, the pair returned to Isola Farnese. What was extraordinary about this gathering was that most of the guests were from families employing Scottish nannies, and not only spoke perfect English, but appeared to prefer to converse with each other in this, rather than in Italian. Several of them had been reduced to destitution by the war and its aftermath, surviving now with considerable grace on less, probably, than one of our villager's income by doing odd jobs round the ministries in Rome, preparing well-written persuasive applications for government posts and correctly filling in the forms required in the case of foreign residents for even such prosaic operations as buying a new car. One of these, immaculate in his attire and with the presence of a functionary at the Papal Court, owned a castle within sight of Tarquinia which he offered to sell me, as he admitted with little more than a forlorn hope, for the equivalent of £5,000. His description of it was stunningly frank. 'Let me say that only one room is habitable,' he said. 'Even then not in winter. I am happy for my neighbours to keep chickens in the rest, for which they repay me with a dozen eggs from time to time.'

After dinner the Count and Alice went off in a hurry back to the excitements of Rome leaving Zo-Zo with

Annunziata. This proved to be a mistake. For some reason Bruno was off the scene at this time, but Annunziata agreed to look after the girl, who preferred to stay in Isola Farnese, and to give her a bedroom in her house. For several days all was quiet, and then at about eight in the evening of the day before her parents were due back, the shrill and tocsin-like bell of the telephone the Count had just presented us with rang for the first time. It was a panic-stricken, hardly coherent aunt ringing from Rome. Zo-Zo had telephoned her from the castle of Isola Farnese to say that she was about to commit suicide. The woman had been unable to reach the parents whom she believed to have gone to the theatre. There was no reply from the police at La Storta, and I was the only person she could appeal to in the crisis.

The problem now arose of my complete ignorance of the geography of a vast building of which I had only seen an extremely small part. The ground-floor rooms were roughly rectangular and without complication. When first the possibility had existed of our occupying the principal wing the Count had taken me up to the first floor to point out the bedrooms that went with it, and I noted then that access to these along passages and up and down sundry flights of stairs was dark and labyrinthine. These rooms in the upper storey were small but numerous and I remembered that there were two wings of the castle in which I had not set foot, and if it came to a search for the suicidal Zo-Zo it now occurred to me that this was an operation into which the whole village population would have to be enlisted.

The agonizing choice was whether to go for help in a case when a few minutes delay could have been fatal, or to drop everything and get to the scene of whatever was happening as fast as my legs could carry me. I chose the second alternative and rushed up to the castle where I found the small door protected by security devices giving access to the family's apartments significantly open, and the lights in the entrance hall switched on. Through this I plunged into the enormous principal room, a blaze of light and a distorted uproar of rock music belting out from loudspeakers suspended under the ceiling. At the far end of the room a wide staircase led to a landing where it divided to continue to the first floor. Lamps stood at each side of the foot of the staircase, and on the landing had been switched on as if in preparation for the arrival of guests for a splendid party. I ran up the staircase, down corridors, through a library, a billiard room, a chapel, bedrooms, a room where theatre props had been stacked, a laundry, through medieval nooks and crannies of every size and shape, lost and found my way again, always in the stark, shadowless illumination of innumerable lamps, and pursued by the moan and clamour of rock singers turned up to the maximum, and the hammering of drums.

There was nothing to be done in the end but to get help. Annunziata and her husband lived at the far end of the village. Our Fiat was parked outside the house a hundred yards away but refused to start. I called to the man who ran the bar, and who was standing in his doorway, 'Trouble with the Count's daughter.' He jerked back his head in a local gesture conveying sympathy without involvement, his hands held together before his chest as if to display an oracular inscription. 'Eh-eh,' he shouted.

I was gasping for breath by the time I reached Annunziata's house, where I found her husband, Ricardo, a

notable idler, sipping coffee. I tried to make him understand the extreme urgency of the situation, but he
remained immutably passive. 'Not a moment to lose,' I
shouted. He took a last gulp of coffee, shrugged his
shoulders and said, 'You don't know her. I do.' We set
off. 'For God's sake hurry,' I begged him. 'They won't
let me,' he said, patting his rib cage in reference to some
obscure complaint that kept him largely out of action.

I waited in the glare and the continuing hubbub of the
big room for him to catch up and we went up the stairs
together and found Zo–Zo in the only bedroom I'd
managed to overlook. An empty pill bottle was tipped
over on the bedside table, and under it had been placed a
farewell note written in a firm hand on a sheet of paper
scrawled otherwise with astromantic signs. Ricardo
leaned over her, as I first supposed tenderly, curled back
an eyelid, then lifting her with one arm round her
shoulders, struck her with some force across the face
with his open hand. He then let her drop back. 'You
have to know what to do, that's all,' he said.

Ten minutes later the ambulance arrived, bringing
with it Annunziata, two white–coated ambulance men
carrying a machine sprouting tubes, and a doctor with a
forked beard and a denunciatory stare. 'Members of the
family?' he asked us. We shook our heads and he shoved
us through the door.

We walked back together. Primo was still at the door
of the bar and we drifted in. Two glasses of foggy white
wine were placed in silence on the counter. 'Nothing
stronger than this?' I asked, and Primo said, 'We've run
out.' They'd picked up the silly habit in the Rome area at
that time of saying 'cheers', which they did with an
Italian rolling of the r. We lifted the glasses and the pair

of them said cheers, and in the next second I felt the sting of the wine in the tiny cracks it had already opened in my lips. Someone had given Primo a cuckoo clock which only worked once in a while, and at that moment the bird popped out and started its insane squawking and Primo cuffed it back.

'People are different,' Ricardo said, 'and they call for different treatment. Like cars, some are trouble-free and some aren't.' It was the only comment on life I ever heard him make.

'Eh,' Primo agreed. 'What happened about the Count's girl?'

'Had one of her turns,' Ricardo told him. 'They're taking her away, but she'll be back the day after tomorrow.'

And she was.

Spring came early in Isola Farnese, and was in full flower by early March, although it was the silent spring of which Rachel Carson had warned, and which in leaving England we had hoped to escape. The migrant birds that had come under such concentrated fire on their way south in autumn customarily avoided the Rome area on their way back to the north. A few sportsmen hung about at points of vantage in the hope of intercepting a bird that had wandered off course, and the grocer and his friends managed to stage a successful ambush of a pair of crows that had been sighted in a local coppice, and shot the hen on the nest. Otherwise wild life in the Latium was at an end. Even a rabbit was an extreme rarity and the last to be snared in Isola Farnese some two years earlier, having been stuffed, now peered down wistfully from a shelf in the priest's study at villagers who called upon him in search of godly advice.

Nevertheless with the coming of the warm weekends Roman families sallied forth in droves to picnic by the roadsides of the Cassia and the rest of the highways leading in all directions from the capital. With the demise of winter the winds had swung round, and now blew strongly from the south, in our case with the slight inherent disadvantage that the surrounding fields soon became plastered with rubbish from the northern suburbs. Lay-bys and side turnings on these northern roads were soon deep in refuse, and the view was often spoilt by the sight of plastic bags by the hundred trapped in bushes, or caught up in the lower branches of trees.

At about this time the faintest of unpleasant odours was detected in Isola Farnese itself. In the beginning this was so slight that when we sat down to the evening meal in the little grassy plateau overlooking the scene of past greatness, half the family members refused to admit to its existence, and thereafter days might pass before someone was seen to sniff the air doubtfully once again. On windy days it was certainly absent, neither was it ever noticeable in the early mornings, but on an airless evening when spring had gathered strength, the odour was back, and although it remained vagrant and slight it was generally admitted now that it was not imaginary.

I spoke to Annunziata about it and she showed surprise. 'I agree with you that there's a stink, sir, but personally I don't notice it. It comes from all that stuff they throw into the ravine. You may find it unpleasant at first, but I assure you you'll get accustomed to it as the year goes on. Let me explain: it's warm and it's been raining. That's the trouble. Quite frankly after the summer rains it stinks like a cesspit. But then again it doesn't often rain in summer, so why lose heart? Believe me, sir, you'll get used to it like anybody else.'

'Doesn't the Council ever do anything about this?' I asked.

'The Council?' she laughed. 'If you expect the Council to do anything you're living with your head in the clouds. Last year they were going to work on it this year. Now they say it's top priority for next. Better accept it as it is, sir. The Council isn't going to do anything for you.'

Dr Pecorella agreed to accompany me, reluctantly, I suspected, on an inspection of the ravine, where endless black sacks lay one upon the other, spilling their contents and spreading a sullen fetor among the splendours of the ancient woods.

'The smell. Rather off-putting these days.'

'Eh,' he said. My secret hope had been that he might have offered in his position to alert some appropriate body to a danger to public health. The Italian language provides many phrases employed in support of passivity. One is *è così*, a vague comment translatable as 'that's the way it is'. '*È così*,' Pecorella said, thus accepting what he saw as an inevitability, and hoping I would do so too.

'And the Council don't want to know about it,' I said.

'Of course not.'

'Can you suggest any other body that might be induced to interest themselves?'

'My dear friend, Rome is rich in bodies that have been set up to deal with every conceivable abuse. Those in charge accept exceedingly low salaries in the knowledge they will be called upon to do roughly nothing whatever. You will be inundated with sympathy and assurances, and there the matter will rest. To obtain a positive result you would be required to put forward a petition signed by every member of the community, and passed to a minister through various intermediaries, all of them suitably rewarded. There is one drawback.'

'And what is that?'

'Nobody would sign the petition.'

'Why?'

'A contractor dumps the rubbish here. He is rich. They are poor. We have a proverb. "No one says of the lion his breath smells".'

'So it's a waste of time?'

'Well naturally. A complete waste of time.'

The doctor was looking down into the ravine, his nose held lightly between thumb and forefinger. Although his English ranked with that of the Count he was liable in emotional moments to break into Italian. '*Che bellezza*,' he said. 'I always feel an extraordinary freedom in these surroundings. Let us walk as far as the old Etruscan bridge.'

'I'm told they throw unwanted furniture over it into the river these days,' I told him.

'I know,' he said. 'Fortunately there's a tremendous spate of water in November and that breaks up whatever's there and carries it away. That excellent book of yours describes the view as the finest in this part of the country.'

We reached the bridge finding that an old Fiat van had been parked on it within a foot of the edge which was protected by a spindly wooden balustrade. It bore no number plates, the seats and lamps had been removed, and an open door drooped on its hinges. We stood to one side to enjoy the distant scene. There was no pollution from the hill villages and the meadows above this point. The water spouting and cascading from the face of the low falls we looked over was of crystal clarity, with polished pebbles shining in the bed of the deep pool beneath in which the ruin of a chest of drawers rotated slowly. Ahead the river tunnelled into the evergreen oaks' foliage, perpetuating their rich autumnal glow here among the colours of spring. Anemones by the thousand were clustered round their roots, and from where we stood the black sacks were no longer in sight.

'So this lot will go over the top,' I said.

'Undoubtedly,' the doctor said. 'They've not quite done with stripping it down. They'll have ducked into the bushes to wait till we've gone. The wheels must be worth something to them. It'll go in tonight.'

'No amount of autumn spates is going to get rid of this.'

'I'm afraid you're right. A problem,' he said. 'I wonder if it could be blown up if necessary? We shall have to see.'

It was at this point that certain doubts surfaced as to the permanence of the Roman venture. From some viewpoints it had been a huge success. To live in an Italian village in close and happy contact with the children of another race was an experience which we believed ours would never forget. Life here was freer than in England. Some sort of a class division existed but it was a mild affair compared with the English version, as was exemplified by the Count's philosophical attitude to his daughter's love life. After further observation I was to conclude that this was no more than an exceptional example of a liberalism that was widespread.

From this aspect the venture had been an undoubted success. Life in Isola Farnese offered the prospect of weekend exploration of so many beautiful cities that were easy of access. There was the endless fascination of the great cemeteries of Tarquinia and Cerveteri where the tombs reproduced the domestic environment of a mysterious nation, married couples in effigy exchanged conjugal smalltalk on the lids of their sarcophagi, a young man raised himself on his elbow to confront infinity with startled eyes. Viterbo, an hour away by car, where the Popes held out for three centuries against Rome and a rapist had recently been hanged from a hook, was of endless interest. The Gran Sasso D'Italia, greatest natural rock-garden in Europe, was within easy reach, as was L'Aquila with its celebrated fountain of ninety-nine jets at the entrance to the wilderness of the Abruzzi, which we had yet to explore. Finally, the inexhaustible splendours of Rome, hardly investigated by us, waited at the end of the Cassia, only a half hour away.

These were some of the powerful pluses, the richness of experience that so easily outweighed the environmental drawbacks of which we sometimes complained. But more serious objections were beginning to emerge. It was becoming clear that the children would never be bilingual following this move to Rome. After seven months in Isola Farnese they had picked up a smattering of Italian, but it was of a rustic form – almost a dialect, although on testing senior pupils who had been studying the language at school they seemed to have learned even less. It had possibly been the worst moment to arrive in the school's short history. The horrific accounts of Paul Getty's kidnapping and mutilation had started a panic among parents who had supposed their children to be out of harm's way in Rome, and had gone about their business elsewhere with a quiet mind until this storm blew up. Flower Power was seized upon by the press as the scapegoat for these happenings, and *Forza Dei Fiore* featured for week after week in the Rome headlines. Eventually the Italian translation was dropped and Flower Power, as in English, was accepted into the Italian language as the inspiration for the drugs and sex orgies supposedly conducted by depraved seventeen-year-olds of British or American origin.

With the exception of the Count, Dr Pecorella and Don Ubaldo, the priest, no one in Isola Farnese read the newspapers, but all the details of the scurrilous facts they reported, nevertheless, were discussed there within an hour or so of the appearance of the evening editions. It was normal for these to be presented in exaggerated and even mendacious form. Paul Getty was photographed in a T-shirt bearing the lettering *Cocaine, It's The Real Thing*, in imitation of the famous Coca-Cola logo. Although it was false to allege that such garments could be worn while at school, the villagers were emphatic in their belief that this was so. Moreover the sad example of Zo-Zo was always before their eyes. As Annunziata put it, 'We got rid of the pagans here a couple of thousand years ago. These people are shits. With respect, sir, why send your precious offspring to a place like that for their education when Don Ubaldo would be willing to train them in the fear of God for a couple of hours a day and ask next to nothing for it?'

It was inevitable that the impact of these calamities

should have affected the fortunes of the school. The liberalism of the current dispensation came under attack by the board of governors, and in an attempt to establish a more conventional framework of discipline a new headmaster arrived to take over at St George's. His firmness of purpose evoked bitter resentment among the staff, and passive resistance led finally to a full-scale rebellion. When this failed a number of teachers broke away and announced plans to open a school in competition some few miles away. This prolonged tussle for control could only have an unsettling effect upon the pupils. For us it was all the worse in that a member of the staff had introduced us to the school, and we were on extremely friendly terms both with him and several other dissidents. The situation was that should we decide to soldier on in Rome, life at St George's was likely to be less pleasant than before. The disadvantage in the case of the new school was that it was too far away for comfortable day attendance. In either case nothing could convince me that the *Forza dei Fiore*, or whatever came to replace it, would not continue to await pupils who reached the upper forms, whichever school they attended.

Thus after interminable heart-searchings, discussions, hesitations, changes of mind – after many postponements, and finally looking backward with huge regret, a decision was reached to return to England. With this, all the pleasures great and small of the past months came into sharp focus as Isola Farnese, from which we were about to banish ourselves, refurbished memories and clothed itself in last-minute attractions.

Annunziata, without prompting, carried out a light-ning campaign to restore spick and spanness to the dusty surfaces of our rooms. On inspecting the result, as requested, we remembered that scorpions in the baths were a thing of the past, and that the expression of the Count's samurai, once seen as threatening, had now, through daily familiarity, become conciliatory. Some of the obscurities in the fourteenth-century fresco had been sponged away and freed of the grime of ages, sprightly figures were now visible where before there had been murk. Not only was the house suddenly more inviting on the eve of our departure but mysteriously the smell from the valley was no longer there. Visiting the garden for the last time I discovered unexpected developments there, for the unique brand of parsley sown by the Count on our patch of vegetable garden had not only germinated but burst through a panoply of weeds.

In every way Isola Farnese freshened its image. By some mistake the bar had come by some wine that was not of local production, and in consequence so drinkable that I called for a second glass. While I was there Dr Pecorella came in in a state of excitement because one of the numerous chips of broken pottery passed to him for inspection had not faded instantly, but retained a few square inches of indelible pattern including what might have been a fold of a woman's robe. This he proclaimed without doubt to have been part of a vessel imported from Greece. Where had we found it? We did not know, and it was too late now to go back and search over the area where it might have been found.

This was a Sunday afternoon and the Mafia from Rome had arrived as usual for their Sunday lunch, but, said the Doctor, there were fewer than usual. The village had found a way of making it known to them that they were not welcome.

'They give us a bad name,' as the grocer had complained. Pecorella thought he knew the men of respect well enough to assure us they'd go quietly. 'They never bother themselves over petty matters like this.' We strolled together down to the restaurant where a little group of village men stood watching two black Alfa Romeos parked outside with tyres let down. Ten minutes or so passed and the owner of one of the cars came out. A fair-haired girl tripped on high heels at his side as cautiously as if crossing stepping stones over a brook. The man looked down at his tyres. He cupped his fingers of a right hand oscillating gently from his wrist. Neither spoke. They went back into the restaurant and Pecorella said, 'He was angry, but he smiled. Now we may hope for a change for the better. You should have stayed longer.'

We walked back together. 'So now you're leaving us,' Pecorella said. 'Have you profited from your experience in our village in any way?'

'Yes,' I said. 'It's corrected my view of Italy based wholly on eighteen months among the Neapolitans. The Romans are different.'

'They are,' Pecorella said. 'But tell me, in what way?'

'The Neapolitans are lovable,' I said. 'They promise more than they give. The Romans are colder, but they give more than they promise. I've studied and admired your imperturbability. For reasons of temperament it remains beyond my reach.'

'Be assured it is largely a pretence. A matter of appearances. It is better to remain as you are.'

'Then again I've learned to speak without words. An accomplishment I'm proud of. Pity I shan't have the chance to put it to use.'

We had reached the bar. 'When are you taking off?' Pecorella asked.

'In about an hour,' I told him.

'Time for a last drink together, then.'

We went in and the glasses awaited us. 'Is this the new stuff?' I asked, and the owner jerked his head back and clicked his tongue. 'Nobody wanted it. They said it had no bite. I sent it back.'

I sipped the local vintage, controlling the grimace I would have made in the first weeks. 'How is it?' Primo asked.

'Eh,' I said, in a way that absolved me from commitment of any kind.

Pecorella nodded his approval. 'Spoken like a Roman,' he said.

In the same week we found ourselves back in East Anglia, a homespun Arcadia of dun coloration and flat horizons, providing at best an interlude of monotony in which to plan the tapestries of the future. The children were put to an earnest local school sponsored by an organization of a religious kind, and here, although there was some drug-taking and pupils were notorious for their shoplifting forays into the town, kidnapping could at least be ruled out. Nevertheless we thought it imprudent to allow Kiki the freedom of the streets after dark which she had enjoyed in Isola Farnese. Fresh from the Italian experience we saw England with new eyes. We had returned to an environment where the separation of the social layers appeared absolute. The filth and disorder of our inner cities was depressing indeed by comparison with Italy, yet the rural scene was a tidier one. The

English shot birds in large numbers, too, but execution in this case was conducted out of earshot in private woods.

In the physical sense we were back where we started, among sober, honest and reliable country folk almost as silent as the Romans, although, unlike the Romans, dragooned by memories of a past that had taught them to keep their opinions on all subjects strictly to themselves. Whatever slight contempt they may have felt for the fecklessness and incompetences of ex-urban settlers nothing of this ever showed through an exterior of tolerance and courtesy.

During the war I had spent a year in Naples within the sight of the tomb of the poet Horace. Notwithstanding his doubts on the topic of immortality he had chosen to be buried in this spot on a hillside overlooking the sea, corresponding then as now to the average citizen's view of it as a foretaste of the heaven in which the poet could not quite bring himself to believe. Even men of education among my Neapolitan friends, all of them devourers of marvels, believed in the leakage of mysterious influences from the tomb, fostering an even more relaxed view of life in its vicinity than that prevalent elsewhere in this wonderful city. It was a compliment of the sincerest kind when my neighbours assured me of my inclusion in these benefits.

Of Horace it has been said that he rode to a fame not of his seeking on the back of his poems. As a follower of Epicurus he devoted himself apart from the pursuit of his muse to the cultivation of reasonable and easily obtained satisfactions. The Emperor Augustus, whose secretary he laughingly refused to become, took strongly to him. He sat at the Emperor's left hand at table when in Rome,

and they sipped Falernian wine together and discussed
ways of dodging the stings and arrows of fortune. Of
the poet's literary work what remains most in my
memory is his chiding in verse of a friend whose contin-
ual journeyings he found too restless for his own good.
This, having spent half a lifetime in endless peregrinations, I was inclined to apply to my own case. 'You go
in ships in search of bliss,' Horace wrote. 'Yet what you
seek is here at Ulubrae, you'll find, if to your search you
bring a balanced mind.'

Could it be that Essex was my Ulubrae?